Trust God AND KEEP YOUR POWDER DRY

American folk version of saying originally attributed to Oliver Cromwell.

★

We have learned the answers, all the answers:
It is the question that we do not know.

Archibald MacLeish: "The Hamlet of A. MacLeish" (1928).

Also by MARGARET MEAD

★

COMING OF AGE IN SAMOA

GROWING UP IN NEW GUINEA

SEX AND TEMPERAMENT

—FROM THE SOUTH SEAS (*A 1940 republication, in one volume, of the three preceding titles*)

MALE AND FEMALE

SOVIET ATTITUDES TOWARD AUTHORITY

NEW LIVES FOR OLD

AND KEEP YOUR

POWDER DRY

An Anthropologist Looks At America

A NEW EXPANDED EDITION OF A CLASSIC
WORK ON THE AMERICAN CHARACTER

BY MARGARET MEAD

NEW YORK · 1965

WILLIAM MORROW AND COMPANY

To the Memory of my Grandmother

MARTHA RAMSAY MEAD

1845–1927

and the Future of my Daughter

MARY CATHERINE BATESON

1939–

ACKNOWLEDGMENT

*

THIS BOOK is presented as one part of the program of the Council of Intercultural Relations which is attempting to develop a series of systematic understandings of the great contemporary cultures so that the special values of each may be orchestrated in a world built new.

CONTENTS

★

Preface—1965

★

THIS BOOK was written in 1942 as a social scientist's contribution to winning the war and establishing a just and lasting peace. It was frankly and completely partisan. In writing it, I attempted to use all my experience gained through the study of primitive societies, where distance provided objectivity, to present the culture and character of my own people in a way they would find meaningful and useful in meeting the harsh realities of war. The highest compliment I ever received on this book was implicit in a question asked by a slightly aggrieved adolescent: "How did Margaret Mead know how my mother brought me up?"

Unlike many anthropologists whose energetic learning of the cultures and the languages of other peoples has had its source in extreme dissatisfaction with or disappointment in their own culture, I have always enjoyed my own culture—just as I like my own name and enjoy being a woman. My reason for spending so many years away from the United States on Pacific islands is that field work has given me access to materials out of which we might gain a different understanding and the hope of achieving a valuable new consciousness in the modern world.

In the summer of 1945 I began to write a sequel to *And Keep Your Powder Dry*. My intention was to discuss the postwar roles of the United States, Great Britain, and the Soviet Union (at that time, anthropologically speaking, quite unknown). But when the atomic bombs exploded over Hiroshima and Nagasaki, I tore up the manuscript. Once we knew that it was possible for a people to destroy the enemy, themselves, and all bystanders, the world itself was changed. And no sentence written with that knowledge of man's new capacity could be meshed into any sentence written the week before.

But this book, written three years earlier, was directed to a consideration of qualities in the American character that have not been altered by the fact of the bomb. Furthermore, we are today entering a period of new hope, shaking ourselves free of the apprehension and apathy of the dismal 1950's. The country is stirring. In the mid-1960's, Americans are making themselves ready for an effort of a kind they achieved in the past only in response to the desperation of the Great Depression or the exigencies of war. Those who can recall the tremendous upsurge of hope and the willingness to endure responsibility during the early 1930's and again in the early 1940's are once more moving into action. And a generation that has grown up with the knowledge of what the bomb means is ready to take over part of the responsibility for action.

My contemporaries, to whom this book was originally addressed, their children, and their children's children are together involved in a tremendous effort to translate permanent danger and unprecedented plenty into a newly ordered world. If the members of these three generations are to understand one another, the younger ones must know what their immediate predecessors felt and hoped for. I have made no changes in the body of this book. To do so would falsify the whole. But I have added a new chapter, written in new hope.

My friends in other countries tell me that the phrasing sounds "too American" for the mid-1960's. In explanation I have included in this edition the preface written "in English" for the Penguin edition that was published under the title, *The American Character*, in 1944. But it was, and it remains, a book written for Americans by an American with a willingness to have the rest of the world listen in.

My colleagues who have been good enough to reread the book critically also say that I must add a reminder about who the enemies were in World War II, for the benefit of those who have grown up in a world in which fiery crosses and swastikas have become indiscriminate symbols of hostility. In World War I, Americans could not (as so many then felt inclined to do) break the phonograph record of *Die Wacht am Rhein* because the *Marseillaise*, the national anthem of our ally France, was on the other side. Yet only a few years after the war many people would have liked to break the record for the opposite reason, and still could not do so.

The story has been repeated. Hostility toward Nazi Germany and Imperial Japan, the enemies who precipitated World War II, has been replaced by assistance to and courtship of the new Germany and the new Japan, while two of the allies who fought World War II on our side, Soviet Russia and mainland China, have been treated as countries with which war—at least cold war —is more appropriate than any real attempt at cooperation. As today's students watch the Nazi propaganda film *Hitlerjunge Quex* or even *The War for Men's Minds*, the magnificent film put together from World War II clips by John Grierson, they are scarcely able to understand the film makers' different intentions. And in 1957, when American children drew pictures of Sputnik, some of them decorated the satellite not with the design of the hammer and sickle but instead with a swastika— now only a symbol of enemy hostility.

The necessity for any reminder may seem very strange to the generation who fought to save the world from the darkest tyranny that had ever threatened it. But it is unavoidable. In this book, when I speak of the enemy, I mean primarily Nazi Germany and secondarily Imperial Japan and Italy, two countries that were our allies in World War I. And when I speak of our allies I mean Great Britain, France, split and occupied by the Nazi enemy, the Soviet Union, and the other countries in the West that were occupied, overrun, or attacked by the Nazi armies—Czechoslovakia, Poland, Denmark, Norway, Belgium, the Netherlands, Yugoslavia, Greece, and Turkey—and also China, split and ravaged by the Japanese armies, Burma, the Philippines, and India. In the midst of war, even for those who have already witnessed the strange spectacle of the rehabilitation of a former enemy and diabolization of a former ally, the sides are clearly drawn. During a war in which whole nations lie crushed beneath the conqueror's heel and whole populations are being bombed, it is not necessary to name the enemy over and over again.

But today when our methods of warfare are so fraught with danger for the whole world that men must pause before they start the smallest brush fire war, the situation is a different one. We are moving into a period in which alliances supported not essentially by weapons but by loans will be even more shifting than in the past, and the old, unstable dichotomies of allegiance and enmity will be replaced by the temporary collaborations of an uneasy, precarious, frequently threatened peacetime. Yet in a world that is totally endangered, nations can work together, more conscious of nationhood than of the separate goals that can no longer be totally defended, not without hope for a more stable peacetime.

MARGARET MEAD

New York
   March 1965

Preface from England—1943

★

WHEN I wrote this book,* in the summer of 1942, I had never sat in an English garden, I had never been protectingly scolded for moving backwards in a queue because I couldn't resist a sunpatch, I had never listened to a voluntary prayer in a woman's gathering in a tiny church parlor in East Dulwich Grove as a tired, black-clad, middle-aged woman prayed, in a voice of unforgettable sweetness, that "all those who are on holiday may be having a grand time." I had never seen a Lord Mayor's chain, nor a Town Clerk waiting in the rain with a rolled umbrella, nor been asked by a small schoolboy in Birmingham, "Do American women wear lights in their hats to stop taxis?" I had never seen the sun rise over Durham city, nor driven through the little sunken roads of Devon, nor seen the harvest standing in patterns as formal as a musical notation in the frosty fields of Scotland. I hadn't sat with the Women's Welfare Committee in a mining town and heard them plan

* *The American Character* (Harmondsworth, Middlesex: Penquin, 1944).

to give a pound to the doctor to "do just what she likes with, for the little things that come up that she wouldn't like to mention," nor heard a member of a conference propose a grateful vote of thanks for the hospitality of a hostel, and include in that thanks some very definite advice on how the picture in the room should be re-hung.

In the last four months it has been my privilege to see and hear all of these things, to see the face of Britain, and to trace, haltingly because of lack of previous sight, just as the blind trace the features of a new acquaintance, the marks of war upon that face. I came to Britain because I was sure that, however many English or Scottish or Welsh people I might meet abroad, and however closely I might come to know them, I would have very little understanding until I stood among them in their own land listening, when they were intent upon their own affairs and I was unnoticed.

I have been lecturing, lecturing in canteens and public meetings, visiting aircraft factories and mines, responding to the ceremonious welcome accorded me by officials and official hosts. But in between all this I have been listening to and watching the ordinary life of Britain. I learned a great deal one day in a crowded train when a little boy, returning with his mother and his aunts and a host of cousins from a day's holiday, planted himself upon my lap in order to see out of the window without looking around to see what sort of face went with the lap that made this view possible. After I had puzzled over it, I came to understand the outraged virtuosity of the taxi driver who wouldn't say

thank you for a tip because I had let him take me past
my destination by giving him an imperfect direction.
I began to wait for the negative warnings which accompanied every direction— "You'll come to a church
but *don't turn there*. Go straight on. You can't miss
it"—warnings which anticipated a rootedness in old
familiar ways which had to be sharply interrupted to
become conscious at all. I watched mothers handle their
babies like small innocent animals, confining them, by
a sheer curve of the arm, within a narrow realm in
which even a playful bite was permitted. I heard a
seventy-year-old Nannie who was looking at a snapshot
of my own small daughter, ask with the sureness of long
years of tender observation, "What sound is she listening to?" and heard that same old Nannie deny that any
of her many babies had ever shown a possibility of
becoming black sheep. Officials in ministries have explained to me over and over again the powers which
they never use. Teachers have told me a plan by which
children could say grace each in their own classroom,
so as to be able to eat their school meal piping hot—and
a wonderful scheme in which schoolchildren might go
swimming under the dual protection of trained swim-
mers and "responsible persons who might not themselves
be able to swim." On trams, in buses, on darkened rail-
way station platforms, in country lanes when my driver
had lost her way in the blackout and two boys on bi-
cycles rode miles to put us right, I have been the witness
and many times also the recipient of a thousand "little
unremembered acts of kindness and of love." Out of it

all I hope to carry back a pattern and a fragrance, a quickening understanding of the people of this country and the way they conduct their relationships. Always I have learned most when I could listen unobserved and absorb this harmony undistorted by any foreign note.

I wrote this book for my own countrymen to add what I had of knowledge and love of them, to armor them for the conflict of the years ahead. For the first time in my life I asked my publishers to set the book in American spelling. I deliberately turned from writing, as I have always done in the past, for the general English reading world, where many eyes are jolted rudely by the absence of the *u* in labor or the presence of the *z* in realize, to writing specifically for my own country, making full use of our own idiom. For I was talking to Americans in America about our share in the job of fighting the war and winning the peace. If we are to fight it well, and put our shoulder equally well to the tasks of the postwar world, we need, I feel, to know ourselves, to measure our strengths and guard against our weaknesses, to know whence we came and where we might best be going. Because this is a book written by an American to Americans it is no apologia, it does not slur over those aspects of our character which other peoples find most trying, nor does it mute the tones of optimism and confidence in our voices which might have been muted had I been worried lest an observer from an older civilization should find us bumptious and too confident.

One or two of my American friends, over-sensitive in the unwholesome atmosphere of appeasement which sometimes surrounds the exacting details of wartime cooperation, and so becoming unduly worried by the probable result upon Anglo-American relations of the behavior of American soldiers who fail to eat the crusts of tomato sandwiches at a party, even suggest that it is unwise to publish a book at all which discusses us so frankly. Shouldn't something, they ask, be written expressly for a British audience, taking their special biases and preoccupations into account? But just as I think I have learned most about the people of this country when I have been allowed to listen-in unnoticed, so I think you, the British people, may want to listen-in sometimes when Americans talk together among themselves. The type of news selection exercised by the Press today often deals with the bizarre, the spectacular and at times even the damaging, and thus affords you little opportunity really to taste the savor of American discussion about the war. The films, the art of a people who are too newly come to their nationality to be able to delight in any accurate picture of its diversified realities, again provide no portrait of American life. It is difficult for you to understand our soldiers who cluster on the street corners of your great cities, as they were accustomed to stand on the street corners of prairie villages farther from any city than Edinburgh is from London. You find our soldiers rather outspoken in their surprise that the word "lake" refers in this country, whose history was sung in song and story when America was still almost untouched by the hand of man, to stretches of water so much smaller than those which we call "lake," that some land made known to them by legend, prose and poetry may yet be crossed from end to end within the day. Our soldiers have learned to be concerned oftener with results and less often with process, oftener with what gets done, seldom with how it is done and what are the implications of the doing. Perhaps, therefore, the story of how their characters have developed, in a country in which only three times the population of yours is spread over thirty times the space, may be useful.

If I were writing a book for you and telling you something about us, and our soldiers in your midst, I would write differently. I would try to give you an understanding which would help point the way to a genuine, trustful, friendly cooperation with Americans as the great work begins of building the world anew. So a book written especially for you would contain many other points, would try to show, although words are singularly clumsy tools with which to do it, something about the difference between the way in which we think in single sequences, each unit quite simple and clear, while you seem to think in units which are so very complex that it would be quite impossible to put all of their multiple dimensions into words. I'd want to say something about the contrast between the way in which people from any one part of the country over here can take pride and pleasure in the distinctive characteristics of some quite different part, the white cliffs of Dover, Snowdon, or the Lake District—the Tower of London or Princes Street, Edinburgh—and the way people in America have to feel instead that their own town, their own state, have been directly responsible for some accomplishment before they really feel a right to be proud of it. And if I were writing in 1943 I would want to say a good deal about the particular fashion in which the British people are meeting the Americans—what Hollywood calls "boy meets girl." I'd want to explain why the American boy seems so forward at first, because he has grown up with girls and had dates with girls, his own age or a little younger, since he was thirteen or fourteen, and so lacks any endearing shyness. He just wants girls to go out with and is puzzled when he finds his casual wise-cracking approaches, which worked so well at home, regarded either as insults, as invitations or as proposals. There are many points like this which are important, and which it would be most necessary to discuss in a book written about America, for you in 1943.

But this particular book was written for Americans. In spite of the many critical notes in it, I offer it to you without a comma altered, or a figure of speech toned down, as I wrote it, as I felt it. It was written with a profound faith in the strengths of my own people and in a belief—a belief which will find an echo, if I am not mistaken, in every British mind—that every nation does best to cultivate its strengths and watch warily over its weaknesses, denying neither, accepting both. It was written in the belief that only by each people developing their separate genius to the full as they cooperate more and more with each other can a culture develop which will take all these themes, not only those from Britain, the United States and the Dominions, but from China

and Russia, from France and Burma, from India and
Italy, from Yugoslavia and Japan and Germany, from
the glory that was Greece and the future dream of an
ordered world society of peoples, in which each may
stand in his own appointed place and find it good.

MARGARET MEAD

14 Woodfall Street, Chelsea
17th October, 1943

Introduction—1965

★

And Keep Your Powder Dry grew out of the experiences of the period between the outbreak of war in Europe in the summer of 1939 and the entrance of the United States into the war after Pearl Harbor in December 1941. From the first we felt it was only a matter of time before this country would be drawn into the conflict, and we hoped to put our growing knowledge of the human sciences at the services of the Allied fight against Nazism. Today, living in a world in which the dangers are so much greater and the only means at our disposal for protecting the world's peoples is the prevention of war and the protection of our enemies in spite of themselves and even against their will, I find it hard to realize how urgent it seemed then to take part in the struggle. But in the 1940's, when we contemplated the consequences of a victory by Nazi Germany in Europe and of the establishment of the Japanese Co-prosperity Sphere in Asia, it seemed very important for men's freedom everywhere in the world that we should win the war. And it also seemed very important that

Americans should win with a good conscience, so that we could play a full, responsible part in the postwar world.

Born in 1901, I belong to the group of those who came of age in the 1920's, in the period when, having refused to join the League of Nations, the United States failed in its commitments to international order and in doing so contributed heavily to the breakdown of that order. By standing aside we helped to create the situation in which Mussolini, Hitler, and Japan could make their naked bids for world power. My contemporaries, English and American alike, lived through the grim days of the Great Depression. Our experiences made us realize not only that modern societies needed more help from the human sciences, but also that the older sciences of history, political science, and economics needed to be supplemented by the newer disciplines of anthropology, sociology, psychology, and psychiatry.

My own group was not caught up in the fashionable radicalism of the 1930's with its roseate views of the Soviet Union. As anthropologists, we were very much concerned with the intricate meshing of means and ends and we were not engulfed in a desperate preoccupation with totalitarian panaceas for the woes of a capitalist society in travail. For this reason we were spared the paralysis that gripped so many liberals who were stunned and confused by the Soviet-German pact. My contemporaries in England also had smarted over Chamberlain's return from Munich. But from 1939 on, we were free to address our energies to the question of how our particular anthropological understanding, developed almost solely on the basis of the study of small groups of primitive peoples, could be used constructively in the conflict that clearly lay ahead.

Here, when I say "we," I am speaking primarily of the group of four anthropologists who worked with the Committee for National Morale. The impetus for this book grew out of the anthropologists' efforts to work with the large number of other human scientists on the Committee as well as with other anthropologists, notably Ruth Benedict and Geoffrey Gorer. The focus of our joint efforts was the application of anthropological methods to the study of modern societies, many of them cut off from us by the conditions of war after the summer of 1939.

My own interests had always turned on the relevance of the study of primitive peoples to our understanding of our own customary behavior and our attempts to modify it. Ruth Benedict had called anthropology the science of custom. And I had been in the habit of ending my books, which dealt with the ways faraway South Sea peoples worked out universal human problems, with a discussion of how some of my results could be applied to the modern world. But in 1939 we had no formal rules to go by in our new undertaking. We did not yet know how to combine anthropological detachment, which was achieved by traveling to and studying intensively a people distant in time and place, and awareness of our own culture in which we ourselves had a place. Extraordinary difficulties in coming to grips with the problem of bias had plagued earlier attempts to adapt an anthropological model and anthropological methods to the study of our own culture in such works as *Middletown*, the Yankee City research (which had not yet reached publication), *Deep South*, *The Children of Bondage*, and *Caste and Class in a Southern Town*. The Lynds lamented the Middle West of their childhood. Lloyd Warner fashioned the analysis of social class in the United States into a tool that later came to be used in destructive mutual denigration. The studies of the American Southeast fiercely indicted the old South.

Today, twenty years later, we know a great deal about how to speak and write about our own culture—as anthropologists. It is still perhaps easier for those who are deeply and happily at home in their own culture to write about it than it is for those whose principal emotion is outrage or repudiation. But this is true also when one works with a distant culture, very different from one's own. Vivid appreciation and delighted laughter are the emotions from which good ethnographies flow felicitously, as in Colin Turnbull's *The Forest People*,* while empathy and compassion provide a different kind of insight of the kind found in Oscar Lewis's *Childen of Sanchez*† or Jules Henry's "passionate ethnography" of contemporary American life, *Culture against Man*.

*New York, Simon and Schuster, 1961.
†New York, Random House, 1961.

We know now that if one can get a cultural description exactly right it will have the effect of making those who are characterized by it laugh harder and more warmly than they would at a similar characterization in some other culture. We know now that we must address ourselves to whole human beings both in our descriptions of people and in our relation to those we are speaking to. In writing about a culture and a people it will not do either to single out the disallowed emotions or to harp continually on the articulate ideals. And we know how fully we must specify our own position vis-à-vis the culture—and our situation in the culture—we are discussing. When he reviewed this book, John Chamberlain was able to applaud certain points in it. Six years later, when Geoffrey Gorer, an anthropologist who wrote as an Englishman about the United States, referred to some of the same points, Chamberlain condemned them vigorously. And even the careful specification of one's position may not make a descriptive point tolerable when the vehicle is wit instead of humor.

All this is hindsight, based on twenty years of hard thinking and hard work by those of us who have continued to relate our work to the problems of the contemporary world and have not retreated to the ivory bomb shelters of minute and entrancing specialist problems of kinship systems, templates, and mentifacts. In an age when paperback publication is bringing new life to old books, one of the rewards of a long professional career—and mine began forty years ago—is the periodic opportunity to look back and say what one thinks, oneself, about what one has done. I have left the body of this book just as it was written and published in 1943. My daughter, to whom it was dedicated, was then too young to read the book, but realizing that it was somehow different from other books she took it to bed with her. What value this book has now lies in the way it places a period—a period in American culture and a period in our developing understanding of our own culture.

I have written a new final chapter that maintains the book's original purpose of giving Americans a sense of their particular strengths as a people and of the part they may play in the world. The gulf separating 1965 from 1943 is as deep as the gulf that separated the men who became builders of cities from Stone Age men. Yet those who were living in 1943 and are living now know both sides of the gulf and our chances of arriving at a new understanding of the world we live in are far greater. But the danger in which contemporary man lives is greater also. We shall need every bit of understanding we can muster among ourselves and among all the other peoples of the world if mankind is to survive this period in which we live surrounded by the constructions we know very well how to make but are only beginning to learn how to control.

CHAPTER I

Introduction—1942

★

SIX TIMES [1] in the last seventeen years I have entered another culture, left behind me the speech, the food, the familiar postures of my own way of life, and sought to understand the pattern of life of another people. In 1939, I came home to a world on the brink of war, convinced that the next task was to apply what we knew, as best we could, to the problems of our own society. There was no more time to go far afield for the answers which lay crystallized in the way of life of distant, half-forgotten peoples who, for thousands of years, had been finding quite different and various answers to those problems which all human beings must solve if they are to continue to live together in groups. For a few short years the methods of anthropology had been used to explore social problems; and now, with such increased knowledge as the study of other cultures had given us, we had to tackle the enormous problem of a world on the verge of social self-consciousness, a world on the verge of a new period in history.

This did not mean that I, or any other anthropologist,

3

was now to treat our own society exactly like a primitive society. The dispassionate study of culture, of the whole way of life of a people seen as a dynamic pattern, is dependent upon a degree of detachment which no one can attain concerning his own society and remain a normal, participant member of that society. My own culture, the language and gestures, the rituals and beliefs of Americans, will always be to me something more than materials for study, to be catalogued side by side with the practices of Samoans and Balinese. Where the Samoans and Balinese may have developed a pattern of life which disallows in cruelest fashion some special capacity of the human spirit, I can record that fact with clarity and a minimum of personal involvement. For my own culture, this cannot be. The obligation of the scientist to examine his material dispassionately is combined with the obligation of the citizen to participate responsibly in his society.[2] To the investigation of social materials to the end that we may know more, has to be added the organization of social materials that we may *do* more—here—now—in America towards fighting the war in a way that will leave us with the moral and physical resources to attack the problem of reorganizing the world.

Although the anthropologist never looks at his own culture and his own people with quite the clear, objective appraisal he is trained to give to South Sea Islanders and Indians, nevertheless, if those South Sea Islanders have been studied carefully enough, the anthropologist wears forever another set of lenses, a new set for each primitive culture which has been examined. With these lenses, acquired in the long months in which he minutely studied strange ways of life and held reflectively small wriggling babies—for the babies of each society wriggle in a slightly different way, and one learns from observing the differences—the anthropologist sees different things about the home culture from those things which others see who have never had to submit to this special discipline.

What the anthropologist sees is different from what the traveler sees. The American who has lived for many years in Paris or London, in Moscow, or Berlin, or Shanghai, comes back with freshened vision: notices how tight the Faculty wives' mouths are at the old university; how nervous the bridge club members are; how no one speaks to anyone else on a train in the East any more. Peculiarities in manners, which those who stay at home take for granted, show up when the eyes and ears of the returned traveler are turned upon them. Pearl Buck, returning to a world which she had dreamed of as a true democracy, saw, with a sharpness denied to most of those who have lived in America instead of having heard about America in China, how far from her dream—from our dream—we were. Men who fought in Spain, men who have gone through months of London in the blitz, or men who have seen the Russian front come back with eyes which see more clearly, more fiercely, than our own.

It is not these things that the anthropologist has to offer. The anthropologist is trained to see form where other people see concrete details, to think in terms which will bring together a wedding in a cathedral and a ceremony on a small South Sea island, in which two middle-aged people with three children sit down and solemnly eat one white chicken egg.[3] Seen in terms of the social history, both are marriages: both are socially-sanctioned ways of recognizing that two people, a man and a woman, now publicly assume complete responsibility for their children; although in one society the children are born before the ceremony, while in the other the ceremony must come first. Where the advocate of better housing worries about the moral effects of a whole family living in a trailer, the anthropologist knows that it is not the small space, nor the poor sanitation, which is crucial. The anthropologist has seen people live with complete dignity and morality under conditions which would make a modern trailer look like a palace, or even a share-cropper's cabin look like a substantial and prosperous dwelling. Behind the small space of the trailer and its possible effect upon the morals of adolescent children is seen a system of family relationships which depends upon privacy, upon doors and bathroom keys. People trained to depend upon such details of house construction to preserve incest taboos cannot do without them easily. So the anthropologist does not disagree with the housing expert, but the problem is seen in a different perspective against the background of shelter and tipi and pile house set in a shallow salt lagoon.

Speaking from a platform to a women's club, if one is

merely an experienced speaker at women's clubs, one notices whether the audience is smartly dressed, and how smartly. If one is an American sociologist, one may add observations about the probable class level of the audience and the proportion of professional women—lawyers in sober suits seeking to tone down their sex, social workers in pleasant but serviceable headgear, civil servants with clothes that look like uniforms or clothes that aggressively do *not* look like uniforms. But I never completely lose a still further point of reference—the awareness that my audience wears clothes, and several layers of them; the consciousness that this is a great group of women of child-bearing age, and yet nowhere is there a baby crawling at its mother's feet or begging to be fed; the knowledge that, if there were a breast-fed baby in that audience, it would have to go hungry. I do not cease to observe whether this is a patriotic group of women, valiantly and self-consciously wearing last year's hats, or an afternoon group of women who are homemakers, or an evening group of women who, whether they are homemakers or not, don't do homemaking in the daytime—but this other consciousness: "These people are completely clothed," stays with me to widen my perspective.

In the chapters that follow, I do not present a study of America. This is not a *Middletown* [4] or a *Yankee City* [5] or a *Hollywood*,[6] although the detailed observation recorded in the pages of those books has been very valuable to me. This is not an indictment of America in the style of Grant Allen's *British Barbarians*,[7] in which the British are held up to ridicule because they have taboos and fetishes and totems. This is not an "Are We Civilized?" in which the random pieces of better behavior among primitive peoples the world over are cited to deflate our spurious complacency. This is not an attempt to take off American's clothes. I prefer Americans with clothes, just as much as I prefer South Sea Islanders without them. It is an attempt to say: In the last seventeen years I have been practicing a certain way of looking at peoples. I bring it—for what it is worth—to you, to us, at this moment when no American can escape the challenge to use what special or accidental skills he has.

A score of years ago, the British invented a special use for anthropologists as advisers to the government. In colonial countries, where a small colonial staff has to administer large areas filled with native people speaking diverse languages and practicing a large number of strange and diverse customs, there are always administrative problems: Why is there a sudden outbreak of headhunting in the gold-fields? Why have all the men in a certain area suddenly all gone away to work, or all refused to work? What will be the response of a tribe of two hundred fishing people if the government moves them to other land? How is it possible to stop a sudden messianic cult, which is sweeping from tribe to tribe making everyone kill his pigs and neglect his gardens? These are recurrent situations, and some governments retained anthropologists to find immediate answers to these vexatious questions. Trained to get the outlines of a situation quickly in cultural terms, the anthropologist was asked to find the source of the trouble and to suggest satisfactory answers. His answers had to be within the rules of the colonial administration as set up: he couldn't recommend cannibalism as a substitute for headhunting. Education was too long a process. Some change had to be made quickly which would stop headhunting, yet leave the natives able to initiate their young men into manhood. He had to recommend something like pig-hunting; explaining, for instance, that for this given people, boys couldn't grow to full manhood without killing something, that this was a tribe which couldn't get on without some form of long pants.

So, in our own society at present, the anthropologist can comment on particular problems, based on a special type of experience. The war is putting new strains on men, women, and children; [8] on teachers; [9] on young people; on old people; on social workers; on factory owners; on farmers. The war is posing new problems for which there is desperate need of solutions. Most of the ideas in the chapters which follow were developed in answer to definite questions brought to me by groups of people hopeful that a different experience and training might throw light on their problems. The research, the detailed objective recording [10] of human behavior, which lies back of this discussion was not done in the United States, but in the South Seas. On the basis of that study I have looked at America; I have thought about Americans. I have offered certain diagnoses to Americans, who have found them, by virtue of their very strangeness, illuminating.

But one serious difficulty confronts the anthropologist. When writing about some strange South Sea culture, there is the persistent difficulty of translating strange native ideas into English, until one wishes passionately that it were possible to describe Samoa in Samoan and Arapesh in the Arapesh language. English words, no matter how skillfully used, do not convey accurately the meaning of a Balinese word like *tis,* which means not to be hot when it is hot, and not to be cold when it is cold. It's a lovely word, and it takes some fifteen English words to translate it even partially. But the anthropologist, writing about his own culture in his own language, suffers from the opposite difficulty. I wish to say different things from the things that have been said before, to look at America in a way that has not ever been attempted. But all the words are old; they have been used by novelists and journalists, by columnists and Fourth of July orators. It is extremely difficult to differentiate between a "glittering generality" and a careful statement arrived at by scientific means. Unless the reader follows the *kind* of reasoning, rather than the old familiar words in which the reasoning is perforce clothed, he is likely to turn away thinking, "Just some more remarks about the American way of life."

And there is an even more serious trap. As America has a moral culture—that is, a culture which accepts right and wrong as important—any discussion of Americans must simply bristle with words like *good* and *bad.*

Any discussion of Samoans would bristle with terms for awkward and graceful, for ill bred and "becoming to those bred as chiefs." Any account of the Balinese would be filled with discussions of whether a given act would make people *paling,* the Balinese word for the state of not knowing where you are, what day it is, where the center of the island is, the caste of the person to whom you are talking, or being in trance or drunk. Similarly, when I talk about what Americans must do if they are to use the full resources of their character structure, I will be making highly technical statements, and they will often sound exactly like a Sunday-school lesson.

If I were writing about the way in which the Germans or the Japanese, the Burmese or the Javanese would have to act if they were to win the war, I would not need to use so many moral terms. For none of these peoples think of life in as habitually moral terms as do Americans. Only by remembering this, by pausing every time that a sentence in this book seems to sound like a Fourth of July sermon and realizing that Fourth of July sermons are, after all, what little Americans are made of—among other more temporary ingredients such as Mickey Mouse and Superman—will it be possible for the reader to realize that this is a scientific discussion and that it sounds familiar, not because the points are old and familiar ones, but because it is expressed in the words and ideas of our culture with which we are all familiar. When automobiles replace outrigger canoes, apples replace mangosteens and papayas, and boxes of chocolates are substituted for octopus pudding as a suitable gift to take on a date, the whole incidental paraphernalia of strangeness which I could use to convey the cultures of other peoples is gone. Only by remembering that when I look at a box of chocolates I see it as just one item in one form of courtship—instead of a cigarette containing love magic, an octopus pudding, the heart of a coconut or a bunch of lotus stems in as many different systems of courtship—and that where I use the words *good* or *just* here, I might be using the words *status,* or the *"honor of the Emperor,"* or *"keeping the world steady,"* will it be possible for the reader to appreciate what I am trying to say, instead of being swamped by a barrage of old words, each one struggling to convey a new point of view.

If we were not at war, if the whole world were not at war, if every effort of each human being were not needed to ask the right questions so that we may find the right answers in time, I would not be writing this book. I would be on a ship, bound for some South Sea island to continue my study of rapidly vanishing primitive peoples in the belief that the knowledge thus accumulated would some day give us adequate guidance in building a good society. But even in a world relatively at peace, a world which gave a breathing spell for scientific work, I would have been bringing back whatever hints [11] and guesses seemed relevant to our own problems in need of solution. Now there is no longer time to go to any more islands, to study any more languages, to find any more cultures which might turn our traditional beliefs upside down. We are caught in a situation so dangerous, so pressing, that we must use what tools we have.

There are those social scientists who are unwilling to use tools which they know to be as clumsy, when measured against what we may some day develop, as a stone ax against an electric drill. They fear the fellow scientist who may review their work. The man who hit on the idea of a stone ax was free to use it because he could imagine nothing better. Because we know that we might have better tools and, in fact, are that much wiser than Stone Age man, there is no reason for us to become weaker because wiser, to be ashamed to use our stone axes. Nor need we wait passively for starvation and destruction, proud that we know that more precise tools of thought are available. Some of us feel that with every increase in knowledge—even with our wider vision of what Science may some day be—we should become stronger, not weaker; bolder, not more craven; freer to act.

Recently, I sat at a meeting to which a government official posed a question, a question for which there was insufficient data to give a full answer. At that meeting sat a nationally known psychologist. He objected: "We ought to do some research." The answer was: "You have a week in which to answer this question. Then *some* action will be taken." The nationally known psychologist sat up. "You mean we have to stick our necks out?" "Yes!" "Okay," and he squared his shoulders.

Anthropology was made for man; not man for anthropology. In peacetime we labor to increase anthropological knowledge, to construct a systematic picture of how human culture works, to provide the scientific basis for building an ever better world. In wartime we have three courses—to retire into ivory towers, protect our scientific reputations, and wait, on the chance that peace will come without our help and leave us free again to go back to our patient labors; or, we can do something non-anthropological, satisfy our patriotic consciences by becoming air-raid wardens, working in an area where no colleague will review our works. Or, we can say quite simply, with such knowledge and insights as we have, we will now do what we can, as anthropologists, to win the war. We can come out into the marketplace, work in the dust of the traveled road, laying aside the immunities of the ivory tower, and try to ask the right questions, secure in the faith that, whenever in all his history Man has asked the right question, he has found the answer.

CHAPTER II

Clearing the Air

★

THERE ARE MANY WAYS in which a country may reckon its assets and its liabilities, for war, for peace after wars, for building an order in which war and peace shall become as outmoded as alternations of famine and plenty, plague and health were on their way to being outmoded in the western world. We may count over our natural resources—and a great many experts are busy doing just that. We may make an inventory of our idle stock—in warehouses, in the rusting rails of abandoned trolley tracks or the pedestals of our less-loved public statuary. We may draw maps and calculate distances as they were when men sailed the seas, as they are not when bombers have a range of thousands of miles. We may even count noses and match them up with the number of sub-machine guns we can manufacture or the number of assembly lines which we can complete by March 10th or 12th or 15th, in 1943 or 1944 or 1945. What we have available on or under the earth, what we have made and are not using or need not use, where we are and how much trouble it will be for other people to get to us or we to them, laden with either bombs or food—these are familiar problems.

But there is another problem which is just as relevant to the question of winning this war and playing an effective and decent role in the post-war world which people have taken less seriously. Not the problem of what we have, where we are and how many of us are available to use how many machines and weapons, but the problem of *what we are ourselves*. When the statesman or the general utters the words "total war," either as a threat to his own people or a threat to the enemy, he means that, to all these other questions of matériel, geography, and sheer numbers, has been added another —the quality of a people; their national character.[1] The youngest child, its physical stamina, its psychological security, may be a factor in the resistance, in the total effort of a whole people, for if great numbers of children die—or even refuse to eat—under the stress of total war, the courage and the energy of their parents will be by that much lessened and depleted. The old grandmother, bed-ridden and half blind, also becomes a factor. Does she insist upon others leaving more important tasks to care for her, or does she fall half out of bed urging her children and her grandchildren to get on with the business of life and never mind even leaving her a sleeping draught beside her bed? The simplest mountain farmer may live on a remote spot where a parachutist drops; whether or not he is a real representative of rugged individualism may turn the tide of battle. Upon the alertness of some unskilled laborer in a great aeroplane factory may depend the prevention of a major act of sabotage. The chairman of the Senate Committee who inaugurates the wrong investigation may play a greater role than the general who gives the wrong command. Just as any tree or bush, any village or suburb, is as possible a target for a bomb as is a forest or a city, so total war stretches out the human beings who form a nation into a great straggling chain, as strong as their ability to join hands rapidly again if one drops out.

This is the measure which total war takes of a nation's character. It tests our ability to work together, to compensate quickly for errors and miscalculations, to fight a battle so that it leaves one strong enough to gather up the wounded, rally one's own troops, stop fires which may have started in the neighborhood, order new supplies, sleep soundly, and rise to work—if there is no more fighting to do—on the morrow. And it tests our enemies and our allies, and our ability to co-operate with our allies in the same way. So in wartime people begin to think again in terms which had fallen into disrepute in the last quarter of a century, in terms of national character. What is an American, a German, an Englishman, or an Australian? What are his strengths and his weaknesses, what is his peculiar pattern of strength and weakness, invincible under one set of conditions, infinitely vulnerable under another? In a last-ditch war, these will be the imponderables that count. And can we hope to build any sort of world order which does not take account of them? Was it not one of the errors of

Versailles that it assumed that peoples are really all alike, merely suffering to greater or less degree, from sets of obsolete political institutions or equally obsolete piratical leaders? The whole League of Nations plan assumed that grown-up people, people bred under strongly contrasting family organization,[2] different religious emphases, people who sat and slept and talked and made love entirely differently, would nevertheless behave in quite similar ways, if they all had a chance to sit around a conference table and vote by secret ballot. All the shibboleths, that we are not fighting against the German people but against their Kaiser—or their Dictator, their military clique or their Nazi party—against their hierarchical and undemocratic political institutions, but not against them themselves, obscure the connections between a people and the institutions under which they have been reared, between the leader and the led, between a culture and the human beings who carry that culture.

Just because we repudiate with all our strength the idea that a man's manners or his morals, his IQ or his capacity for democratic behavior, might be limited by race, that the color of a man's skin, the shape of his head or the waviness of his hair might carry with it either an ability or a disability, there is no reason for going to the opposite extreme and insisting that because we cannot explain the consistent occurrence of certain traits among the majority of the German people, or the Italian people, or the English people, by their Race, that those traits aren't there. We need not believe that the inhabitants of Hamburg or Essen, or Naples, or Plymouth are all just "people like ourselves." One reason why the theory of Race has been given such wide acceptance is just because the inhabitants of Hamburg are *not* like the inhabitants of Plymouth or Naples, and the man in the street, who hadn't spent his life checking up on the social processes by which babies become adults, just couldn't believe that these groups of people could have turned out to be so different, if they had started out—as babies—with the same kind of gifts and the same kind of limitations. In America, as we watched one wave of immigration after another hit our shores, it was much easier to refer the startling differences between the Southern Italians and the Poles to their "blood" than it was to realize that not only the Italians and the Poles but even we ourselves have been shaped by our social environment—that the language one speaks, the religion one professes, the code of ethics by which one judges and is judged, one's taste for wine or beer or vodka, or one's preference for paprika or snails or French-fried dragon-flies can all be referred to the culture within which one is brought up. It is hard to believe that the same children who can eat food seasoned so highly with red pepper that it burns our tongues for hours after, would have indignantly repudiated that "horrid highly-spiced foreign food" if they had been adopted at birth by people who ate tasteless food. But just because we know—on the basis of modern anthropological findings—that this is true, that it is not blood, but upbringing which determines all of these ways of behaving, does not mean that we then have to sit down and ignore our discovery.[3] If people, potentially similar at birth, can be developed to look so very different, to walk and talk differently, quarrel and make love, drive a bargain and mourn a relative, race a horse or shoot a rabbit—so differently—we must also recognize that they—the Germans, the Italians, the English—and the Americans—*are* different now. It is nonsense to say that Versailles failed because "the Germans lacked democratic machinery," just as it would be nonsense to say that a steam engine lacks a magneto. The Germans lacked democratic machinery because their way of life lacked those emphases and attitudes on which democratic machinery can flourish. Democratic procedures are not something that people have, like automobiles or hot-dog stands or a way of building roads. Democracy is not something which can be added or subtracted; it is not one of an array of items found on closet shelves, in stores or text-books, not just one more detail in a hodgepodge of furniture models, written laws, and grammar books. The way in which people behave is all of a piece, their virtues and their sins, the way they slap the baby, handle their court cases, and bury their dead. It would be impossible suddenly to introduce "democracy" which is a word for a type of behavior and an attitude of mind which runs through our whole culture, through our selection of candidates for office, our behavior in street cars, our schools and our newspapers, into an undemocratic society—as it would suddenly to introduce feudalism into a modern American city.

We *are* our culture. The culture of 100 years ago was the behavior of those who lived a hundred years ago. The odd bits and pieces of that way of life which we have conserved, in books, in pictures, in samplers, in old wives' tales, is not their culture but part of ours. Culture is an abstraction in the mind of the social scientist, but each people for whom he can make this abstraction behave in certain ways, are certain kinds of persons, were reared in a given fashion, and have a given character. Character is also an abstraction, a way of talking about the results in human personality, of having been reared by and among human beings whose behavior was culturally regular.[4] So, in every culture, in Samoa, in Germany, in Iceland, in Bali, and in the United States of America, we will find consistencies and regularities in the way in which new-born babies grow up and assume the attitudes and behavior patterns of their elders—and this we may call "character formation." We will find that Samoans may be said to have a Samoan character structure, and Americans an American character structure. Banishing the bogies of racism [5] and its related insistencies does not mean that we must end up by saying that all peoples are alike just because we believe that, within a normal distribution of individual differences and potentialities more or less common to each group, they *could* have been alike under other circumstances. If we once accept the demonstrations that the aggressiveness of Negro children reared in the American South may be explained by the fact that they are inadequately protected from violence within their own race, that the aggressiveness of Negroes in the British West Indies is different—because of the difference in the two white cultures—we must then also face up to the fact that Southern American Negroes and West Indian Negroes will continue to behave differently, or if they alter their behavior, that the alterations may be referred to their previous different training. If one brother in a Russian family brings his children to America and the other stays in Russia, the children of the two families will turn out to be American on the one hand and Russian on the other. The fact that it was a matter of historical accident which brother came—perhaps they even diced for the passage money—does not for one minute change the existing circumstances or make it easier for American Peter, who is a go-getting member of the Junior Chamber of Commerce, to like Stalin, or for Russian Ivan to understand what Americans mean by rugged individualism.

If the Racists were right, if the absolute believers in heredity were right, humanity would be caught in a trap which would—as the Fascists logically enough believe—make Democracy a pipe dream. Because a new-born baby can be brought up to be a Hottentot or a German, an Eskimo or an American, because each group of people seem to be born with the same kinds of individual differences, democracy is not a pipe dream, but a practical working plan. Unless we obscure the point and for "created equal" we substitute "are equal." If differences between *peoples* are to be referred to culture, and to circumstances, events in their past and present situation—and those cultures and those circumstances are different—then the people themselves will be different. Their children may be potentially equal, but they themselves are not either equal or similar. They have been shaped to different forms; in adults these forms are relatively rigid. In order to develop a world order which will give to every child, of whatever race or creed, a chance to develop his fullest potentialities, we must work with what we have now, a world full of people whose potentialities have been very differently elaborated. We aren't going to sit down at conference tables with a set of abstract or infantile potentialities, but with a group of adult people who embody, in every thought and act of their lives, different and often mutually incompatible values. To argue otherwise is to argue that everybody could learn Esperanto and then world communication would be much easier, ignoring the fact that practically no one has learned Esperanto and negotiations will have to be carried on in English and Russian, German and Chinese and Spanish. The Racists obscure the issue by talking as if certain skin colors and certain vowel sounds go together. Their opponents too often confuse the issue almost as badly by talking as if different vowel sounds didn't impede communication.

In the next three chapters the reader may feel that I am going far afield, that with a war on, with American troops fighting on twenty fronts, with half of our home economy dislocated, with shortages and adjustment to shortages, with the threat of inflation and the need of stopping the inflation spiral all staring us in the face, this is no time to stop and examine the way in which American babies are made into Americans.* But if I were writing a book discussing how we could win the war with one type of aeroplane rather than another, I should have to devote parts of the book to describing the weapon which I was advocating. Here, we are going to discuss what are the strengths and weaknesses of the American character—the psychological equipment with which we can win the war. To do this we have to get clearly in mind just what that American character is. The clearest way I know of to do that, is to describe how it is made. Human beings are notoriously difficult to describe, but it is possible to approach objectivity in such a task by narrating the most revealing experiences through which they have lived—highlighting the process which turns a beet-red baby in a hospital delivery room into an American to whom baseball scores and fair play and business and the importance of success all make consummate good sense. If the reader keeps this analogy in mind, keeps asking: how does the fact that Americans are like *this* and like *that* bear on our capacity to fight and to endure, to adjust, to change, to manage a twenty-four-hour day, or stand separation and heartbreak and

---

* Statements about the culture of the United States have to be qualified in many cases, if they are to apply both to the North and the South. The introduction in the South of the bi-racial classification of humanity means that caste [6] is sometimes a directly formative element in developing standards of behavior. The generalizations in this book should be regarded as based primarily on the North, Middle West, and West, and should not be called in question because certain elements of Southern culture differ from them, as this is inevitable. A discussion which overrode the very considerable differences between North and South would often be too abstract to be fruitful.

death, to keep on with the job and see it through—not only through the war but through into a new world—the next chapters will be seen as a necessary part of the task which we are attempting in this book.

There are some who will argue that to sit at any international table, to have a hand in planning the next great step for the human race, we have to win the war first, win it in full knowledge that, while the winning is not enough, nevertheless the winning is essential. So evident is it that, if Hitler wins, this sort of discussion is academic, that many people think we should drop it, get on with the war, beat Hitler at his own game, and then come back to considerations of national character and international social organization. All this comes after, they claim.

In denying their argument, I do not take the position of the newest form of intellectual pest, the person who teeters back and forth as to whether he will save democracy at home or abroad. This book is based upon another premise—the premise that, in total war, national character, what Americans are now, today, in the 1940's, is one of our principal assets, and may nevertheless become, not wisely handled, one of our principal liabilities. We are the stuff with which this war is being fought. If we had been born somewhere else and reared somewhere else, we would be different kinds of people. As new-born babies we didn't differ from German babies or Japanese babies or English babies or Russian babies. Some of us were potentially bright, some potentially stupid. All of us, culturally speaking, were *tabula rasa.* But, as adolescents and adults, we do differ, and we differ for good. There is no time to re-educate us—even to the degree to which re-education is possible. What we are must be enough. What we are must be used. If we make war plans which seek to invoke a kind of courage which we lack, and neglect a kind of courage which we have—we will lose. If we let our generals and our statesmen involve us in international threats and reprisals which fail to bring out the strengths in our character—we may lose. To win we must take accurate inventory—not only of our copper and our aluminum, of the number of skilled mechanics and potential fliers with good eyesight—but of our American character. We must fight and win the war as Americans, not as hastily streamlined, utterly inadequate, imitation Germans or Japs. It's a safe bet that an attempt to make an American adult into an imitation of a Nazi soldier will produce something inferior to a Nazi soldier. We believe that the strength of those who are reared to freedom is greater than the strength of those reared in an authoritarian state. Now, in the strength of this faith, we wish the chance to fight and, if need be, die. Therefore, we must also articulate the other half of the belief—that only as we use the character developed under that freedom, in all its uniqueness, can we win. Freedom's battles must be fought by freedom's own children. We, who have been reared in one dream, who would be pathetic if we made grotesque attempts to imitate the enemy, can be invincible if we fight in our own way.

CHAPTER III

We Are All Third Generation

*

WHAT THEN is this American character, this expression of American institutions and of American attitudes which is embodied in every American, in everyone born in this country and sometimes even in those who have come later to these shores? What is it that makes it possible to say of a group of people glimpsed from a hotel step in Soerabaja or strolling down the streets of Marseilles, "There go some Americans," whether they have come from Arkansas or Maine or Pennsylvania, whether they bear German or Swedish or Italian surnames? Not clothes alone, but the way they wear them, the way they walk along the street without awareness that anyone of higher status may be walking there also, the way their eyes rove as if by right over the façade of palaces and the rose windows of cathedrals, interested and unimpressed, referring what they see back to the Empire State building, the Chrysler tower, or a good-sized mountain in Montana. Not the towns they come from—Sioux City, Poughkeepsie, San Diego, Scotsdale—but the tone of voice in which they say, "Why, I came from right near

there. My home town was Evansville. Know anybody in
Evansville?" And the apparently meaningless way in
which the inhabitant of Uniontown warms to the inhabitant of Evansville as they name over a few names of
people whom neither of them know well, about whom
neither of them have thought for years, and about whom
neither of them care in the least. And yet, the onlooker,
taking note of the increased warmth in their voices,
of the narrowing of the distance which had separated
them when they first spoke, knows that something has
happened, that a tie has been established [1] between two
people who were lonely before, a tie which every American hopes he may be able to establish as he hopefully
asks every stranger: "What's your home town?"

Americans establish these ties by finding common
points on the road that all are expected to have
traveled, after their forebears came from Europe one
or two or three generations ago, or from one place to
another in America, resting for long enough to establish
for each generation a "home town" in which they grew
up and which they leave to move on to a new town
which will become the home town of their children.
Whether they meet on the deck of an Atlantic steamer,
in a hotel in Singapore, in New York or in San Francisco, the same expectation underlies their first contact—
that both of them have moved on and are moving on
and that potential intimacy lies in paths that have
crossed. Europeans, even Old Americans whose pride
lies not in the circumstance that their ancestors have
moved often but rather in the fact that they have not

moved for some time, find themselves eternally puzzled by this "home town business." Many Europeans fail to find out that in nine cases out of ten the "home town" is not where one lives but where one did live; they mistake the sentimental tone in which an American invokes Evansville and Centerville and Unionville for a desire to live there again; they miss entirely the symbolic significance of the question and answer which say diagrammatically, "Are you the same kind of person I am? Good, how about a coke?"

Back of that query lies the remembrance and the purposeful forgetting of European ancestry. For a generation, they cluster together in the Little Italies, in the Czech section or around the Polish Church, new immigrants clinging together so as to be able to chatter in their own tongue and buy their own kind of red peppers, but later there is a scattering to the suburbs and the small towns, to an "American" way of life, and this is dramatized by an over-acceptance of what looks, to any European, as the most meaningless sort of residence—on a numbered street in Chicago or the Bronx. No garden, no fruit trees, no ties to the earth, often no ties to the neighbors, just a number on a street, just a number of a house for which the rent is $10 more than the rent in the old foreign district from which they moved—how can it mean anything? But it does.

For life has ceased to be expressed in static, spatial terms as it was in Europe, where generation after generation tied their security to the same plot of ground, or if they moved to a city, acted as if the house there, with its window plants, was still a plot of ground anchored by fruit trees. On a plot of ground a man looks around him, looks at the filled spaces in the corner of the garden. There used to be plum trees there, but father cut them down when he was a child; now he has planted young peaches—the plot is filled up again. And he can lean over the wall and talk to the neighbor who has planted plums again—they are the same kind of people, with the same origins and the same future. Having the same origins and the same future, they can dwell in the present which is assumed to be part of one continuous way of life.

But for two Americans, chance met on a train or at adjacent desks in a big office building, working in a road gang or a munition plant or on the same ground crew at an airport, there are no such common origins or common expectations. It is assumed, and not mentioned, that grandparents likely were of different nationality, different religion, different political faith, may have fought on opposite sides of the same battles—that great-great-grandparents may have burned each other at the stake. "My name—Sack. Yes, I know that you know that it was likely something else, likely something you couldn't pronounce, but it's Sack now, see? I was born in Waynesboro." "Your name—Green. I don't even stop to think whether that is a changed name. Too many Greens. An American name. Maybe it had a second syllable before. Did you say you had an uncle in Waynesboro? Well, I declare! Isn't life full of coincidences!" And the president of a national scientific society in making his inaugural address, takes five minutes to mention that the president of another great national society who made *his* inaugural address last week, actually came from the same county and went to the same high school—many years later, of course. "Never"—and his voice, which has just been dealing in fulsome phrases with the role of his profession in the war, now breaks for the first time—"never has such a thing happened before in America." Each and every American has followed a long and winding road; if the roads started in the same spot in Europe, best forget that—that tie leads backwards to the past which is best left behind. But if the roads touched here, in this vast country where everyone is always moving, that is a miracle which brings men close together.

In our behavior, however many generations we may actually boast of in this country, however real our lack of ties in the old world may be, we are all third generation,[2] our European ancestry tucked away and half forgotten, the recent steps in our wanderings over America immortalized and over-emphasized. When a rising man is given an administrative job and a chance to choose men for other jobs, he does not, if he is an American, fill those jobs with members of his family—such conduct is left to those who have never left their foreign neighborhoods, or to the first generation. He does not fill them exclusively with members of his own class; his own class is an accidental cross-section which wouldn't contain enough skills. He can't depend upon his golfing mates or this year's neighbors to provide him with the men he needs. Instead, he fills the jobs with men from somewhere along the road he has traveled, his home town, his home state, his college, his former company. They give him the same kind of assurance that a first-generation Hollywood producer felt when he put his cousins in charge of the accounts—their past and his past are one—at one spot anyway—just as in a kin-oriented society common blood assures men of each other's allegiance. The secretary, trying to shield her boss from the importunities of the office seeker, knows it's no use trying to turn away a man from that little North Dakota college that the boss went to. The door is always open to them, any one of them, any day. And a newspaper headline screams: "Rock of Chickamauga blood still flows in soldiers' veins."

European social scientists look at this picture of American intimacy and fail to understand it. In the first place, they cannot get inside it. An Englishman, who has never been in America before, arriving in Indianapolis and trying to establish relationships with an American who has never been in England, finds himself up against what seems to be a blank wall. He meets hearty greetings, eager hospitality, an excessive attempt to tie the visitor to the local scene by taking him rapidly over its civic wonders, an equally excessive attempt to tie in Uncle Josiah's trip to India with the fact that the guest was reared in the Punjab—and then blankness. But if the Englishman then takes a tour in the Northwest, spends a week in the town where his Indiana host lived as a boy and then returns to Indianapolis, he will find a

very different greeting awaiting him, which he may mis-
takenly put down to the fact that this is a second meeting. Only if he is a very astute observer will he notice
how the path he has taken across the United States has
the power to thaw out any number of hosts at any number of dinner parties.

The wife of the European scientist, now living as a
faculty wife in a small university town in Colorado, will
find herself similarly puzzled. She doesn't seem to get
anywhere with the other faculty wives. Their husbands
and her husband have the same status, the same salary,
perhaps the same degree of world-wide reputation. She
has learned their standards of conspicuous consumption; she can make exactly the same kind of appetizers,
set a bridge table out with prizes just as they do—and
yet, there is no intimacy. Only when both have children
can she and some faculty wife really get together. She
thinks it is the common interest in the children which
forms the tie; actually it is the common experience of
the children, who have something in common which
the two women will never have in the same way—the
same home town, which provides the necessary link, so
fragile, and from a European point of view so meaningless and contentless, and yet, for an American, so essential. Later, even if they have lived childlessly beside each
other, should they meet again in Alaska or Mississippi,
they would be friends—with no real accession of common interests that the European wife could see. For she
does not realize that to Americans only the past can

give intimacy, nor can she conceive how such an incredibly empty contact in the past can be enough.

A group of people travel together from Australia to San Francisco: a manufacturer from Kansas City; a nurse from Sydney; a missionary from India; a young English stockbroker temporarily resident in New York; and a jobber from Perth. They form a fair enough table group on the boat, dance together, go ashore together, and separate on the dock without a shadow of regret. Then, to the amazement of the Englishman, he begins to get letters from the Kansas City manufacturer, reporting on the whereabouts and doings of every one of the ill-assorted group. The man actually keeps up with them—these people who shared three uneventful weeks on an ocean liner.

But it is impossible for all Americans who must work or play together to have a bit of identical past, to have lived, even in such rapidly shifting lives, within a few miles of the spot where the others have lived, at some different period for some different reason. Thin and empty as is the "home town" tie, substitutes for it must be found; other still more tenuous symbols must be invoked. And here we find the enthusiastic preferences for the same movie actor, the same brand of peaches, the same way of mixing a drink. Superficially it makes no sense at all that preference for one brand of cigarette over another may call forth the same kind of enthusiasm that one might expect if two people discovered that they had both found poetry through Keats or both nearly committed suicide on account of the same girl. Only by placing these light preferences against a background of idiosyncratic experience—by realizing that every American's life is different from every other American's; that nowhere, except in parts of the Deep South and similar pockets, can one find people whose lives and backgrounds are both identical or even similar—only then do these feverish grabs at a common theme make sense. English or Dutch residents in the colonies will spend hours sighing over the names of the shops or drinks of their respective Bond Streets, creating in their nostalgia a past atmosphere which they miss in the harsh tropical landscape about them. Americans, in a sense colonials in every part of America, but colonials who have come to have no other home, also create a common atmosphere within which to bask in the present as they criticize or approve the same radio program or moving picture actor.

There is also that other American method of forming ties, the association—the lodge, fraternity, club which is such a prominent feature of American life. Lloyd Warner [3] has described our societies of veterans of past wars as comparable to a cult of the dead which binds a community together, with the veterans of the most distant war lowest in the social scale. Seen from the point of view which I have been discussing, each war creates a magnificent common past for large numbers of men. It is not surprising that those who have the fewest ties among themselves—those whose poverty-stricken way of life admits of few associations—cling longest to this common experience.

Social scientists have observed with mild wonder that among American Indians, ranging the Great Plains before the coming of the white man, there was the same efflorescence of associations,[4] that Blackfoot and Omaha Indians were also joiners. But Blackfoot and Omaha, like the inhabitants of Kansas City and Fort Worth, were also newcomers. They came from a wooded land where the rituals of their lives were localized and particularized to the great undifferentiated open spaces where men had not lived before. Like the Palefaces who came later, they needed new ties and based them upon new patterns of group relationship; and those new patterns served at least as a bulwark against loneliness, in a land so great that the myths are full of stories of groups of playing children who wandered away and were never found until they were grown. So the white man, having left his brothers—in Sicily and Bohemia, in New York and Boston and Chicago—rapidly creates new patterns of social kinship, trying to compensate by rigidness of the ritual for the extemporized quality of the organization, so that men who have no common past may share symbolic adoption into the same fraternal society.

Social scientists, taking their cues from Eastern colleges or from Sinclair Lewis, have been inclined to sneer at the American habit of "joining," at the endless meetings, the clasp of fellowship, the songs, the allegedly pseudo-enthusiasm with which "brothers" greet each other. Safe on the eminence of available intellectual ties and able to gossip together about the famous names and the scandals of their professions, they have failed to appreciate that these associational ties give not the pseudo-security which some European philosopher feels he would get out of them if he had to share in them, but very real security. Not until he has been marooned —his train missed, no taxi available—and driven sixty miles across bad roads in the middle of the night by someone who belongs to another chapter of the same national organization does he begin to realize that the tie of common membership, flat and without content as it is, bolstered up by sentimental songs which no one really likes to sing but which everyone would miss if they weren't sung, has an intensity of its own; an intensity measured against the loneliness which each member would feel if there were no such society.

If this then, this third-generation American, always moving on, always, in his hopes, moving up, leaving behind him all that was his past and greeting with enthusiasm any echo of that past when he meets it in the life of another, represents one typical theme of the American character structure, how is this theme reflected in the form of the family, in the upbringing of the American child? For to the family we must turn for an understanding of the American character structure. We may describe the adult American, and for descriptive purposes we may refer his behavior to the American scene, to the European past, to the state of American industry, to any other set of events which we wish; but to understand the regularity of this behavior we must investigate the family within which the child is reared.

Only so can we learn how the newborn child, at birth potentially a Chinaman or an American, a Pole or an Irishman, becomes an American. By referring his character to the family we do not say that the family is the cause of his character and that the pace of American industry or the distribution of population in America are secondary effects, but merely that all the great configuration of American culture is mediated to the child by his parents, his siblings,* his near relatives, and his nurses. He meets American law first in the warning note of his mother's voice: "Stop digging, here comes a cop." He meets American economics when he finds his mother unimpressed by his offer to buy another copy of the wedding gift he has just smashed: "At the 5 and 10 cent store, can't we?" His first encounter with puritan standards may come through his mother's "If you don't eat your vegetables you can't have any dessert." He learns the paramount importance of distinguishing between vice and virtue; that it is only a matter of which comes first, the pleasure or the pain.[5] All his great lessons come through his mother's voice, through his father's laughter, or the tilt of his father's cigar when a business deal goes right. Just as one way of understanding a machine is to understand how it is made, so one way of understanding the typical character structure of a culture is to follow step by step the way in which it is built into the growing child. Our assumption when we look at the American family will be that each expe-

---

* Sibling is a coined word used by scientists for both brothers and sisters. The English language lacks such a word.

rience of early childhood is contributing to make the growing individual "all of a piece," is guiding him towards consistent and specifically American inconsistency in his habits and view of the world.

What kind of parents are these "third-generation" Americans? These people who are always moving, always readjusting, always hoping to buy a better car and a better radio, and even in the years of Depression orienting their behavior to their "failure" to buy a better car or a better radio. Present or absent, the better car, the better house, the better radio are key points in family life. In the first place, the American parent expects his child to leave him, leave him physically, go to another town, another state; leave him in terms of occupation, embrace a different calling, learn a different skill; leave him socially, travel if possible with a different crowd. Even where a family has reached the top and actually stayed there for two or three generations, there are, for all but the very, very few, still larger cities or foreign courts to be stormed. Those American families which settle back to maintain a position of having reached the top in most cases moulder there for lack of occupation, ladder-climbers gone stale from sitting too long on the top step, giving a poor imitation of the aristocracy of other lands. At the bottom, too, there are some without hope, but very few. Studies of modern youth dwell with anxiety upon the disproportion between the daydreams of the under-privileged young people and the actuality which confronts them in terms of job opportunities. In that very daydream the break is expressed. The daughter who says to her hard-working mother: "You don't know. I may be going to be a great writer," is playing upon a note in her mother's mind which accepts the possibility that even if her daughter does not become famous, she will at least go places that she, the mother, has never gone.

In old societies such as those from which their grandparents and great-grandparents came (and it is important to remember that Americans are oriented towards the Europe from which their ancestors emigrated, not to the Europe which exists today) parents had performed an act of singular finality when they married, before ever a child was born. They had defined its probable place in the sun. If they maintained the same status throughout the child's growing life, kept the necessary bit of ground or inheritance to start him off as befitted him, reared him to act and feel and believe in a way appropriate to "that state of life to which it has pleased God to call him," the parents had done their share. Their service to their child was majorly the maintenance of their own place in the world. His care, his food, his shelter, his education—all of these were by-products of the parents' position. But in America, such an attitude, such a concentration on one's own position makes one, in most cases, a bad parent. One is not just restaking the same old claim for one's child, nor can one stake out the child's new claim for him. All one can do is to make him strong and well equipped to go prospecting for himself. For proper behavior *in* that state of life to which it has pleased God to call one, is substituted proper behavior *towards* that state of life to which God, if given enough assistance, may call one's son and daughter. Europeans laugh at the way in which parents pick for their newborn babies colleges which they have never seen. It does, of course, make sense to plan one's affairs so that one's son goes to the same school one went to oneself; but this fantastic new choice—for a squirming bit of humanity which may after all not have the brains to get through the third grade—is inexplicable. Parenthood in America has become a very special thing, and parents see themselves not as giving their children final status and place, rooting them firmly for life in a dependable social structure, but merely as training them for a race which they will run alone.

With this orientation towards a different future for the child comes also the expectation that the child will pass beyond his parents and leave their standards behind him. Educators exclaim impatiently over the paradox that Americans believe in change, believe in progress and yet do their best—or so it seems—to retard their children, to bind them to parental ways, to inoculate them against the new ways to which they give lip service. But here is a point where the proof of the pudding lies in the eating. If the parents were really behaving as the impatient educators claim they are, really strangling and hobbling their children's attempts to embrace the changing fashions in manners or morals, we would not have the rapid social change which is so characteristic of our modern life. We would not go in twenty years from fig leaves on Greek statues to models of unborn babies in our public museums. It is necessary to distinguish between ritual and ceremonial resistances and real resistances. Among primitive peoples, we find those in which generation after generation there is a mock battle between the young men and the old men: generation after generation the old men lose. An observer from our society, with an unresolved conflict with his father on his mind, might watch that battle in terror, feeling the outcome was in doubt. But the members of the tribe who are fighting the mock battle consciously or unconsciously know the outcome and fight with no less display of zeal for the knowing of it. The mock battle is no less important because the issue is certain.

Similarly, on the island of Bali,[6] it is unthinkable that a father or a brother should plan to give a daughter of the house to some outsider. Only when a marriage is arranged between cousins, both of whose fathers are members of the same paternal line, can consent be appropriately given. Yet there flourishes, and has flourished probably for hundreds of years, a notion among Balinese young people that it is more fun to marry someone who is not a cousin. So, generation after generation, young men carry off the daughters of other men, and these daughters, their consent given in advance, nevertheless shriek and protest noisily if there are witnesses by. It is a staged abduction, in which no one believes, neither the boy nor the girl nor their relatives. Once in a while, some neurotic youth misunderstands and tries to abduct a girl who has not given her consent, and as a result the whole society is plunged into endless confusion, recrimination, and litigation.

So it is in American society. American parents, to the extent that they are Americans, expect their children to live in a different world, to clothe their moral ideas in different trappings, to court in automobiles although their forebears courted, with an equal sense of excitement and moral trepidation, on horsehair sofas. As the parents' course was uncharted when they were young— for they too had gone a step beyond their parents and transgressed every day some boundary which their parents had temporarily accepted as absolute—so also the parents know that their children are sailing uncharted seas. And so it comes about that American parents lack the sure hand on the rudder which parents in other societies display, and that they go in for a great deal of conventional and superficial grumbling. To the traditional attitudes characteristic of all oldsters who find the young a deteriorated version of themselves, Americans add the mixture of hope and envy and anxiety which comes from knowing that their children are not deteriorated versions of themselves, but actually—very actually—manage a car better than father ever did. This is trying; sometimes very trying. The neurotic father, like the neurotic lover in Bali, will misunderstand the license to grumble, and will make such a fuss over his son or daughter when they behave as all of their age are behaving, that the son or daughter has to be very unneurotic indeed not to take the fuss as something serious, not to believe that he or she is breaking father's heart. Similarly, a neurotic son or daughter will mistake the ceremonial grumbling for the real thing, and break their spirits in a futile attempt to live up to the voiced parental standards. To the average child the parents' resistance is a stimulus.

On the east coast, people grumble about the coming of winter, lament over the wild geranium which marks the end of spring, and shudder noisily away from the winter that they would not do without. Occasionally, someone takes this seasonal grumbling seriously and moves to Southern California; but for most people, born and bred in a north temperate climate, the zest and tang of the too cold winter is as essential a part of life as the sultry heat and wilting flowers of the too hot summer. If one were to do a series of interviews among immigrants to Southern California, one would go away convinced that Americans had but one aim, to escape from the dreadful rigors of the north temperate zone into the endless health-giving, but eventless balminess, of a Riviera climate. This would be quite wrong. It would be equally wrong to suppose the Southern Californian insincere in his passionate climatophilism. Just as the flight from the bruising effects of winter to the soothing effects of no winter at all is a part of the American scene, so each generation of Americans produces a certain number of fathers and sons who make personal tragedies out of the changing character of the American scene; tragedies which have their own language, music and folklore, and are an inalienable part of that American scene.

By and large, the American father has an attitude towards his children which may be loosely classified as autumnal. They are his for a brief and passing season, and in a very short while they will be operating gadgets which he does not understand and cockily talking a language to which he has no clue. He does his best to keep ahead of his son, takes a superior tone as long as he can, and knows that in nine cases out of ten he will lose. If the boy goes into his father's profession, of course, it will take him a time to catch up. He finds out that the old man knows a trick or two; that experience counts as over against this new-fangled nonsense. But the American boy solves that one very neatly: he typically does not go into his father's profession, nor take up land next to his father where his father can come over and criticize his plowing. He goes somewhere else, either in space or in occupation. And his father, who did the same thing and expects that his son will, is at heart terrifically disappointed if the son accedes to his ritual request that he docilely follow in his father's footsteps and secretly suspects the imitative son of being a milksop. He knows he is a milksop—or so he thinks—because he himself would have been a milksop if he had wanted to do just what his father did.

This is an attitude which reaches its most complete expression in the third-generation American. His grandfather left home, rebelled against a parent who did not expect final rebellion, left a land where everyone expected him to stay. Come to this country, his rebellious adventuring cooled off by success, he begins to relent a

little, to think perhaps the strength of his ardor to leave
home was overdone. When his sons grow up, he is torn
between his desire to have them succeed in this new
country—which means that they must be more American
than he, must lose entirely their foreign names and
every trace of allegiance to a foreign way of life—and his
own guilt towards the parents and the fatherland which
he has denied. So he puts on the heat, alternately
punishing the child whose low marks in school suggest
that he is not going to be a successful American and
berating him for his American ways and his disrespect
for his father and his father's friends from the old
country. When that son leaves home, he throws himself
with an intersity which his children will not know into
the American way of life; he eats American, talks American, dresses American, he will be American or nothing.
In making his way of life consistent, he inevitably makes
it thin; the overtones of the family meal on which
strange, delicious, rejected European dishes were set,
and about which low words in a foreign tongue wove
the atmosphere of home, must all be dropped out. His
speech has a certain emptiness; he rejects the roots of
words—roots lead back, and he is going forward—and
comes to handle language in terms of surfaces and
clichés. He rejects half of his life in order to make the
other half self-consistent and complete. And by and
large he succeeds. Almost miraculously, the sons of the
Polish day laborer and the Italian fruit grower, the Finn-
ish miner and the Russian garment worker become
Americans.

Second generation—American-born of foreign-born parents—they set part of the tone of the American eagerness for their children to go onward. They have left their parents; left them in a way which requires more moral compensation than was necessary even for the parent generation who left Europe. The immigrant left his land, his parents, his fruit trees, and the little village street behind him. He cut the ties of military service; he flouted the king or the emperor; he built himself a new life in a new country. The father whom he left behind was strong, a part of something terribly strong, something to be feared and respected and fled from. Something so strong that the bravest man might boast of a successful flight. He left his parents, entrenched representatives of an order which he rejected. But not so his son. He leaves his father not a part of a strong other-way of life, but bewildered on the shores of the new world, having climbed only halfway up the beach. His father's ties to the old world, his mannerisms, his broken accent, his little foreign gestures are not part and parcel of something strong and different; they are signs of his failure to embrace this new way of life. Does his mother wear a kerchief over her head? He cannot see the generations of women who have worn such kerchiefs. He sees only the American women who wear hats, and he pities and rejects his mother who has failed to become—an American. And so there enters into the attitude of the second-generation American—an attitude which again is woven through our folkways, our attitude towards other languages, towards anything foreign, towards anything European—a combination of contempt and avoidance, a fear of yielding, and a sense that to yield would be weakness. His father left a father who was the representative of a way of life which had endured for a thousand years. When he leaves his father, he leaves a partial failure; a hybrid, one who represents a step towards freedom, not freedom itself. His first-generation father chose between freedom and what he saw as slavery; but when the second-generation American looks at his European father, and through him, at Europe, he sees a choice between success and failure, between potency and ignominy. He passionately rejects the halting English, the half-measures of the immigrant. He rejects with what seems to him equally good reasons "European ties and entanglements." This second-generation attitude which has found enormous expression in our culture especially during the last fifty years, has sometimes come to dominate it—in those parts of the country which we speak of as "isolationist." Intolerant of foreign language, foreign ways, vigorously determined on being themselves, they are, in attitude if not in fact, second-generation Americans.

When the third-generation boy grows up, he comes up against a father who found the task of leaving his father a comparatively simple one. The second-generation parent lacks the intensity of the first, and his son in turn fails to reflect the struggles, the first against feared strength and the second against guiltily rejected failure, which have provided the plot for his father and grandfather's maturation. He is expected to succeed;

he is expected to go further than his father went; and all this is taken for granted. He is furthermore expected to feel very little respect for the past. Somewhere in his grandfather's day there was an epic struggle for liberty and freedom. His picture of that epic grandfather is a little obscured, however, by the patent fact that his father does not really respect him; he may have been a noble character, but he had a foreign accent. The grandchild is told in school, in the press, over the radio, about the founding fathers, but they were not after all *his* founding fathers; they are, in ninety-nine cases out of a hundred, somebody else's ancestors. Any time one's own father, who in his own youth had pushed his father aside and made his own way, tries to get in one's way, one can invoke the founding fathers—those ancestors of the real Americans; the Americans who got here earlier—those Americans which father worked so very hard, so slavishly, in fact, to imitate. This is a point which the European observer misses. He hears an endless invocation of Washington and Lincoln, of Jefferson and Franklin. Obviously, Americans go in for ancestor worship, says the European. Obviously, Americans are longing for a strong father, say the psycho-analysts.[7] These observers miss the point that Washington is not the ancestor of the man who is doing the talking; Washington does not represent the past to which one belongs by birth, but the past to which one tries to belong by effort. Washington represents the thing for which grandfather left Europe at the risk of his life, and for which father rejected grandfather at the risk of his integrity. Washington is not that to which Americans passionately cling but that to which they want to belong, and fear, in the bottom of their hearts, that they cannot and do not.

This odd blending of the future and the past, in which another man's great-grandfather becomes the symbol of one's grandson's future, is an essential part of American culture. "Americans are so conservative," say Europeans. They lack the revolutionary spirit. Why don't they rebel? Why did President Roosevelt's suggestion of altering the structure of the Supreme Court and the Third-Term argument raise such a storm of protest? Because, in education, in attitudes, most Americans are third generation, they have just really arrived. Their attitude towards this country is that of one who has just established membership, just been elected to an exclusive club, just been initiated into the rites of an exacting religion. Almost any one of them who inspects his own ancestry, even though it goes back many more generations than three, will find a gaping hole somewhere in the family tree. Campfire girls give an honor to the girl who can name all eight great-grandparents, including the maiden names of the four great-grandmothers. Most Americans cannot get this honor. And who was that missing great-grandmother? Probably, oh, most probably, not a grand-niece of Martha Washington.

We have, of course, our compensatory mythology. People who live in a land torn by earthquakes have myths of a time when the land was steady, and those whose harvests are uncertain dream of a golden age when there was no drought. Likewise, people whose lives are humdrum and placid dream of an age of famine and rapine. We have our rituals of belonging, our DAR's and our Descendants of King Philip's Wars, our little blue book of the blue-blooded Hawaiian aristocracy descended from the first missionaries, and our *Mayflower*, which is only equaled in mythological importance by the twelve named canoes which brought the Maoris to New Zealand. The mythology keeps alive the doubt. The impressive president of a patriotic society knows that she is a member by virtue of only one of the some eight routes through which membership is possible. Only one. The other seven? Well, three are lost altogether. Two ancestors were Tories. In some parts of the country she can boast of that; after all, Tories were people of substance, real "old families." But it doesn't quite fit. Of two of those possible lines, she has resolutely decided not to think. Tinkers and tailors and candlestick makers blend indistinctly with heaven knows what immigrants! She goes to a meeting and is very insistent about the way in which the Revolutionary War which only one-eighth of her ancestors helped to fight should be represented to the children of those whose eight ancestors were undoubtedly all somewhere else in 1776.

On top of this Old American mythology, another layer has been added, a kind of placatory offering, a gesture towards the Old World which Americans had left behind. As the fifth- and sixth- and seventh-generation Americans lost the zest which came with climbing got to the top of the pecking order * in their own town or city and sat, still uncertain, still knowing their credentials were shaky, on the top of the pile, the habit of wanting to belong—to really belong, to be accepted absolutely as something which one's ancestors had NOT been—became inverted. They turned towards Europe, especially towards England, towards presentation at Court, towards European feudal attitudes. And so we have had in America two reinforcements of the European class attitudes—those hold-overs of feudal caste attitudes, in the newly-come immigrant who carries class consciousness in every turn and bend of his neck, and the new feudalism, the "old family" who has finally toppled over backwards into the lap of all that their remote ancestors left behind them.

When I say that we are most of us—whatever our origins—third-generation in character structure, I mean that we have been reared in an atmosphere which is most like that which I have described for the third generation. Father is to be outdistanced and outmoded, but not because he is a strong representative of another culture, well entrenched, not because he is a weak and ineffectual attempt to imitate the new culture; he did very well in his way, but he is out of date. He, like us,

* Pecking order is a very convenient piece of jargon which social psychologists use to describe a group in which it is very clear to everybody in it, just which bird can peck which, or which cow butt which other cow away from the water trough. Among many living creatures these "pecking orders" are fixed and when a newcomer enters the group he has to fight and scramble about until everybody is clear just where he belongs—below No. 8 chick, for instance, and above old No. 9.

was moving forwards, moving away from something symbolized by his own ancestors, moving towards something symbolized by other people's ancestors. Father stands for the way things were done, for a direction which on the whole was a pretty good one, in its day. He was all right because he was on the right road. Therefore, we, his children, lack the mainsprings of rebellion. He was out of date; he drove an old model car which couldn't make it on the hills. Therefore it is not necessary to fight him, to knock him out of the race. It is much easier and quicker to pass him. And to pass him it is only necessary to keep on going and to see that one buys a new model every year. Only if one slackens, loses one's interest in the race towards success, does one slip back. Otherwise, it is onward and upward, *towards* the world of Washington and Lincoln; a world in which we don't fully belong, but which we feel, if we work at it, we some time may achieve.

CHAPTER IV

The Class Handicap

*

IT HAS OFTEN been said that America is a middle-class country,[1] that our behavior, our ideals, our manners are middle-class. This statement has been made to mean a variety of things. Sometimes it means that if the average American is compared with a group of Englishmen, his voice and vocabulary, his tempo and his style of life will be more like those of the middle-class Englishmen than like the styles in a peasant hut or manorial hall. It has been taken to mean that if one made a statistical survey of the American people, a majority of them would express aspirations which might be labeled "middle-class." It has been made to mean that we are developing more and more of a class system,[2] or that we are developing less and less of one. It is a statement worth examining.

What is it that distinguishes the middle class [3] in a European country where the class system is a direct modification of a former feudalism? First, the emphasis upon mobility, the expectation that life is a sort of race, a challenge to one's thrift and one's industry, a race in which one can only win if one displays the necessary aspirations and the necessary skill. The member of the upper class rests upon his birth; born a gentleman, only his own act can take from him something that birth and breeding have given him. The member of the lower class rests in a sense on his birth also; born to a certain way of life and without the education which would give him an ambition to change it for the better, he conducts himself in that state of life to which it has pleased God to call him. But the true member of the middle class denies this fixity to which both upper and lower are committed. Life depends, not upon birth and status, not upon breeding or beauty, but upon effort, effort that will be rewarded in riches, in material goods which are the sign that the effort was made, that one has in the language of childhood been "good." The member of the middle class—a class which is historically spoken of as "rising"—is taught from birth that upon his own effort will depend the valuation which is placed upon him.*

* Another aspect of "middle-class character" as it is found in England, and to an exaggerated extent in almost all American families, is that children are brought up by their mothers and taught how to behave towards those mothers by those mothers. Upper-class children are reared by nurses and governesses who teach them indirectly how to behave so that they may enter that vague world in which their parents move. The children of working-class mothers in England are brought up to know how to behave to their betters, but the busy mother has scant time to emphasize how they should treat her. The working-class father may insist on silence, or upon his daughter coming home at a given hour, and threaten or give a beating if he is disobeyed, but the whole thing is impersonal, he is enforcing his right to make his children behave, not teaching them specifically how to behave towards him. But the middle-class mother—to an increasing extent *every* American mother—teaches her child how to

In old and stable societies, where the remnants of feudalism and symbiotic relationships between one class and another linger on, even into the twentieth century, second and third generation members of the middle class borrow from the ideology of feudalism, and think of their position as a birthright instead of a workright, think of it as something to be conserved and consolidated, and as a result we find a "middle middle class" in England, that is, a class of people who no longer see it as their job to push upward, and who are well enough entrenched to lack any deep fear of falling downwards.

behave to her. Whether she says "I won't have you speak to me like that" or "Don't you love mother at all, to go and break that glass," or "I didn't think *my* little boy would forget what he'd promised his mother," she is stressing behavior to a person towards whom one is in warm immediate contact, not illustrating a set of rules as to how other persons are to be treated.

This has various results. Where European children chafe under the authority of a father, and must fight it or throw it off, Americans chafe less against the father but also escape less from the subtle influence [3] of the maternal voice and hand. To be good, is to follow Mother's instructions, most of them prohibitions; and the average American man thinks of good works, town planning, clean politics, etc., as feminine. He never throws his mother's influence off entirely—to do so would be to throw away his most precious childhood relationship—but he chafes under it. Especially in wartime, when he is trying to be a man and really tough with a serious enemy, he becomes very impatient with what he regards as feminine frills, day nurseries, "things for children." In the spring of 1942 there was a sudden almost pathological outburst against the social welfare program of the Office of Civilian Defense, which swept the country like a forest fire. The flames of this outburst were of course fanned by politics and fascism and general reaction, but the outburst originated in the disgruntlement of men who were not in the army, in the bad news from the fighting fronts, in the American man's impatience with the kind of "goodness" which is identified as feminine. As America is a "middle-class" country in this sense of the greater role of the mother in rearing the children and in the peculiar attitudes towards "goody-goodyness" and "frills" which this result, this must also be taken into account in talking of America in "class" terms.

We find the Mittelstand of Germany, in which occupation was as precious as birth as a sign of caste position, and where the threat of factory work to a small shopkeeper or petty official was a threat of social death.

Class thinking, derivative as it is from caste thinking, defines one's own position in terms of one's group. One is a gentleman, or a member of the Mittelstand, or of the Petit Bourgeoisie, etc. Those attributes of the self which serve to classify oneself with a group of other people are jealously guarded and insisted upon. Clothes, address, occupation, invitations to dinner are the signs that one belongs, that one is continuing and will continue to be classified with a given group. Choices are made on a class basis, often inarticulately, but none the less definitely. To make one's son a gentleman is a possible ambition in England for a man who is not a gentleman himself; the right schools, long enough and intensively enough, can do it. A father who is not a gentleman may set his back to the task of providing the wherewithal and paying for the job. When the job is finished, the son and the father do not belong to the same class—their character structure is different.

In America, especially in the old communities of the Eastern seaboard, it is possible to find quite a considerable echo of the European system. Enough people have lived there long enough to establish themselves in a stratified position, to which they do or do not admit newcomers, according as the latters' manners and pocket-books appear to approximate those of the people in possession. Within such a community, where pedigrees are remembered, it is difficult to cross the tracks. This can be done more easily by going to another city, where the exact residence and occupational status of one's parents is not remembered. Furthermore it is possible to make a study of the inhabitants of any *one* community and classify them as: upper upper, lower upper, upper middle, lower middle, upper lower, lower lower,[4] and give a long series of characteristics by which each group may be identified within that community. The overlap is considerable, and it is probable that without our thinking oriented in European terms these three main divisions would not have been chosen as classifications. Even with the European orientation, middle upper, middle middle and middle lower are missing. The lack of these middle positions shows at once that the American system is really a classification based on a ladder, up which people are expected to move, rather than upon orderly stratification or classification of society, within the pigeon-holes of which people are born. What is "an upper upper"? In England, someone born into the families whose titles confer highest rank in a hierarchy. In America, someone whose only possible social movement is downward. Taken the country over, they have no distinguishing manners and no distinguishing morals and no distinguishing occupation or lack of it. They are simply people whose family arrived at the top of a particular ladder long enough ago so that no one whom they will ever encounter will be able to demote them by references to railroad tracks. They can enter any house they

like, and have, in fact, nowhere to go that is up—
unless they go outside this country and try to get themselves fitted into the hierarchical system of the English Court, where, be it noted, they immediately lose
their upper-upper, their unassailable position, and start
to move again.

Because this upper-upper position lacks any definition beyond its place at the top of a shifting ladder,
Americans have developed a very slight set of ethics to
define the obligations of class. The young man of upper-
upper birth is faced with the choice between picking an
occupation in which he will have to work as any middle-
class young man would, and playing. Since America
lacks a feudal system and any pattern of behavior derived from a fixed caste system, when one is at the top
one is at the top, and that is all.

Not that being at the top doesn't give one a point of
view, a character structure, somewhat different from
the rest of the people in town. The sense that even if
one gets as drunk as a lord people will still recognize
one as a Livingstone has its security-giving points, permits a casualness in dress and manners which is denied
to all of those who are still climbing the ladder. The
absence of effort and the confident security is apparent.
Recently I asked a large group of college students to
write papers comparing their own families' way of life
with the way of life in some South Sea culture, in Samoa,
or New Guinea. When asked to give their class, they
classified themselves as upper class, as upper middle
class, or, in the few cases of girls who came from small

rural communities, merely in terms of the parental occupation—"My father is a lawyer." They listed the details of their way of life, number of bathrooms, of motor-cars, of servants, of who got together the supper on Sunday night and who used the back stairs, but it was impossible from such lists to distinguish the group which had called themselves upper class from the group which had called themselves upper middle. There was only one distinctive difference; most of the "upper class" girls simply studied the style of life of the top-ranking family among the primitive peoples they were discussing and then with considerable flexibility and imagination compared their own upper class family with the Samoan or Manus family of rank. But the girls who had placed themselves as "upper middle" displayed instead a moral and disapproving attitude; there was no way in which they could compare themselves with those horrid savages, who had no sense of privacy, or did not bathe at the right moment. They demonstrated in their moral valuation of life how completely they saw life in terms of moral behavior and its rewards, rather than as a hierarchy or structural system within which one had an established place. The security of those who have arrived and now have nothing else to do but sit, was lacking.

Just as the American "upper upper" is defined by having got to the top of the ladder, so also the American "lower lower" is someone whose position cannot be bolstered by finding anyone lower than himself within a given community. If he lives in a community without

Negroes, the first Negro who enters the community will give him a lift in his own eyes. If he has lived in an old American community where everyone spoke English, the first foreign accent in someone of comparable occupational status is a step up for him. If his English is still faulty and his low status is merely a function of his being the most recently arrived member of the laboring group, the next arrivals, with English even less adequate than his, will give him shoulders on which to mount. His position is purely relative; it has no content. No one can say what a lower-lower class man in the United States will eat, or wear, what religion he will profess, whether he will be law-abiding or a thief, whether he will be literate or illiterate. No one can sketch the gesture of obeisance with which he will acknowledge superior status; it may be a "Sir," it may be a scornful spray of tobacco juice in the general direction of the man of higher social status. There is no difficulty within any given community in identifying him, by a simple process of arranging everyone on a scale and lumping together at the bottom those people who do not claim much superiority to each other, and over whom all others will claim superiority. But if one tries to put side by side a lower-lower from a New England city and a New England village, a middle western town, a mining camp, a summer resort, a mill town and a cotton ranching country—only by keeping one's eye clearly on the ladder, only by asking the original question, "Is anyone lower than he?" can one arrive at the classification.

True, careful studies, such as those of Warner and

Lunt, Gardiner and Davis,[2] make it possible for us to predict the social position of an individual about whom we have any one of a number of classifying data, in the given community or region which they have studied. It is reasonably safe to guess that a member of the Episcopal Church, in certain parts of the East, will claim and be accorded higher status than members of the Baptist Church or the Methodist Church. If one adds to such a datum, occupation, type of house, schooling of children, and magazines read, it is possible to arrive at the classification which was originally derived from just such data. It is even possible to make such very pretty correlations as Warner's finding that if one examines the auxiliaries of patriotic societies, one finds the average status of the women in them to be one sub-class lower than the average status of the men in the main society. In other words, men slum for various professional and political reasons in patriotic societies, women do not. Such a regularity is very pretty and consistent. But still there probably is no single item in the distinguishing marks which one can array for the various "classes" which is reliable by itself. Even those which are grounded in income, such as ownership of a yacht or playing polo, only place a man on certain several rungs of the ladder. And if a member of the upper upper class of Baltimore should turn up in shabby clothes with ten cents in his pocket in Billings, Montana, he would find it very difficult to document his position, unless there happened to be some other member of the upper class of the Eastern seaboard about. Former residents of Baltimore might be able to identify him if they had known him personally, but not by his bearing and accent, as would be the case in England. The very facts that only among those with whom they habitually associate can upper-uppers put on cheap clothing without fear of being taken for just anyone at all, insulted by doormen and refused entrance to clubs, and that lower-lowers properly clad can go anywhere where one does not require a pedigree or a personal invitation, demonstrate the lack of any absolute class standards in this country.

In this respect American society is very like a fish society, based as it is on length of residence in a community rather than upon original antecedents or special personality characteristics. Among chickens and cows and monkeys, a strong animal will take up a position related to its own strength; when it is moved into a new flock or herd or horde, it will experiment to find out which animals it is strong enough to knock around and to which animals it must submit. This sort of pecking order or butting order gets established in old societies, so that certain individuals carry in their voice and gesture a statement that they have a certain privileged position, a hereditary right to peck or liability to be pecked. But among certain species of fish,[5] the only thing which determines order of dominance is length of time in the fish-bowl. The oldest resident picks on the newest resident, and if the newest resident is removed to a new bowl, he as oldest resident will pick on the newcomers. Social dominance in these fish societies is not a function of strength or intelligence or beauty, or least of all of course birth, but of the situation. So, in the United States, within a given community, at a given period, accurate classifications can be made, classifications of where the Joneses and the Pierces and the Elliotts belong, and as long as members of these families have to operate inside that community, these classifications will hamper their movements or facilitate them. When they or their offspring leave those communities, the memory of those old positions will cling to their voices, giving an extra assurance to the manner of those whose classification was high, an extra anxiety to the voice of a man who is now a successful lawyer but whose father was a janitor. The fluid moving society which is America often petrifies and crystallizes long enough to leave a mark, both in the character of some individuals and in the ideas of many others. So the knowledge that if one moved to Philadelphia one would not be invited to the Assembly can be used as a symbol to embitter the life of a successful climber in Wichita, and the knowledge that one's parents ate and still eat in the kitchen can jeopardize the pleasure with which a university professor enjoys the rosy candlelight and old linen at the college president's table, and can give enormous relish to the discovery that the college president's wife's father kept a garage.

Almost every American, the newest immigrant and the member of an old, old family, carries with him, in some facet of his mind, the mark of these petrified pecking orders. Yet, with extraordinarily few exceptions, when a host or hostess tells the special guest about the people he is going to meet, the information supplied is not who their families were, but what they or their husbands do. Only in those centers of American life where the rites and observances appropriate to the precarious attainment of social petrifaction are observed, does "She was a Brammerly" supersede "He's just been elected Vice President of National Brands."

Class in America is in fact part of the success game. "How much did you have to start with? Hm, not much, started with a big handicap. And how far did you get?" "How much did he have? Oh, didn't you know, he is one of *the* Gordons. Hm, born with a silver spoon in his mouth, I suppose every step of the way was smoothed for him." "And, my dear, she never got in. Not with all his millions and her looks and everything. She never got *in*." One point down for her. It just shows that her success so dazzling, so almost complete, needn't make the speaker, who is in and unsuccessful, or out and unsuccessful, feel quite as inferior as she otherwise might. For the American success system, in which each man plans to die in a position higher than the position in which he was born, and which therefore robs our upper-uppers of a zest for living because it is relative, carries with it an unfortunate need to depreciate the success of others at the same time that one maximates the success which one has attained oneself. So, as two opponents in a game may count up points and honors, one opponent scores for what he has, by birth, which the other can't get, while the other scores for what he has got by effort without birth, for the fact that he has outdistanced other men in energy, in the display of that virtue which alone makes success tolerable.

It is possible to describe the American system without mentioning class, to talk instead of the premium on success, and to go directly to the dynamics of character formation which lie back of the American will to succeed. If our European observer, who has haunted these pages, could be eliminated, I think that is the way it would be done. An observer from a country without a feudal past, or an observer from a country still in the feudal state, would find our whole bewildering network of pecking orders and temporary crystallization of status to have so little form as to be unworthy of primary mention. But that hypothetical European observer is no accident, but a continuing part of our lives. Since the first colonists began to move back and forth across the seas, Americans have looked at themselves, anxiously, appraisingly, through European eyes. "Is there such a thing as an American gentleman?" The question asked in the eighteenth century has never been answered to the complete satisfaction of any American, and so some protest too much and some attend too little. "Are share-croppers peasants?" And another question gets under the skin of those of us who have been led to believe that all the ancestors fought and suffered to build a country in which no such thing as a feudal system could exist. "Will the middle class, threatened by modern streamlining, go fascist?" Newcomers from Central Europe shudder over the revolutionary possibilities of taking shops away from shop-keepers, and ignore the steady procession of school teachers (surely a "middle-class occupation") who are racing each other for employment in bombing plants. "The problem will never be solved until the working class tackles it itself," say the labor leaders who have read deeply in European political literature. "Seattle is a strange town!" exclaims the new-comer from the East. "Why, here you have a worker in Boeing's living right next door to a superintendent of a store, and a *big* store too." Echo after echo, question after question from Europe, resounds through American ideology, and class, one of the principal ways of conceding or withholding recognition from other people, is used freely as a social weapon. Anyone who is conscious of class, or whose position theoretically identifies him as interested in the subject—this includes social scientists, visiting Englishmen, newcomers to a town who are asking for guidance in the local labyrinth —will be supplied with an endless amount of comment on the subject. Anyone in America can be made uneasy by invoking some class point, even though one may have to go to the Court of St. James to get the necessary symbol, or make a phonograph recording to demonstrate a vulgar accent.

Yet, when I say that class is not dynamic, I mean something very definite. People can be made afraid by class, they can be reassured by class, they can suffer because of class-typed behavior, but they do not act because of class except in pathological cases where this special form of mobility has become an obsession. Goals are not stated in class terms, but in pecking order terms and in terms of the outward and visible signs of success. To get ahead, to make good—these are the goals which are impressed on American children—to go some place else, get on with it, count your success by the number of less handicapped that you have passed on the road. Where an English upper-class child is reared to *be a gentleman,* an absolute term, an American child may sometimes be brought up to be a member of a given family, an Adams, or a Lowell, in other words to perpetuate someone else's success, not to be a success, which is a relative statement. How can you tell that a man is a success? Only by knowing how far he has come, how many he has passed, what he has in the way of power and possessions. What he is—as a person—is irrelevant, for to be a success is to have done something, rather than to have been a kind of person. Pride at being at the top is soured if it is based on someone else's climbing, and so the sons of rich men are driven back into harness, back to the office to show what they have in them.

When the European thinks about America, he asks questions like: What is happening to the middle class? Will the proletariat revolt? Is the American class system becoming more rigid? Is it tottering? Is it not, however, more relevant to ask: Has the American scene shifted so that we still demand of every child a measure of success which is actually less and less possible for him to attain? Have we made the symbols of success so definite and so clear—measured in houses and motor-cars and fur coats and expensive college educations—that it is impossible to shift them with a shifting economic system? Have we made it a condition of success that a man should reach a position higher than his father's, when such an achievement (for the many) is dependent upon the existence of a frontier and an expanding economy? Have we given the moral accolade only for material success and so condemned to a sense of failure and ignominy all of those who were plunged downward by the Depression? [6] If we demand that a man must succeed to be regarded as good, how difficult do we dare to make that success without running the risk of breaking the hearts and minds of the many who fail? Not: Is the American class system likely to crack or crystallize; but rather: Is the American success system flexible enough to adjust to changing conditions? That is the question.

CHAPTER V

The European in Our Midst

★

THE EUROPEAN, whose comments, whose bewilderment and whose special interpretations of American culture have cropped up time and again in this attempt to sketch in some of the most characteristic and most puzzling of American attitudes, is not, as he might easily be thought to be, merely a fictional personality, a straw man or a whipping post. All through American history, from the day the first colonist set foot on his section of stern and rock-bound coast, we have seen America through European eyes, first the landscape, the savages and the foodstuffs, later the manners and customs which the earlier colonists developed in response to the new country and its new demands. Always two standards of value, what we thought of the people who were less American, less placed, less equipped with American ancestry than ourselves; and the other question, what the European writer, visitor, or critic thought of us. Life has become a sort of circle in which our highest critics and our humblest residents both stem from the same civilization, and the same people who cringe before a

Czech playwright or a French poet will exclaim against "that impossible woman, why, she speaks broken English. We can't have people like that in the Chapter!" Parvenus from the standpoint of Europe, we regard as parvenus all Europeans who come here to stay. The same woman who would rather die than have her daughter marry someone who was only second generation, will think it distinguished for a daughter to marry someone who grew up in Europe and came here trailing the remnants of the class structure behind him.

Gradually a dichotomy has developed between those things in terms of which we permit Europe to look down upon us, and those things in terms of which we look down on Europeans: art, "culture," music, "things of the spirit," "the suavity of diplomats and statesmen," "mellow maturity"—these we concede and meanwhile we reserve the material and moral worlds for our own superiority—better plumbing, friendlier personal relations, more moral marriages, more interest in children, a "healthier, more normal," younger and more robust form of life. We have more democracy and more peace, more freedom. America is a new man's country—or God's! Europe is old and effete, and so it was left to the women of America to cultivate the arts, arts in which Europe was conceded superiority. The longer women cultivated them, the surer the men became that they were feminine and effete.

This is old history. Generation after generation, the voice of the European traveler has boomed and patronized. Students have left this country for the Left Bank of the Seine for so long that it is hard to think what it must be like to have grown up in a student generation in which no one wanted to go to Paris. Russia replaced France in the idealization of the students and the deviants, and because France had stood for the arts and Russia stood for politics, it was not recognized that here again Americans, dissatisfied at home, were turning back to Europe for something to which to give allegiance. The habit of giving deference to other people's ancestors—which we have practiced so long on the founding fathers—became complete. It was not a question of those of French descent turning back to France or those of Russian to Russia. Experience in America had broken, more surely than ever before in history, the tie between blood and ideals, between land of birth and land of political dreaming. Most radicals, in literature, in art, in politics, were Americans who depended upon a European inspiration. As such they have been fought in America with a fury which cannot be explained by mere references to bourgeois mentality. Precariously balanced against a sort of political background which has never been developed before and for which there are inadequate sanctions, the American is specially frightened of these artifact nostalgias for the Left Bank or the Soviet Union, and is especially cruel in his persecution of them.

For three centuries we have been living through this paradox by which all Europeans who were dissatisfied with Europe, or with whom the ruling powers of Europe were dissatisfied, came to America to embrace a new way of life and a new idealism. From the flexibility of this new idealism, its lack of geographical and genealogical roots, there arose new idealisms, and their exponents turned back on their forebears' tracks, and went looking for the things which were lacking in America—as well they might be, America having been constructed by people who ran away from them in Europe. Order, form, discipline, style—all of the attributes of old and settled culture where the same gestures which are found in 12th century statues of the saints recur in the hand postures of the townsmen today —these the Europeans told us were lacking in our lives, and we, trained from childhood to feel that dissatisfaction was a prelude to searching for that which we lacked, kept going back to Europe to look for the missing solutions.

For all our lives, our own and those of our ancestors who lived in America, have been spent in measuring up to an unknown standard—learning to live in a world that did not exist for us yet, finding no clues where all other peoples have found clues—in the behavior of our parents. You must be a success. What does that mean? Doing what father did? Certainly not, any more than you would like to drive a 1913 model of a Stanley Steamer. Driving a 1962 model? More like it, much more like it. But a 1962 model of what—an automobile or an aeroplane? There's the rub. Meanwhile, what did that fellow say the other day about the 1942 model and its defects—how it still compared badly with a Rolls Royce or Renault?

It's a bleak and lonely business looking into the future, modeling one's life on an undrawn blueprint. It was all very well when one was first generation; learn English, learn to dress and eat and walk and gesture like an American. Learn the intricacies of ward politics and the big leagues. It was all very well in the second generation, going to college, making the "right friends" moving in circles one's parents couldn't have entered. That was what they expected and that is what one did. It was pretty good in the third generation—an American now, without effort, taking it in one's stride, doing better than one's father, planning for one's son to go further still.

If the first generation started poor enough and had bad enough luck, the American dream could last more than three generations before it became an empty myth, before the sharecropper, tied to his land in ignorance and hopelessness, came to feel that he had always lived there and always would. Something of the optimism of the first generation attitude could survive to make people humble and uncritical and accepting— even of the terrible starvation of the Depression. After all this is not quite our country, once fair and prosperous, now conquered and depressed. It is, for every one of us, somebody else's country—Columbus' or the Indians' or God's; or it belongs to the *Mayflower's* complement of passengers; or it belonged to Sir Walter Raleigh or Pocahontas or perhaps Balboa—he saw the Pacific first. We came here, of our own accord, in great pride over what we could do with these endless plains and forests. If we've failed—well—it is we who have failed. There is no one else to blame, no dynasty of Bourbons, no Junker class, no Hanoverian kings, no entrenched Church, no landlords who had oppressed man through the ages. This was a free country with free institutions, where each man could hew his way up to success, barefoot and out of any log cabin. This belief that "any boy can be President" has been described by John Dollard as a euphemism for "dog eat dog." But it is something more. It is the final statement of moral responsibility for success. The gibe which always comes so rudely from the lips of "Americans" speaking to "foreigners"—"If you don't like this country, go back where you came from!" is not as unfair as it seems, for the people who live here have accepted, in the very quietude with which they lived through years without bread, the terrible burden of choice. The man who does not riot, when after years of conscientious toil he is laid off overnight without an explanation, has a sort of right to turn to the foreign-born rioter and say: "Why do you, who came here of your own accord, think that you can throw a stone through the window of a house you did not help to build, just because the roof leaks this week? Why didn't you stay home and fix the leaky roofs in your own country? Why generation after generation have you run away to this country, and left your own in a parlous state, if it was revolution you wanted instead of just a chance to work?" It does not matter that he is also talking to himself, quieting his own doubts, stilling any revolutionary stirrings in his own breast.

"You say there isn't any democracy in this country, don't you? You who were carried here in the arms of parents fleeing from a pogrom or a massacre. Sure, we ain't perfect. We got a long way to go. But the way to get there is to make something new, not break something old. Just push the old stuff aside, get on out and hustle and go places and stop brooding. More business makes more jobs and more jobs mean more cars and more cars mean everybody is going places—that's the American way. Let's go places."

But for the fourth generation American who is the fourth of a line of successful men—and here I speak symbolically and not for purposes of accurate description—the "places" which he is all dressed up for are undefined. He keeps the moral purpose, the assurance that it is his business as a human being somehow to play a role in a world that is better than his father's and his grandfather's. He realizes, as the third generation did not, that the cars and bath-tubs and refrigerators are not substance but symbol of the good life, and that the good life has still to be built.

But what is he to do? He is an American. Americans have traditionally given of their energy and their devotion in the service of someone else's dream. "Aye, call it holy ground, the ground where THEY first trod." So when there is new dreaming to be done, we do not think of looking inside our own heads for the plans. Young Americans go back to Europe, to Russia, if their dream is based upon a happier human life; to Germany or Italy, if dark specters of hostility and need for power darken their minds. They may even go looking somewhere else inside America.

For regionalism, American folk art—all the efflorescent search for a real American way of life—is often just that, looking somewhere else inside America instead of somewhere else outside, for a pattern, a clue, a line against the sky, a hay barn or a barn dance, or a boll of cotton. Not our barn, our street corner, our town hall, but that of some other part of the country. The city man goes to the small town, the small town man to the wilds, the Northerner to the South, the Southerner to the West, looking for clues to inform this way of life gone suddenly stale in their hands. We are ourselves willing vessels, but with what shall we be filled? We have been schooled so long in the need to succeed in mastering someone else's way of life and then ardently claiming it as ours, not by birth but by right of arduous capture, by right of immigration and the painful learning of new vowel sounds and new gestures. We have moved towards the future wearing always the guise of the past, and become good Americans who accepted Washington, good Americans when we learned the meaning of Valley Forge.

Schools, seen first as a way of making one's children in America the literate and educated men which they could not be in Europe, became very quickly a way of turning other people's children into a closer version of one's own. With the next turn of the wheel they became a way of turning everybody's children into something that the parents were not.[1] But where to go? The teaching of the arts is a vivid example of the dilemma. Our art schools have sometimes enshrined tradition and taught the child to draw from casts and models of the studios, to imitate an Old Master's line. But that line remains to him dead in all its loveliness because it has no relation to his immediacy of feeling, because if the child learns to love it he himself will die to all that moves the men around him and wander forever lost among ghosts. That is one way. Other schools have left the children free, given them great lush brushes packed with raw color, given them pots of paint and let them use their sensitive inquiring fingers to map out the dimensions of their hearts, on very large sheets of paper. They have given them no tradition, no pattern, no single constricting instruction. And what do we find? From the little child on whom the traditions of his society still rest lightly, beneath which his own peculiar undisciplined rhythms still thump with recognizable vigor—we get again lovely lines. But then as the shades of the prison house begin to close about the growing boy—and close they will as for his own spontaneity he learns to substitute a posture and gesture which nine times out of ten would not have been his by choice—he loses this communication with his own heart, and there is nothing left. Out of the grandiose and beautiful and pathetic drawings of the nursery school, no new art develops.[2] Freedom is not enough. Freedom that is its own goal has no design, but is only an impulse, an impulse in the case of Americans that is so strong that it eats at our vitals—a stolen fox hidden against our hearts.

The European is in our midst, either learning our ways and becoming like us, an American who is morally devoted to success in an endless race, or not learning our ways, scorning us and turning his eyes back to the Europe that has disowned him. We cannot shake him off, we cannot ignore him, we have assimilated into our national character both his patience and his eagerness in the face of American life, and his scornful impatience of its lack of design. The humility of the immigrant stays our hand when we would rise up and denounce patronizing comment upon our way of life which brings us only humiliation. This paradox is woven into our speech, into our use of phrases like "old-world beauty" as approval and "foreign" as disapproval, into an eternal ambivalence towards ways which are older and more definite, less atomistic and more patterned than ours. With our insistence upon the importance of building something new, we have combined a tremendous valuation upon anything which someone else has finished. Innovation is our ideal but conformity is our mentor. How to blend them for a New World which lies not in the New World, is not entirely of it, and yet could not have been without it?

CHAPTER VI

Parents, Children and Achievement

★

THERE ARE SEVERAL WAYS of studying a culture. We first look at the behavior of the human beings who are representatives of that culture, and from their behavior we arrive at a systematic description—which we call their "culture." We then must ask how does that type of behavior become part of those human beings, how in fact do they, once unco-ordinated bits of newborn humanity, acquire this particular set of patterns which we are now able to discern? We can either ask the question: What are Americans? and get for answer a flat or static picture, or we can ask: How does one become an American? and the answer to this second question will give us a picture of the changing and growing individual. As we follow the newborn baby through babyhood and schooldays, through getting a job and leaving home and setting up a home of his own, we get a glimpse of the dynamics of the American character.

There is a third question which many people ask but which will not be asked in this book: *Why* are Americans as they are?—a question which looks towards a few historical causes. It may be argued that such historical phenomena as immigration, as the wide frontier and the unpatterned landscape have been invoked. But these have been invoked as descriptions of the current American character, as a means of indicating what he preserves of the past in his present behavior. Why these particular items of the past, this selection of the conspicuous circumstances of the settling of America, have left their residues, and others, themes which have no present embodiment, have disappeared, we do not ask. As each new generation worked out its adjustments to the American scene, an imprint was left on American institutions which those individuals embodied and perpetuated.

The American language may be taken as an example. In areas where English immigrants brought with them the speech of sixteenth and seventeenth century England, we find a language more archaic in syntax and usage then present-day English. Cut off from the main stream, these pockets of English have survived. But the American language, as written in the newspapers, as spoken over the radio, as captioning the movies, is not the language of those whose ancestors have spoken Elizabethan English for generations, nor is it the language of those whose scholars have gone back each generation to Latin and Greek sources to refresh their sense of how their language has developed. It is instead the language of those who learned it late in life and learned it publicly, in large schools, in the factory, in the ditches, at the polling booth, at the post office and the savings bank. It is a language of public, external relationships. While the American-born generation was learning this public language, the private talk which expressed the overtones of personal relationships was still cast in a foreign tongue. When they in turn taught their children to speak only American, they taught them a one-dimensional public language, a language oriented to the description of external aspects of behavior, weak in overtones. To recognize this difference one has only to compare the vocabulary with which Hemingway's heroes and heroines attempt to discuss their deepest emotions with the analogous vocabulary of an English novel. All the shades of passion, laughter close to tears, joy tremulous on the edge of revelation, have to be summed up in such phrases as: "They had a fine time." Richness in American writing comes from the invocation of objects which themselves have overtones rather than from the use of words which carry with them a linguistic aura. This tendency to a flat dimension of speech has not been reduced by the maintenance of a classical tradition. Our literati themselves are coming to have little Latin and no Greek, and our words lack both the depth of meaning which comes from early exercise in expressing delicate and deep personal relationships, and the formal precision which comes from awareness of past and different usage.

This change in language has come about because the language was used, was spoken, was written, by those who had learned it in a particular way. But today, the American who uses American in this characteristic fashion may well be a tenth generation descendant of English stock, living in Iowa or California. Individuals with a certain type of experience have left an imprint on the way in which one of the fundamental American institutions is used, and all Americans have come to share in the change. It is in this sense that the contributions of first, second, third and fourth generation Americans have been discussed. Their contributions, their versions of the American way of life, have become part of a common heritage, shared by the majority of American children, so that in the voice of the great-grand-niece of a revolutionary lady, there echoes the peculiar sentiment, the stridency, the insistence of some first generation immigrant, just as surely as in the voice of an immigrant's baby there are tones and phrases which may be attributed to the influence of the lady's forebears two hundred years ago. When we ask how babies become Americans, we are asking how all these precipitates, in the American language, in American jokes and American songs, in American attitudes towards politics and the world and the universe, which were originally created by the attempt of many diverse peoples to assimilate themselves to a pattern which others would accept as identical with their own, have been re-created in the upbringing of the growing child.

The American baby is born into a family which is isolated from both paternal and maternal lines of kindred.[1] His parents typically live in a house by themselves. If they do not, they seek to create some sort of social isolation to recompense themselves for the presence of relatives. The mother dreams in secret of the day when "John's mother won't have to live with us any more," and the father hopes that "One of Mary's brothers will be able to take Mary's mother before long." This attitude is conveyed to the baby. He learns that only his father and his mother are really relevant to his life, that grandparents should live at a distance if at all, and are not really necessary. There is no occasion on which their presence is essential. If they are all dead, he experiences no sense of loss, no feeling that his own place in the world is compromised or incomplete. But he learns that parents—a father and mother—and a sibling of opposite sex—a little brother for a girl, a little sister for a boy—are essential to make up a "family." [2] As his baby fingers scuffle through the pages of the *Saturday Evening Post* or the *Ladies' Home Journal*, he sees picture after picture of a family, the family for which a man takes correspondence courses, buys life insurance and puts money in the savings bank, the family which now in wartime is working together on the farm to feed a soldier and a sailor, the family which is the other part of the sailor far away on the high seas. When mother and children occur alone in a picture, the father is implied, coming home from work, away defending them, working for them, thinking of them. Every picture a child sees, every skit over the radio, every song or popular phrase, reaffirms the importance of having a family, that one is not either safe or sound without one. Meanwhile, when he goes to school, sometimes before he goes to school, he encounters the phenomenon of adoption. Some children don't belong to their families at all—they are adopted. The people who mention the subject to him are very mixed in their feelings on the subject. His mother is far less tolerant of the bad behavior of her friend's adopted child than of the behavior of another friend's own child. The adopted child carries with it the stigma of belonging to some other family, an unknown, disintegrated, probably immoral family, the kind of family which vanishes off the map and leaves its children all alone. And some children don't know they are adopted. That he learns also. The scene is set against which he can come to doubt and question his own place in his own family.

In old societies when the extended family or the clan is still an important part of the way of life, the child moves easily among many relatives, many of whom bear his name, with some one of whom he can almost certainly find a community of interest and even a common physique. But in America, with the family whittled down to father and mother, a child may often feel he is like neither of them. The fact that two parents are all the anchors he has in a world which is otherwise vague and shifting, over-emphasizes the tie and brings it into question. And so the phantasy of adoption develops, the fear which grips so many children's hearts that they are adopted, that they don't really belong anywhere at all. The day comes when both father and mother seem strange, forbidding figures, enforcing some meaningless moral code in a meaningless world. At first it gives a fine feeling of rebellion to say: "I don't care what you say.

I am not your child anyway. My father and mother were a king and a queen and you are nothing but gypsies who carried me off," or: "I won't listen to a word you say. I am not your child. I don't look like you. I don't think like you. I don't feel like you. And I won't come out from under the bed," but afterwards, when the anger has worn off, the child is left with a terrible fear that maybe the words spoken in stubborn rejection are true. The children who are adopted, the children who have feared they were adopted, all serve to exaggerate for each American child his dependence on his father and mother, of whom there is only one edition in the whole world. From broken homes come our delinquents and our neurotics; from unbroken homes come the ordinary Americans, terribly impressed with the fragility and importance of those homes which made them into regular fellows, not children about whom other children whispered and whom teachers and neighbors commiserated.

From this curious structure of the American family, from the fact that two young people, often of quite diverse backgrounds, are sent out into the world together to make a way of life, with no oldsters by to help them, with no guides except the movies, the pulp magazines and the fumbling experiences of those very little older than themselves, it follows also that each child's experience will be different from each other's. However much his mother may study the daily specials, may deck his baby carriage in the type of tailored cover in style this year, and dress him in the most approved sun suit or slacks, beneath the outward conformity there lies always the mother's sense of difference. How does her marriage compare with that of the other women who stroll beside her with their impeccably dressed babies? She doesn't know, she doesn't dare to ask, even if she had words in which to ask such a question. The questions themselves might betray her, might betray some peculiarity in her own make-up or some inadequacy in her husband. The endless query: "Am I happy?" can in part be translated into the question: "How close am I to what I should expect to be?" Back of her lies her single experience with family life—her view of her own parents. She lives in the only other experience she may ever have. She cannot know how her worried version of life compares with the average, with the normal, with those who are "really" happy. And her voice is sharp as she admonishes her child if he deviates from the public behavior which is common for all of the children of the block, if he fights when they don't or fails to fight when they do. The basis of her life, her membership in her new family, like her membership in her old one, is secret, and probably deviates in a thousand ways from that which others would respect and envy—if they knew. To compensate for this, she insists on conformity. Their house, their car, their clothes, their patterns of leisure time, shall be as much like other people's as possible. Her face cream, her powder, her lipstick, shall be publicly validated. But inside the walls of that home, there is no one to tell her, or to tell her husband, whether their expectations are too high or too low, no one to quote from the experience of other generations, no yardstick, no barometer.

Some of this desperate uncertainty is conveyed to the baby, as she dresses him to take him out, as she undresses him when she brings him in. Just as virtually no American family is completely certain of its social antecedents, or can produce a full complement of unblotted escutcheons, so also no American family is sure of its position on an unknown chart called "happiness." The mother anxiously searches her baby's face. Are his "looks" something which should make her happy, is his health something which shows she is a good mother, does he walk and talk early enough to be a credit to her, to prove to others and so prove to herself that she has a right to be what she wants to be—happy? From the day when self-conscious fathers stand outside the glass-walled hospital nursery and anxiously compare the shape of their own babies' heads with those of the other babies, the child is valued in comparative terms, not because he is of the blood and bone and "name" of his parents, but because of his place on some objective (but undefined) rating scale of looks and potential abilities. In his parents' every gesture, the child learns that although they want to love him very much, although they hope they will love him very much—for loving your children is one of the things that books say parents do—they are not quite sure that he will deserve it, that when they check him up against the baby book and the neighbors' baby he will come out A-1 and so worthy of complete blind love.

Each civilization conveys different things to its children. The Balinese mother [3] mimicking a desperate fear as she calls the wandering child back to her side teaches him forever after to fear the unknown, to cling, he knows not why, to well-trodden paths. *"Aroh!"* she shrieks, "Wild cat!" or "Witch!" or "Snake!" or "Fire!", making no effort to adapt the scare word to the circumstance. If she screamed "Snake" when the child went into the grass, and "Scorpion" when he climbed the wood-pile, he might learn to look and find patches of grass without snakes and piles of wood without scorpions. But instead any scare word in any context will do; the child gets no chance to test reality out, he remains frightened of an unknown.

"He's so strong," says the Iatmul [3] mother. "He runs so fast. I can't catch him." "When I catch him I will hit him and kill him," she says, as she pretends to chase and fails to catch her erring two-year-old. She acts as if the child were as strong and fleeter of foot than she, and the terrified baby, pushed beyond his endurance into an assertive role for which he is not ready, learns that safety lies in stamping and shouting and pretending to be bigger and stronger and fiercer than one really is.

Not with a single phrase or a single gesture, not with one punishment alone, but in every tone of the voice, in each turn of the head, these nuances are conveyed to the child, and as the Balinese baby learns that the unknown is always to be avoided, and the Iatmul baby learns to play at being strong, the American baby learns that its parents' love—even if they are his parents and he isn't adopted—is conditional upon the way in which he compares with others. "He's such a poor eater. I don't know what to do with him. I just can't get him to eat like other children." His mother thinks he isn't listening, as he digs with his shovel under the park bench, but the "won't eat" and the depreciating tone in which she says it gets through to him—she is not worrying because her beloved child does not take the food which she has lovingly prepared for him, but because he is showing himself inferior at being a growing child. At his next meal he looks guiltily at his carrots. If he rejects them again that same depreciatory note will recur tomorrow in his mother's voice.

So while the child is learning that his whole place in the world, his name, his right to the respect of other children—everything—depends upon his parents and on what kind of a house they have been able to build or buy or rent, what kind of a car they are able to drive, what kind of toys they are able to buy him, he also learns that his own acceptance by these parents, who are his only support, is conditional upon his achievements, upon the way in which he shows up against other children and against their idea of other children. To the anxiety with which small boys in many if not all cultures of the world view grown men and wonder if they will ever be as tall and strong, is added in America, for both boys and girls, the anxiety as to whether they will be successful in keeping their parents' love as children. American girls of college age can be thrown into a near panic by the description of cultures in which

parents do not love their children. Against the gnawing fear that their personal achievement has made them
unworthy of love, they have placed a vague persistent
belief in "mother love," a belief that somehow or other
their parents won't be able to get out of loving them
some—because they are parents, and theirs. Any evidence that destroys their faith in this "maternal instinct" is profoundly disturbing. They know they are
not worthy; if the modicum that was to be theirs forever, even without worthiness, is taken away—what is
there left of which they can be sure? Their own children? No, because what if they are imbeciles? The
brightest people, college professors especially, have im-
becile children. "If your skirt turns up in back, your
mother loves you better than your father. If your skirt
turns up in front, your father loves you better than your
mother." "She loves me, she loves me not," is a game
that Americans do not wait to play until they are in
love.

So the young American starts life with a tremendous
impetus towards success. His family, his little slender
family, just a couple of parents alone in the world, are
the narrow platform on which he stands. If he becomes
an orphan, or a half orphan, if his father deserts his
mother, or his mother his father, if any of the things
happen that happen all the time in the movies, in the
papers, on the radio, he is already half defeated. To succeed after such an event he would have to overcome a
dreadful handicap. "He lives with his uncle. His
father's dead." "She hasn't any father and mother; she

lives with some people who were just neighbors." "He lives with his grandmother and she's deaf as a post." "Poor Jane, she is a little queer, but then you know her grandparents brought her up." "He's just boarding there—some charity pays for him." This is what he may expect. And when he has got his family intact, down to a kid sister, he can't be sure of keeping his place in it, just because he is himself. "No one," remarked a famous American educator, "no one can love unconditionally a child with an IQ over 90." A normal child must earn his parents' love.

Recently, students of comparative education, philosophers of improved family relationships, have made this point articulate and begun to scold American mothers because they do not love their children unconditionally. This has merely added to the confusion. It is only possible to love a child, as part of oneself, unconditionally, if one loves oneself in a certain sense unconditionally. The unconditional mother must have once been an unconditionally loved child, taking into her own soul part of the approval which was showered upon her. The peculiarity of the American version of "To him that hath shall be given" lies in this, that the child who, because it was bright or strong or beautiful, did receive great approval from its parents, is in turn able to love friends and lovers and children as parts of its highly approved self.

For the obverse of the whole system obtains. If parents can persuade themselves that their child is wholly admirable, they are then given license to love it fatuously, without the reserve or the precautionary bows to Fate appropriate in other societies. Although the anxiety that one will not be worthy is never entirely lacking, the assurance of the successful American child can be very great, and that in turn he passes on to his children.

This whole emphasis upon achievement in order to deserve that parental love which is so essential, in a world where everything else is shifting, where one's home is a number of a street, where one may change schools every year and move always among half-familiar faces, is further sharpened by the parents' inability to applaud themselves in their children. In societies where the father rears his son to his own trade, it is possible for him to feel a fine thrill of identification and pride the first time the child manipulates the tools of the trade with a distinguished touch. "Ha, a chip of the old block!" says father. "My child shares my skill." But in America, with the rapid rate of change, most parents know that the child will not do what the parent did, but something different. A parent cannot think back to his own boyhood and simply make an inaccurate comparison. When he was a boy, it was his pride to ride a bicycle thirty miles a day, not drive a car four hundred miles a day, to tap out a few words on a home-built radio set, not to build a model aeroplane of beautiful accuracy and new design. He must applaud in his son something which he did not do himself, and something which he has no way of judging. If he knew more than his son about building model aeroplanes, then he could judge his son's model on its merits. As it is, he vacillates between fatuous attacks of paternal pride, for whose undiscriminating nature his son despises him, and anxious requests as to whether the model has won or will win a prize, and so give him the right to be proud. Any approval which he does give must be necessarily ill-informed and not of the sort to win his son's respect. Only from outside sources, from school grades, competitions, rises in salary, prizes, can he learn whether this son whom he has reared is really as good as he hopes that he is.

Yet the further the child goes from standards that his parents know, the greater is his need for success. He is leaving them, he is giving up every concrete thing which they did, he will neither eat like them, nor dress like them, nor have the same standards as to what is appropriate to say to a girl or how he should plan his life insurance or where he should take his vacation. In big things and in small, in all the habits of life through which they taught him what the world was like, he will leave them, he will in a sense betray them. All he can offer in return is success. As a high school principal said recently to the parents of the graduating class: "They lay their success, their achievement, before you, a thank-offering for all that you have done for them."

When we see this situation dramatized in the immigrant father, himself with no book learning and hardly an English word, pathetically delighted because his son has won some academic honor, we are touched with the pity of it, of the father who cannot, himself, realize the

inwardness of what his son has done. We can sympa-
thize with the young research chemist who is offered
a job as the president of a small college—"President!
Now that is something my father and mother would
understand. They don't get this sort of thing I am doing
at all. But a title, a limousine, to live in a big house
called the President's house. They'd know I'd made
good then." And he hesitates and goes back not quite
happy to the research work which his fine mind is so
perfectly fitted to do, not able to be gay in the rejection
of the conspicuous role which would have made sense to
his less schooled parents. These seem to us extreme
cases, part of the drama of immigration, of the rapid rise
from generations of peonage to a place in a free world.
But they are only extreme cases of what happens to almost every American parent, no matter how successful
his son. And we find a curious reflection of this dependence upon externals for the validation of success,
in the anxiety of wives, or of the husbands of professional women, to be assured that the spouse is really
good, really recognized by his or her colleagues. A husband who has regarded his wife's excursions into the
academic world with kindly contempt will grow suddenly respectful when she is offered a fellowship.
"They" have recognized her, she must have something
in her after all.

This anomalous state in which American parents are
forever looking for a right to be proud of, and a right
to love, their children, and forever recognizing that the
proofs of worthiness must come from a world which it-

self has already slipped beyond them, is dramatized also in the relationship between parents and teachers. The teacher, in the American school, is teaching the child something which the parents don't know. If not in sober fact, giving the child a mastery of English grammar of which the parents have never heard, or a facility with fractions which the mother never mastered, still in spirit the teacher is the representative of the changing world in which the children must succeed. The teacher symbolizes a gulf between parents and children which will grow year by year—not the inevitable gulf between old and young, for that, like the seasons, is a circumstance to which man can bow with dignity, but the more dishonorable gulf which results from the parents getting out of date. The children are fast outstripping the parents, and handling daylight saving time with no mistakes at all while the parents are still missing trains. It is hard to find in such a breach between youth and age a place for pride in the young who outstrip the old, not because of greater ability but merely because of being born in a different year. Only those who have made a point of pride out of the very pace of our lives, out of the very fact that those who are born in 1920 start off wiser than those born in 1910, can find pride in such a circumstance. For the majority it is galling to slip behind, for it was one's place in the race which gave one dignity. And the teacher, often younger than the parents, becomes the symbol of this indignity. Children come home from school, anxious to put their parents in their place, and quote the teacher's word against theirs. It is small wonder that American parents retaliate by taking a savage interest in the teacher's character, by surveying her morals with a scrutiny accorded no one else except the minister's wife and the characters of political opponents. In a sense she is the enemy. They have given in, they have turned their children over to her to be made smarter than themselves and to learn a lot of things they, the parents, never needed to know. But just let them find her wanting in some way, failing to teach the children what the parents *do* know—that sacred symbol of the little bit of the Past which is worthy of respect, the Three R's—and they become merciless.

The situation, although difficult for the teacher, can be used to good purpose, if she makes herself the child's ally, the person who helps him take home to his parents the success which they so eagerly demand and upon which their love is contingent. If she is merely the dispenser of grades, she becomes to the child the person who, when she gives out a low grade, is denying him his passport to his parents' love. If she is helping the child to learn, she is helping him gain the coveted approval. She is in no sense a parent, but always she is professionally concerned with success, and this concern may be phrased in various ways. She may give or withhold, or she may turn with the child by her side to some impersonal power, which says whether the task was well done, and, if it was not, help again. In more static societies where there are schools, it is the duty of teachers merely to represent the parents, teaching what the parents would have the children learn. The teachers are the custodians of the past, the preservers of tradition. In America, the teacher is, in fact, never the representative of the parents—hardly even in those Eastern schools and colleges which attempt to imitate English institutions—she is always the representative of the future into which the parents are anxious that their children should enter, and enter well prepared.

CHAPTER VII

Brothers and Sisters and Success

★

AMERICAN PARENTS looking at their children—theirs to feed and clothe and educate for an unknown future, theirs for such a little while before they pass beyond their ken, not into a heaven where they could be envisaged as remaining ever the same, but into a living world that knows their parents not—are faced with a strange task. In other societies, where parents were bringing up children for their own way of life—a way of life seen as static or changing so slowly and each change so heavily grudged by the living that it was hardly perceptible—the job was reasonably clear. As you sat, so you taught your children to sit. Or, if you lived in a class society and hoped to push your child up a peg or two, as somebody else sat, so you taught your child to sit. The young mother either treated her baby as her mother had treated her, or she gave the best imitation she could of the way in which a nurse or a mother would treat a baby of higher social order, whether that treatment was seen as involving feeding by the clock, or lace cushions in a leather baby carriage. A given mother might be rather inept about it, might not know what to do when the baby ate green apples or green mangoes or raw snails, or drank the tattooing oil or the ink. But somebody knew, and back of the ignorance and ineptness of any individual lay the sureness of folkways, of the crystallized successful habits of centuries of survival and expansion.

American motherhood and, less completely, American fatherhood are compound of two attitudes, that of second and third generations trying to learn THE American way of doing things and trustingly accepting recipes from the smug lips of anyone who claims the authority to speak—advertiser, radio announcer, columnist, or lecturer—and of what I have called the fourth generation knowledge that the job of mastering the current American scene is completed and that the next task is to master an unknown future. For the question: How can I bring my child up to be a successful American among Americans? is substituted: How can I bring my child up to be successful in an unknown 1962? For such knowledge as this one can no longer go to the columnists and the text-books—the medicine men who hand down the lore of the "American way of life"— but must go instead to prophets and seers, which means incidentally a good many calls on quacks and charlatans, without the test of time to sift out one from the other. But because all of us have a large component of second and third generation attitudes in our make-up, we add to the kind of vigorous striking out into the future that goes with consulting a prophet, the sort of slavish humility that goes with following the instructions of the medicine man. So here again we find a paradox. We find new schools of education, new schools of diet, new schools of human relations, sprung up like mushrooms, new, untried, rank like skunk cabbages in early spring. And we find serious, educated people following their dictates as a hundred years ago they followed the laws of rhetoric laid down a thousand years ago by Aristotle, unchanged since because no one had known enough to change them.

If one travels slowly across the United States, one finds in various parts of the country examples of these various attitudes: in New England, traces of an old world point of view in which the past has come to have a validity of its own more reliable than the future; in the South, veneration for a past which has the validity of the age of Irish Kings, a fable more powerful than any present-day reality; in the Middle West, a third generation emphasis upon conformity, on doing it in what is believed to be the "American way"; while in California, one finds the epitome of the fourth generation attitude, the religious veneration of the newly manufactured solution, hoarfrost sprinkled on new-laid eggs.

Meanwhile, the children grow, and their weight and height are measured against a scale for other children of the same part of the country—or maybe a scale for the whole country. The very best pediatricians translate the current fad in baby feeding into challenging statements to the anxious young mother—"All the smartest 15-month-old babies I know can feed themselves." A little "under weight," a little "retarded in speech," a little "advanced in his talking"—her baby stands always against a frieze of those of his own age or a little older or a little younger than himself. The picture of her own babyhood, of her husband's own babyhood, is not allowed to enter in—things were different then—food was different—the fact that she knows that they walked late or talked early is irrelevant. Even the behavior of babies ten years ago—when her sister had a baby—isn't relevant. Why, in those days, babies didn't get raw carrots at all. And people were just beginning to know about allergies. There weren't any serums for whooping cough and measles. No one knew about feeding expectant mothers on vitamins, etc., etc. Obviously, the present ten-year-olds and her own baby are not comparable, just as those ten-year-olds and their predecessors of ten years before were not comparable. The idea is developed while the child is still an infant that the only valid comparisons by which one can judge one's baby are those with his near contemporaries. Brothers and sisters within five years of the same age; cousins near of an age, neighbors near of an age, even strange babies chance met in a park, of some other nationality group and whose parents speak a foreign tongue, may be more like one's own child—owing to the orange juice and carrots and well-established taboos on pacifiers, which now occur only in the slums and among the very modern Park Avenue practices—than any past and gone babies.

A mother learns to see her child in terrifically flat

perspective. Practically, as she wishes to believe in his potential strength and achievement, she can refer him to no absolute standard, only compare him, shoulder to shoulder, weight for weight, with the baby next door. In old static cultures, one can find a standard of behavior—a child will be judged a baby until it can walk, or a small child until it has lost its teeth or learned to pass kava or take the cows to pasture. Some reach these classifications earlier than others, but the standard of behavior is fixed. It is each baby which does or does not measure up to the standard. But in America, there is no such fixed standard—there are only this year's babies. "No one worries any more if a baby isn't trained by eighteen months." But that wasn't true ten years ago. It may not be true ten years from now. Only by keeping her eye on this year's fashionable dicta about this year's crop can the anxious mother get any security at all.

With this habit of mind deeply ingrained, American parents send their children to school, to nursery school or kindergarten or first grade, to measure up and to be measured against their contemporaries. "How does John compare with the other children, Miss Jones?" That is the question, not: "Has my child the tongue of a poet, or the eye of a painter, or the voice of a leader?" Not that, unless of course it is a very special kind of school for the children of intellectuals, and then, although the question may be put as: "How is John's finger painting, Miss Jones?" it usually means, "How does my John compare with the Allingham's Willy who

they are always saying shows such artistic promise?"
Marks! Marks! Mrs. Smith's little girl gets all A's. Mrs.
Brown's little boy gets such good grades. Why doesn't
our Bill get them? The European in our midst points
the finger of scorn. Americans aren't interested in content. They don't ask what the child is learning. They
don't ask how well he is learning it. They only ask:
What are his marks? This is the only thing they *can*
ask. The standards of content and learning shift and
change—spelling matters terribly, spelling doesn't matter at all, penmanship is important, cursive script has
gone out altogether and manuscript writing come in—
and "My children can't read the letters I write them.
I've had to get a typewriter." But an A, when only three
children in the class got A, that is a least common denominator which any father and any mother, confused
and puzzled by the intricacies of educational fads and
fancies, can understand, and to which they cling. How
does my child stand in relation to his age mates? becomes the only question which can be asked with any
hope of an intelligible answer.

And just as so much of our so-called objective science
is merely an apologia for the current climate of opinion,
so the psychologists have provided a final symbolic form
in which to express this attitude towards achievement
as an index of where one stands in a horizontal series, in
a world with no past that is known and no future that
can be predicted. This is known as "marking on the
curve." Human beings, say the statisticians, if measured
for any given trait will distribute themselves in an ap-

proximation of the "normal curve of distribution," that is with about 50 per cent of the cases falling above the average and 50 per cent below, and with most of the cases clustering around the average. Therefore, when we have a class in English literature or ancient history, let us treat their achievement as we might treat their heights and weights. Mark their papers, arrange them in serial order, and give a certain fixed percentage of them A's, and a certain percentage E's, and most people C's. This means that if Mrs. Jones' Mary happens to be in a class where everyone is bad in mathematics, she may get an A. If she has the measles and misses half a year of school and so gets into another section, or if the class is unusually good at mathematics, she may only get a C. All absolute values have vanished from the scene, and for them has been substituted one's position in regard to an accidental set of contemporaries. Occasionally, there is a break in the system. I remember the case of a professor, a devotee of the "curve," who was confronted by one student who did work which was unexpected for his class. The conscientious and perplexed professor finally gave that student an "A plus"—there was no such grade—and then "marked the other students on the normal curve."

When the schools, like the pediatrician and the child health center, can offer American parents only a relative standard, parents cling to it; they punish and reward in its name. We find the cartoon of Jimmy, fists dug into cheeks, glooming over the dining room table, while his mother stands over him, her arms piled high with his school books. "If your cousin Johnny could skip the fourth grade, so can you if we have to stay here all winter." Keep up with the others, keep up with the record of the just older brother or sister, keep ahead of the achievement of the just younger brother or sister, don't fall below the pace of the group. Our puritan forefathers were admonished to "Hitch your wagon to a star," but we can't do that, because the other children might be hitching theirs to a different star, and it wouldn't be possible to compare the rate of speed. If it is to be stars this year, then someone must decide on the star, and everyone must get teamed up.

This attitude towards success is expressed in the American version of sibling rivalry. The human family provides,[1] in every culture of which we have knowledge, not only the ground plan on which personal relationships are learned, but also particular themes and plots. In Bali we find the mother borrowing another baby to tease her own unweaned child, and so refocusing her baby's attention on herself. To the Balinese child, his younger siblings become rivals for his mother, to be treated well enough, as siblings, but pushed away, if possible, from the mother's breast. Later, when as adults the Balinese express their obsessions in art, they paint the same scene, the baby at the breast and the child on the ground reaching passionately up towards an unresponsive mother. Among the Iatmul of New Guinea, the older baby's attention is focused on the mother as a rival, not on the baby. The knee baby * wants to have the new baby for himself; as he formerly competed with his mother for every bite she ate, and screamed with rage if she dared to pop a bit of coconut into her mouth before his hunger was satiated, now he reaches for the baby and follows the baby about. When a stranger takes the baby, he leaves his mother and goes to the stranger, now interesting to him because of the baby. Among the Zulus, there is a formal ceremony in which the knee baby is introduced to the new baby. Every culture has formalized the relationship between the new possessor and the dispossessed in a different way.

Characteristically, the American sibling position is one of competition, not for the mother's person, for her breast and her soft arms, but rivalry for her approval, and her approval has to be got by one's achievement. When child psychologists discuss the trials of having a younger brother or sister—in America—one of the great difficulties for the older child is seen in that the baby is not scolded for the things for which the older child is scolded. To win his mother's approval, the two-and-a-half-year-old must be dry, must feed himself, must go to sleep quietly with no one there; otherwise, the loving approval vanishes from his mother's voice. Very well, he has learned, sometimes sorrowfully, sometimes eagerly, to do all of these things, to take steps upward and outward towards greater independence of his

* Knee baby—a Southern American term for the next to the youngest.

mother's delicious care. And then, along comes this small insignificant interloper, who can't do any of the hard things for which he has been praised, for failing to do which he has been denied his mother's love—and the creature is petted and loved and not expected to do them at all. Undoubtedly this is a central drama in the life of many American children. The betrayal, for so it seems, in which mother gives her love in one case and withholds it in another, is a seed out of which grows the bitterness towards all those who "have it soft," "get by," "get away with murder," a bitterness combined with envy. The baby sibling was in just that position— he didn't have to hold the spoon and laboriously gather up recalcitrant bits of meat which slipped and slid about his plate until they were worn and uninteresting and cold—he just lay there with his mouth open and got food poured in. "I've worked for everything I've got. But he had it easy from the start."

This does not mean that this familiar American attitude, that it is better to come up the "hard way," better because by it one gets in the end the sense of self-righteousness which is the echo of a mother's approving voice, and that all those who "have it easy" are to be both despised and envied, depends in every case on having been an older child who watched a younger sibling get away with it. The mechanics of culturally determined character are subtler than this. Every boy or girl who has felt this situation strongly, strongly because of being the child of American parents who stressed success, adds his bit to the accepted phrasings of relative success and failure. If one were to ask a group of casual passers-by their attitude on the subject—as the Enquiring Fotographer of the *Daily News* did recently—everyone who spoke with either bitterness or conviction would not necessarily have been an elder brother or sister—there are a thousand other items of standardized behavior which also elicit and reinforce such an attitude towards other people.

It is against this background of "conditional love" that one must understand the sort of audience reaction to programs like Professor Quiz which Herta Herzog[2] describes, in which people rejoice if the uneducated beat the educated, if the younger or poorer or less equipped triumphs over the person who should have been able to succeed without effort. All through American childhood, love is meted out—or so it seems to a child—to those who because they are older shouldn't be praised so much because it's easier, or to those who because they are younger are allowed to get away with things one isn't allowed to get away with oneself. The initial condition inserted into the mother's simplest kiss, that "I will love you only if you achieve as much as other people's babies. I CAN'T love you if you don't," survives into every competitive situation in life. What was his handicap? Ha, and nevertheless he made it? To European eyes, it seems terribly hostile and destructive of values, this indiscriminate gloating over the failure of the mighty and the success of the humble. To the European unconscious mind, the nearest analogous attitude is not directed towards a brother, but towards a father, towards the terrible, strong, hated father who is the child's rival for his mother's love. In the true patriarchal family, where the child's attention is focused in upon his parents, where all his intense child-ish effort is directed towards becoming part of their rela-tionship, the type Oedipus conflict is often intense and terrible. There a brother is either an ally against the father or else a surrogate for the father, and the child's deep repressed hatred of his father as a rival shapes any hatred of his brother as a rival—in an absolute sense—for his mother's love. But in the American family, the child's eyes are focused upon the outside world. He wins praise and approval as he displays that he "loves mother" not by loving her, but by eating his carrots and growing to be the tallest boy of his age on the block. He and his father are not measured against each other on the same scale for his mother's personal love—they aren't in the same class. True, some American fathers regress so badly that they begin to compete with their small sons for their wives' approval, placing their wives entirely in their mothers' former role. But the type situation does not place son and father as rivals, as they are in a patriarchal society. "My father is a policeman." "Hmp, my father is a baseball player!" "That's nothing, my father works in a bank!" are state-ments of one boy to another, in which father's role is merely a counter for doing down a contemporary. Mother isn't comparing Jimmy with father, but with Jimmy's elder brother and Jimmy's younger brother and with the neighbors. Her love isn't conditional on whether he can throw a baseball farther than father. But it is conditional on his achievement in the outside world.

There are undoubtedly many individual cases where sibling rivalry becomes so intense that it colors a whole life or distorts it forever. But for the most part it is a mistake to judge American sibling rivalry which is directed out towards success in the outer world, in the same terms as those European sibling rivalries which are directed inwards towards actual personal relationships inside the family group. The American position is often transitory. Mother praises Jimmy this term, but Johnny the next. Jimmy used to get all the smiles when they were both in grade school, but then Johnny learned to make model aeroplanes and started getting prizes, and "Gee! Wasn't Mom proud." The terrible hopelessness of the situation when a child of two or three decides that another is loved better than itself, is replaced in America by the relative cheerlessness of not getting much love this month—with a report card like that. Sharply as the deviant cases stand out, pairs of brothers who enter the same profession and spend their lives rivaling each other, men who pick other men as rivals and devote a lifetime to emulation in the hope of finally outstripping them—these are the exceptions rather than the rule. The rule is that in order to by-pass your father, you choose another skill than his; in order to by-pass your brother or your sister, you again choose another road to success. Where success in general, not success in particular, is demanded, this is the line of least resistance. Perhaps the areas in which sibling rivalry hits hardest are those of athletic prowess in boys and beauty in girls—where the idea of achievement is most unfair. By making even beauty something which "any girl can have" and athletic prowess a matter of effort rather than a hereditary gift of muscles, we lay a burden of bitterness on the unbeautiful and the puny which is not laid in a society which treats these gifts as coming unsought from the gods. It would be easier for a girl to forgive a sister her satiny skin if she didn't have to listen to lectures on how nice her skin would be if she stopped eating candy, creamed it every night, put on mud packs, and really tried to make something of herself.

So to the American only the very near contemporary is a potential rival or a potential stimulus. Stories of the heroes of other days, or of the exploits of his parents when they were young, are merely boring. Taught to measure himself on a flat narrow scale, he keeps his eyes where he has been trained to keep them, on others who can be compared to himself, and he has many devices for doing this. One of them is money. If you are a bicycle speed artist, how can you compare yourself with a movie actor, a banker or a congressman? Why, by the money they make. And if the money you make, though it's big-time money for your racket, isn't big-time money in there, then translate the money back into a relative scale. You are the best-paid bicycle racer of the year, and he is the best-paid movie actor, or the richest banker. That won't do for the congressman. Then get another common denominator—how often one of them has his name in the paper, or his picture. "Boy, just look at those clippings. Do you know there were only two members of Congress who had their pictures in the paper last year as often as I did! Baby, who says this country doesn't appreciate sport?" Horrible, shudders the European. Reducing every sort of talent to a single gross scale, to dollars or clippings or fan mail, to some meaningless, quantitative scale, on which all human beings become comparable and so inevitably cheap. Yes, that is one way of saying it. But there is another way. We can recognize that yearning for achievement which is planted in every American child's breast by his mother's conditional smile. Success that can be measured. When he reduces a poet to his proceeds, he does not mean to devaluate him. That is not his primary aim; he means instead, if possible, to get into the same class. So does the group of Middle Westerners who have been invited to meet a famous traveler, and who perplex the traveler by spending all the time telling him how their aunts and cousins and acquaintances took trips of much less scale and grandeur. Are they trying to cheapen his trips by comparing their cautious and lazy excursions on tour ships to his dash up the hidden Shangshi? It certainly looks that way, and it may bring about just this result: the children who listen to the conversation may fail to distinguish later between a Raymond-Whitcomb tour and a journey around the world in a tramp steamer. But that failure to look with any awe on the tramp steamer trip, because after

all "Aunt Susan took trips too, Mother said so," may
have another result—the listening boy may decide that
he will do something a jot more daring, go around the
world alone in a ketch. Bringing the great and the
small, the qualitatively incomparable together on a
single cheap little scale of ohs and ahs and dollars and
cents, at once constricts and enlarges the imagination.
If the American lacks the respect that he should show
for the genius, he also lacks the paralyzing inferiority
which comes from too much recognition of genius.
While mother, with her tireless flat anecdotes, reduces
the famous traveler to the level of Our Town, she
brings him automatically within the scope of her
Jimmy.

The Balinese, one might claim, really know the value
of learning, of knowledge, in a way which Americans,
real Americans, don't. They respect books so much in
fact that on the day sacred to books, everyone must ab-
stain from reading them. Every man in Bali knows that
others, because they can read, or because they have read
more, are wiser than he. Everyone is afraid to venture
an opinion. "I dare not speak lest I make a mistake."
But the American familiarity with greatness has its daring side. In no other country does the business man
who has finally decided to write directly to the President, lean back in his chair to watch the respect which
should dawn on his stenographer's face as he noncha-
lantly dictates the Presidential address, only to have her
answer: "Yeah, I wrote him a letter last week."

CHAPTER VIII

Are Today's Youth Different?

★

IF WE ASK the question, Under what conditions can an American display a full determination to fight and win? there are a series of answers. The other fellows must start the fight. Well, they did. The other fellows must have more breaks than we have at the start. Well, they have. They have so many of them that this circumstance comes in conflict with another requirement for an all-out effort—some victories, some proof that our side is pretty good after all. But there is one further absolute necessity if Americans are not only to start fighting well but keep on fighting, on a world-wide front and at home, in factories and in submarines and in the air: to win this war, we must feel we are on the side of the Right.

The insistence that "triumph we must for our cause it is just" has come in for a great deal of cynical debunking in the last twenty-five years by a generation who betrayed their own ideals, whose moral muscles went flaccid after a sudden too violent stretching, who stopped their fight in the middle and went to playing the stock market. No one sneers more readily at love than disappointed lovers, and Americans from 1918 to 1940 were in that position. We had had a dream, the kind of dream in which you suddenly solve every problem, untie every knot, become a very god of goodness and wisdom. Then we woke up in the morning to find that dream was too much work, that we hadn't the guts and the imagination to try to carry it out. We decided to let the Dead Heroes rot in Flanders Fields. In fact— as it was a little inconvenient to think of them as heroes —why heroes?—why not just dupes and fools, just cannon fodder for Wall Street? We had been going to save the world, the Yanks were coming bringing liberty and justice for all in their knapsacks. All that we had hoped to accomplish in the New World, we were bringing back to the Old—we had all the answers, all the good will, all the willingness to suffer and die to make Europe as Holy Ground as New England had become. We were going to show that Europe, which our ancestors had rejected and which was always rejecting us, just how much better our way of life was than theirs. The Liberation of Europe, from all the old dark wars and ways of life, that was the Cause in which we were willing to die, or let others of our best die for us. Why did we welch on that Vision, refuse to play, go home like sulky children insisting the adults had used the very same adult vices which we had accused them of having, Outwitted our Innocents at the Conference Table? And when we ask why, what sort of an answer do we want? Do we want an historical answer, well documented with

the personal qualities of Mr. Lloyd George, M. Clemen-
ceau and Mr. Wilson, with Mr. Lodge and Col. Lind-
bergh's papa scuttling the ship from behind? Do we
want statements about international banking, the big
interests, the fear of Communism in the bourgeois
mind? From the standpoint of this book, these are answers for other disciplines to provide.*

For us, discussing the character structure of Americans in 1942, it is sufficient to point out that men who
are twenty in 1942 were reared by members of a generation which betrayed a Cause which they had believed to be worth fighting for, a generation which
spent twenty years heaping obloquy on those who had
been fools enough to believe in it—especially on themselves. For the first time in American history, we have
had a generation reared by parents who did not see
themselves as knights of a shining cause, albeit often a
very materialistic sort of cause. Each generation before
had been reared by moral paragons, men whose singlehanded virtue had killed the Indians, fought the French
and the Red Coats, conquered the Confederate Armies,
built railroads through the deserts, developed the great-

---

* The answers to the problem of why we welched, cast in the terms
of this book, would involve such considerations as our lack of preparation for the job. We were told we had only to win the war to make
the world safe for democracy. It was presented to us as a quick fight
to the finish; no allowance was made for the long slow job of construction, alteration and maintenance. We had been told to go all out
for a quick victory; we stretched our spiritual muscles, even if we did
not have to work very hard or suffer very much—and when the armis-
tice came, they relaxed. The job was done—so we had been told. The
affairs of other nations still seemed infinitely remote; the very act of
going to fight on foreign soil seemed enough for us to have done.

est Machine Civilization on earth, developed a standard of living in which there was a car in every garage and a chicken in every pot. Such were our parents and we were expected, generation after generation, to go them one better. The World War, a crusade back finally to rearrange the country of our origin, fitted in very well indeed. It was just a bigger and better Woolworth Building, topping the Cathedrals of the Old World, whose glass was somehow of a rarer quality, but whose towers were much smaller. It was going to be as easy as all the rest had been: "Good-by, Broadway, Hello, France, It won't take us long." All our past history, shorn of the work, shorn of the hardship and the suffering which had marked it, as generations of stern, determined and adventurous men and women had marched farther and farther into the wilderness, was presented to us like a huge birthday cake, and the A.E.F. was just the frosting on the cake. The cheap, shoddy slogans of the commercial world, hastily pressed into service to rally a surprised nation to arms, debased our idealism, gave it a false, meretricious ring. With no suffering to mark our souls, nor hardship to mar our bodies, we came out of the last war, and sold our birthright for a mess of pottage.

And what of the results? There are many million young Americans who were brought up by a parent generation who had first welched on the greatest moral responsibility any people had ever shouldered, and second, had seen the Lord God of Plentifulness, who had always rewarded the American people, turn away His

eyes. Betrayal of the Peace, then the punishment—
whether it was cast in terms of a morality play or in
economic determinism—the connection was inescapable.
We no longer walked proudly, as a people beloved by
God, for we knew only too well we didn't deserve to be
loved and apparently weren't. And meanwhile the children were growing up, exposed to a moral peril such as
no group of Americans had ever been exposed to before. Whether they were the children of parents on relief, or the children of parents who thought relief was
an unnecessary measure concocted to keep the returns
on their securities down—it didn't matter. The parents
on relief feared they had failed and so lost much of their
dignity. The parents who weren't on relief brought up
their children to a determination to get something for
nothing—as these others were getting. Recently a dean
of men in an Eastern college, arguing against the wicked
policies of the New Deal, mentioned the large number
of conscienceless young men who got jobs in the summer and collected unemployment insurance after returning to the college in the autumn. "And these are of
course young men from poor families whose morality
has been undermined, as you suggest, by years of relief?" I asked him. "Oh, no," he answered indignantly.
"That's the worst of it, they come from well-off homes
where they didn't need that money at all." To which
the obvious answer is: "Whose morality has been undermined, those who received the relief or those who
morning after morning, across a well-furnished breakfast table, heard father inveighing at the effects of

pauperizing people?" Of course the answer is, The morality of both has been determined—not by relief, but by the need for it. Those who were bred to believe that if one was good, one got work and was able to support one's family, and who then found there was no work and so could not support their families, received a severe moral shock. The moral structure of the universe tottered, and relief grudgingly paid for by men who, although their incomes were halved, insisted upon believing themselves still "good"—and therefore chosen of the Lord and not responsible for other men's sins— did not restore that structure. The old puritan belief—a belief which was only tenable in a country with a great and expanding economy—that wealth was the inevitable reward of virtue and industry, and failure the penalty for unworthiness, had taken a body blow.

Now the thesis of this book has been that the experience of generations of men, in a changing world, leaves its marks upon the culture, in the very bodies and souls of the next generation, that the behavior of those of us who live today carries traces of other behaviors, themes developed under other stresses. There is no American race with an inalienable moral inheritance, an inalienable strength and purity—just as there is no other racial carrier of reliable human or superhuman virtues. Our behavior, good and bad, our strengths and our weaknesses are the resultant of the choices, voluntary and involuntary, of those who have gone before us. Americans are what they are because they have been reared in America by parents with certain ways of behaving. Those ways have changed during the last quarter century. Failure and Betrayal, not Success and Faith, became the watchwords of a people unwilling to admit that they had sinned, and looking instead for impersonal devils, Economic Forces, International Munition Makers, Communists, on which to blame their defeat. For a generation, the most crucial area in American character formation, parenthood of children under twenty, has been manned by people who were willing to crawl out of their responsibilities by blaming somebody else—these have been the fathers of those upon whose strength the present battle and what comes after must rest.

Have we marred them? It's a serious and important question, every bit as important as the question which is asked so much oftener—What about the Nazi Youth? Has Hitler made such a thorough job that he has produced millions of young people absolutely unfit to live in a decent world? Have we—not of willful deadly purpose, indoctrinating for world conquest, but out of a failure of will and of purpose—produced a generation unfit to lead in building a new world? Americans should make good leaders in such an undertaking. They know, by experience, that many things which Europeans still believe impossible, can be done. They have even watched Europeans do them—on American soil. They are committed to the future, not to the past, to experiments, to adventures, to new ways of life. They represent an historic break with Old World habits. The narrow craftsman or specialized hedger became the

American farmer—who had to do everything himself. Later the American farmer became the American manufacturer, who, lacking specialized skills, invented machines to do the job. In the Old World, the machine replaced the feudal masters, enslaving men. But in America, it replaced the laborer when the American farmer hadn't enough hands for the multiplicity of his jobs. In America we started to move towards an era in which men were too valuable to do what could be done by a machine—an era which would really free men from soul-destroying labor. It was all here. The point of view, the state of mind, the touch of evangelism and piety, the belief that only by steady pursuit of the good does man deserve to share in this world's goods, the belief in invention, that practical problems were to be solved practically, by men who loved God but used their own wits. "Trust God and Keep your Powder Dry." Is it here, still? Have the moral debauches of the last twenty years left congenital scars on the children's souls which no medicine can cure, no scalpel remove? [1]

There are some (of both generations) who will say that the proof of the pudding must lie in the eating. If our young people enlist or go cheerfully when drafted, fight well, stick it out in the army or the factory or the farm, and when the war is over, don't welch—as their parents did—then we will know that they weren't maimed. They are Americans after all, wiser than their parents who were fooled by too easy victories and too well-disguised defeats; wiser Americans, who can be trusted with a hard job. But here comes a hitch, a very serious hitch in the arguments. The proof of this pudding does not lie in the eating, for young people are no pudding, already mixed now, which can be put away in an oven to come out, crisp and light or heavy and soggy—but beyond our power to change. An essential ingredient in the achievements of Americans has always been that their parents believed in them, believed in their brains and their strength and their energy, believed in their inherent superiority to any generation that had ever trod the earth before. Generation after generation, in America, the fathers have said to the children, "Ye are the salt of the earth," "Boys and Girls of America, you are the hope of the world." On the light and faith in parental eyes, the young people have gone ahead, anxious because they felt the faith was too great and that perhaps they would betray it, but on a lit path. We have no other habit of walking except in this steady light. If we send a generation out now, while we ourselves doubt: "I wonder if they have it in 'em. Been taught a lot of nonsense in the last twenty years. Learned to distrust everything. Don't believe that you can get anywhere by hard work. Don't believe that anything in the world is worth fighting for," and turn our eyes away, we send them out to danger and perhaps to disgrace. The mainsprings of determination in other countries may lie in the sneer with which the overbearing father derides his son's first efforts to be a man; such treatment makes good revolutionaries, makes boys whose holiness lies in killing all for which that father stood. But it is not so here. Young

Americans have no impetus to succeed in order to spite their parents' lack of faith; they have only the deeply ingrained habit of succeeding because of it. It is the very air that Americans have breathed and without it, they may easily suffocate, they surely cannot fight so well.

So we cannot afford to sit back, to wait and see whether the damage we unwittingly did them was too great and too complete. To send troops into battle ill equipped is to send them to death. To ask men to work in factories without adequate food and shelter, is to doom our troops to too little equipment. To ask any young American to give of his best without at the same time giving him our faith that he will give of his best, is to commit the American Sin against the Holy Ghost. Each people has its own form of this Sin; to fail to believe that our children have it in them to better their parents' record is ours.

If it is grossly unfair to ask our young people to go out and bear the greatest responsibility any generation of Americans has ever borne, without giving them the fullest measure of parental confidence, should we not give it? Many preachers and commencement orators have tried to do just that. They swung suddenly round, between June 1941 and June 1942, from berating and accusing the young people upon whose minds and souls they themselves had branded their own cynical failure. Youth became overnight, not the last "scapegoat of democracy," but the white hope of the nation. But such cheap sleight of hand, practiced in other ways to our shame in 1917, won't go at all in 1942. Nobody believes the words, neither the frightened oldsters who pause in the midst of their berating, suddenly realizing that however poor the spirit in which these young men may fight, they are all that stands between us and slavery, nor the serious inquiring young editors of college papers grappling with the problem of "youth" and what "youth thinks." If we are to accord them that confidence, without which they can have no confidence in themselves, we must act on knowledge, not on a wispy will to believe. We must be able to look them in the eye and say: "Despite the mess that we have made of your education, especially during your adolescence and early youth, we know that we failed to rob you of your inheritance. We admit that we have done something which might have crippled you. We taught you to believe that everything that we fought for was a mirage and that we were dopes to have fallen for it. We lacked the courage simply to admit that we had failed. We did not fail in the sense you have been taught to believe. We did not fail in that a proper treaty in 1919 would have saved the world. It probably would not, could not, have saved us from this war. We were all too ignorant in 1919, we thought the job was too easy, and so we were bound to fail. For our ignorance, which was the ignorance of our period, we need ask no one's pardon. But we did fail in that we withdrew our moral effort from the job, and in that we stopped trying. We had put our hands to the plow and turned back. For that we must ask forgiveness. We failed you because we lied to you, forcing ourselves and you to believe that we had no part in the way in which the world was getting steadily worse.

"Still, we can say with a deep thankfulness that we have failed to break you, failed to rob you of your American inheritance. You are still asking the questions that matter: What is right and what is wrong, and for what should we fight and why? You still think life should have a goal, that men should be able to better their social forms, that there is no excuse for standing still or going backwards. In this our final failure, to put upon our children our own weakness, we have failed also, thank God."

But can we say anything of the sort? We know what we have told them. We know why we told them the things we did. We have clothed them in our weaknesses and our cynicism, what can we see in them which can give us such faith?

To answer that question, we must turn to the roots of character, to the early years in which a child learns, from his mother and his nurse, from his father and his brothers and sisters, the shape of the world in which he is expected to move. The way in which a newborn infant is fed and hushed to sleep, or left to cry it out, teased or treated seriously, dressed and bathed and held in the stiff or compliant human arm, gives him these first lessons. This generation of young Americans, like their predecessors, were brought up by American parents with certain patterns for the treatment of children, patterns which were too subtle and deeply ingrained to be immediately sensitive to their executants' attitudes about the Treaty of Versailles or the New Deal.[2] Even parents who had come to believe that life was just a racket in which the New Dealers got theirs, still solemnly told their children: "Never, never tell a lie." "If you don't eat up all your vegetables you can't have any dessert."

For American parents only know one pattern of parenthood, that which they share, though in an intensified form, with all the Protestant world, the pattern by which the parents assume the responsibility of representing themselves to their children as better than they really are. It has become the fashion to disparage this aspect of parenthood, to call people hypocrites who tell their children not to lie while they themselves lie whenever it is necessary or expedient. But this disparagement is made with no understanding of what a special invention this type of parenthood is, and of how much depends upon it. The criticism comes from those who think that a conscience is an inalienable aspect of a human being, like his eyes or his liver. But comparative studies of other societies show us that a conscience, that inner voice which is able so to admonish the would-be sinner that he pauses and does not sin, or if he has sinned secretly knows no peace until he has atoned or confessed, is a very rare and special development. Far from springing up full grown in every human child's heart, only very special types of training can produce it at all. Half the world lives and has lived, not by conscience at all, but by the intervention of external authorities and the fear of external sanctions, or by a

fear which adults share with children that some supernatural power will shatter them if they break its rules,
or merely by the fear of "what other people will say"—
a sanction which vanishes at once when the "other
people" are out of earshot. We now know enough about
some fifteen other cultures outside the Judeo-Christian
tradition to say whether they have conscience in this
sense. Of these, two have this type of character structure
—the Manus of the Admiralty Islands [3] and the Arapesh
of New Guinea,[4] tiny stone age tribes, far outside the
sweep of the great religions. Among these brown
peoples we find the same conscience that we find among
ourselves, a gnawing sense of guilt for the sin committed or the enjoined act which has been omitted, a
sense of guilt strong enough to deter the individual
from most sins and urge him towards amends for those
which he has committed.

We can compare the way in which Manus children,
Arapesh children and American children are brought
up, find out what the similar elements are which shape
human materials in such similar ways, and from this
derive an understanding of what makes the American
character, and judge whether we can safely expect
young Americans, aged twenty, to have it, in spite of
lectures on the "Origins of War." We find the following common elements: first, children are brought up by
parents, not by child nurses, servants, slaves, or grandparents, or in large impersonal groups. Second, parents
take the responsibility of punishing children, either by
active chastisement—as in Manus—or by withdrawal of

love—as in Arapesh—when they do wrong, thereby risking the children's hostility and hatred. This is a risk that the parents of very few societies have ever been willing to take; more usually they call in gods, or scare dancers, or relatives to punish their children, unwilling to take the moral responsibility of facing the child and saying, "I call this wrong, no matter how much it may alienate you from me. It is wrong." Only as we watch the brazen hypocrisy with which some Indian parents disclaim any responsibility for the scare dancers whom they have actually paid to come and beat their children, do we appreciate that American parents are actually performing, every day, acts which would seem unthinkably brave to parents of other societies. Third, parents act as if they themselves embodied all the virtues which they are busy enjoining upon the child. In this last respect, the Arapesh have the least in common with ourselves, but among the Manus and in America, parents day after day parade themselves as paragons of the virtues that they have not. The most cynical dissenter from any attempt to improve the world and play a nation's part in international responsibility has held himself up time and time again at the breakfast table as a specimen of someone who always eats what is put on his plate, gets up on time, tells the truth, and does all that is expected of him, is always honorable, brave and reliable. He has done this merely because it is our pattern of parenthood and he knows no other way to behave. In those small sections of the United States where groups of intellectuals have systematically worried about the problem of parenthood, they may have attempted to explain to their children that they themselves were but sorry versions of the ideal man, but this seldom carried over to the breakfast hour, when tardiness suddenly became a dreadful crime, or to bedtime, when obedience became a sterling virtue. Parents have to rear children somehow. Each culture has its own techniques, of bogeymen and initiation ceremonies, scare dancers or scare lies, of the parent who admonishes or the grandfather who scares, or the child nurse who simply drags the screaming baby off the premises. It is quite possible that out of the new self-doubt and moral flabbiness of this last generation of parents, new techniques might have developed. Uncle Don and other radio moralists are in fact one such development. "Better drink your milk, Mary. I hear you haven't been drinking your milk very well lately. And there is a present for you under the piano." "I hear you haven't been obeying Uncle Bill very well, Harold. Gotta obey Uncle Bill, you know. He knows what's good for you." When the Soviet Union was attempting to instill more socialized attitudes into the breasts of remote peasant groups, they used this same technique, denouncing the unco-operative over the radio. It is a method which might destroy conscience, obliterate any sort of internal moral sanction, and replace it merely by a fear of public disapproval—by shame.

For conscience and its attendant emotional attitude, guilt, depend upon very special techniques for their existence. To the little child, struggling with his own impulses and with the rules and regulations of the outside world, the parent says: "This is right and this is wrong. If you do this, I will love and reward you. If you do that, I will withdraw my love, I may in fact chastise you." At first the child learns to be good when the parent is looking, but still snatches the forbidden cake as soon as the parent's back is turned. But the parent finds out. Inexplicably, by clues which the child ignores —crumbs on the carpet, a telltale piece of frosting on the nose, no appetite at supper, or a covert smack of the lips—the sin is discovered, and then the punishment is still more awful, especially if to the original act the child has added a cheerful lying disclaimer. Slowly, to good behavior if mother or father is by, the child adds good behavior when they are not, because it is as if he heard within himself the forbidding voice, and his imagination learns to encompass the inevitable punishment. If he has failed to resist the temptation, then his mind is haunted by what they would say, might say, if they knew, if they found out.

This still small voice, which psychoanalysts call the super-ego, the introjected image of the parent, and which most people simply call a conscience, is developed in the child before he is five or six. It is probable—on the basis of what we know at present—that it could not be developed afterwards. Only in days when the boundaries between the actual and the imagined are dim and unclear can this introjection of the parental image take place perfectly. Throughout childhood, it remains, still not entirely a part of the personality, as children continue to be good because of what their parents will say, more often than to feel that the desire for goodness has become part of themselves.

Then comes adolescence, that period which our culture has conventionalized as a period of stress and strain. At adolescence, all the conflicts of early childhood are reactivated. Sex, which has been in a sense laid aside as not for one so young as I, becomes again an urgent interest. Parents, once the center of the world—who faded somewhat into sustaining and restricting background figures, between six and adolescence—are brought back into the picture. The child's interest in his parents is reawakened, both in its childish form when the parent was the chief object of the child's love, and in the new form, when the parent appears to stand between the child and his reaching out towards new love objects. This means that the parents, those paragons of goodness, in terms of whose moral demands one's smallest misdeed, one's least falling behind in the race, have been measured all these years, come in for a much closer scrutiny again. With more powerful motives for disobedience, and stronger emotional reasons for paying attention, the adolescent really begins to look at his parents, not with the clear detachment of the ten-year-old, whose comment is often relentless but rendered barbless by lack of emotion. Suddenly it matters very much to the adolescent whose parents are restricting his new desire for liberty whether their goodness and wisdom gives them the right to the authority they claim so lavishly. And when he looks them over, when she looks them over, this boy and girl who have felt so guilty when their marks were poor, their clothes unbrushed or the bed unmade, they find their parents wanting. This is inevitable, for the parents have been forced, by the conventions of bringing up children, to pretend to be that which neither they nor anyone else ever is, a perfect practitioner of the virtues which they had to preach. So the adolescent looks them over, finds them wanting and faces the greatest spiritual dilemma of growing up in this culture.

This dilemma, which is not inevitable for human beings, is nevertheless inevitable and valuable in our culture as it is at present constructed. The child's picture of goodness, goodness which is not only greater in quantity, but different in quality—exemplified as it is by an adult vis-a-vis a child—is based on the image of the parent. God and Heaven, and, when Hell is included in the picture, Hell also, have been interpreted in terms of the parents. Father has modeled his voice on the voice of God, and the child has heard God's voice through father's rendering. If the moral order of the world, if the supernatural sanctions which made that order still more awe-inspiring and dignified, all hinge on father and mother as interpreters—what is to happen to that order when the interpreters are found wanting. This is the problem which faces every child in one form or another. In America it has various other overtones connected with the insistence upon success, the demand for conformity to the age group and the standards of the future, etc., but for purposes of this discussion I am reducing it to a skeleton of first principles. Those who have taught us goodness are found to be, in various degrees, neither all good nor all wise.

This discovery is essential to maturity. It may be made earlier than puberty, it may be made much later. It may never be made at all, and a man may remain a perpetual boy scout for life. But for the majority, it is made. And then comes the spiritual crisis, the search for what is the good, which must follow on the first discovery that the parents cannot be accepted wholeheartedly, as in the past. "Is there such a thing as right and wrong after all?" This question is rarely asked, and more often the question is: "What is the right and the wrong? What standard am I, who after all have been shaped to follow standards, going to follow?" Crudely, diagrammatically put, it means: "What shall I put in my parents' place? I can't stand this empty altar," and shuddering memories of what happened to the man whose soul was left empty and swept and garnished echo through the back corridors of the mind. "What shall I aspire to that is better than myself?" Parents? These particular parents have been proved the poor broken reeds that all mortals are, but the belief that there is something better, wiser, stronger, freer, truer, survives their downfall. "They weren't it," says the adolescent, "*I* am certainly not it. How well I know that. But the Truth must lie somewhere."

And here, generation after generation, the belief in Progress is reborn in the minds of the young. Progress, the belief that there *is* something better than our own way of life, that our own fumbling version of how men shall live with men here on earth, rests upon these very special mechanics, in which parents first hold themselves up as good and their children learn the rare and beautiful faith that there can be something better than oneself. In some societies adults teach children to believe, slavishly, in absolute gods by bowing down in their children's presence and drawing their children to their knees beside them. So the children learn to accept a God-of-things-as-they-are-and-as-they-have-got-to-stay. But in the Judeo-Christian system in which man becomes responsible for his own sins and for the sins of his children, we have a technique of child training which ensures that men shall hunger and thirst after righteousness and never be filled.

Progress is not merely the name for something which can be said to have happened in the course of human history. Progress is not merely what the nineteenth century made of it, a means of self-congratulation on present material achievement and a way of disparaging our own past and the present state of other people. It is a double-edged social invention, as important as the steam engine, and in fact very like it. Like the steam engine, it opened up to man a new control over his destiny. With machinery, he could sit down and say, "Now what would I like to make?" With the invention of the idea of progress, he could sit down and say, "Now what shape would I like the world to take?" Whereas in the past all change had to be referred to the whims of gods, the will of God, the ruling of an inexorable Fate or the nature of the universe, suddenly man himself was faced with control of and responsibility for his own destiny. Grant that Man can progress and that the direction is up to him, and you put his fate in his own hands. Whether the direction he will choose to go in will actually be better, in terms of any system of values which someone else might erect, is another matter. But a decisive step has been taken forward when Man thinks that he can ask: "Which next step would be labeled progress? Which step would be a step backward? How can I take the step forward?"

The dynamics of American effort today depend on this relationship between moral parents and gradually disillusioned children who have, however, learned the lesson that goodness greater than their own lies somewhere within someone's reach. It is not a perfect mechanism. The moment of disillusionment when youth finds its parents wanting adds a bitterness which is probably not compatible with completely enthusiastic pursuit of a better world. We may in time be able to achieve a better way of bringing up children and still developing in them the capacity to believe in progress. But we have not yet.

Meanwhile, the issue for Americans in 1942 is whether, during the last twenty-five years, we succeeded in spite of ourselves in bringing up a generation who have in fact fundamentally moral characters. To have a moral character does not mean to be good, but it means to think that goodness is transcendently important,[5] that there is a right and a wrong and that in the end all final decisions must be made in terms of what is right and what is wrong. If they care, if they still believe this question is more important than such questions as "How to win power" or "How to avoid death or poverty," then we need not fear when we entrust our future into their hands.

They may not talk as if they had any faith in morality. They may even ask, as one student did lately: "What is the use of a conscience anyway, *ought* one to have one?" The italics are mine, the italics spring from the deepest roots in American culture. One may query the word "conscience" and in that query, with the introduction of the word OUGHT, the whole weight of our peculiar moral attitude towards life lives over again. Ought one to have a conscience? Not need one, but OUGHT one. As long as youth argues as to whether one ought or ought not to have ideals, or to fight for what is right, we may be sure that they have come through, as Americans, through the miasma of twenty-five years of parents who repudiated responsibility.

CHAPTER IX

The Chip on the Shoulder

★

AT ANY TIME in their history, in expanding days or days of retrenchment, in war or in peace—or in that state towards which we hope to work now, where there will be neither war, nor the absence of war, but a world that is not war-oriented at all—the way in which a people handle the problem of aggression is important. We can find a clue to the way in which aggressive behavior is patterned in America in the recent history of interest in the idea. When I left America for the field, in 1931, although the Depression had been with us for two years the implications of the Depression had not yet penetrated very deeply into American scientific thought. Social scientists were more impressed with the disappearance of their stake in the stock market than with the profound shifts that were occurring in American attitudes towards the moral responsibility for success and failure. Those who were interested in the Freudian approach were still talking about the impulse life as it related to pleasure and, especially, the pleasure to be derived from one's body and from interpersonal rela-

138

tions. They were still busy insisting to a puritan world that quite small children had a type of feeling which we had regarded as appropriate only after adolescence. Then I came back at the end of 1939 to find all interest in pleasure practically wiped out, aggression held the center of the stage. Analysts, sociologists, psychologists—everybody was talking about Aggression and the stimulus to aggression—Frustration.[1] I think this was not an accident. Aggression in the American character is seen as response rather than as primary behavior. A nation-wide experience had occurred of a type which was most frustrating to Americans and which most justified our recognition of aggression. Just as it is more permissible to talk about venereal disease in wartime, because we recognize promiscuity as a normal consequence of large concentrations of men for military purposes—although we make no such recognition for the large concentrations of men which are gathered together by mining or industry—so it was permissible to begin emphasizing aggression during a period which was socially recognized as frustrating and evocative of aggression.

Cultures have patterned aggression in many different ways: they have regarded it as primary and rewarded it; regarded it as incidental and undesirable and extinguished it; regarded it as primary and punished it; regarded it as secondary and developed it. The degree to which one individual will fight, attempt to dominate or destroy persons or objects which interfere with his attainment of a goal, is of very great concern in human societies, and almost all societies of which we know are, in some measure, concerned with the problem, with staying the baby's hand, with slapping the baby's hand, or with reinforcing the baby's aimless slap by a cheer or the comment: "How fierce and cruel he is!" And there is a definite relationship between the expectancy, the fear, the disapproval, the cheer in the parent's voice and the later fighting behavior of those babies grown to manhood.

From any audience to whom one talks about war today, there are bound to come questions about the relationship between aggression and success as soldiers. Are Americans aggressive enough? Can we hope to win without a greater love of fighting? Must we not become as relentlessly dedicated to the lust for battle as our enemies if we hope to survive? The girls ask: "How is a girl to nourish the love of war in her boy friend who seems curiously reluctant to enlist, and should she do so?" The boys ask: "Will marriage before enlistment make a man less free to fight, soften his will, turn his imagination backward towards his wife rather than forward towards the enemy?" These are recurring questions. In time of depression and frustration we were given peace-time license to examine our aggressions, but in time of war they become assets which it is praiseworthy to investigate.

Here again it is important to ask the right question. Not: Are we aggressive enough? as if aggression were something which merely varied quantitatively from high to low, like temperature or blood pressure or the amount of a vitamin stored in one's liver. Such a question gets us nowhere. Let us ask instead: What kind of pattern of aggressive behavior have we, as Americans? When is aggression justified in our eyes and when is it condemned? Who can be aggressive to whom, where? And with the answers to such questions as these we can look at the present world scene which calls for the exercise of certain types of aggression and ask: Have we, as Americans, got the kind of aggression that the present world developments demand? If not, what has to be done to alter the way we see the world—something actually easier to do than to alter the form of American aggressiveness.

A good place to study the American pattern is a playground where each mother is shouting her admonitions at her child. "Stand up for yourself! Don't come crying to me when he takes your shovel. Get it back. You're big enough to look after yourself." "Jimmy! Look out, he's just a little baby, don't hit him." "Well, hit him back if he hits you. Don't stand there like a sissy and take it." "Go on, make him learn he can't hit you without getting hurt." "Tommy, don't pull that little boy's hair. He's smaller than you are. He doesn't know any better. If you want to fight, pick on someone your own size." "Billy, don't tear that nice little girl's dress. Big boys don't hit little girls." "No, I won't ask his mother to make him give it back. Go and get it yourself if you want it. He's not much bigger than you are. Go and take it away from him! Show you've got what it takes." And as each mother leads her dirt-smeared champion home, she thinks to herself either: "He can stand up for himself all right. He can take it, and he can dish it out. He's got what it takes," or in a worried unadmitted undertone: "I wish he'd stand up for himself more. He's brave enough when it comes to teasing kids smaller than he is or pulling the girls' hair, but he won't stand up to anything his size."

When the children get a little older, when it is a teacher instead of a parent, a playground director instead of a nurse, a new note, the notion of rules, enters in more prominently: "Play fair." "It's his turn now." "Let him have it for a while now, Jimmy. You've had it a long time." "No, boys, turn about is fair play." "It's not fair to take the little boy's ball, Jimmy, he's smaller than you are." "Billy! Do you think it's fair to grab everything just because you're bigger than the others? I'm ashamed of you."

Educators commenting on the contradictory threads in our culture have stressed that we confuse children about aggression; that we teach them to be tough and to stand up for themselves, and, at the same time, teach them that aggression is wrong and should be suppressed and, if possible, repressed. But actually there is a pattern which underlies these contradictory orders, and a very clear one. It is obscured, however, in the mind of the educated thinker by his knowledge of Anglo-Saxon institutions. To the educated man who has read thoroughly in English literature, fair play means certain definite things. It means "obeying the rules," and the "rules" are thought of as a device for keeping people from bullying or taking an unfair advantage of the other person. One's character is defined by the way in which the rules are embodied in one's behavior—and "That's not cricket" may be applied to making love to the wife of a man who is in a weaker position than oneself. Our games traditions, although altered and transformed, are Anglo-Saxon in form; and fair play does mean for us, as for the English, a standard of behavior between the weak and the strong—a standard which is curiously incomprehensible to the German. During the last war, articles used to appear in German papers exploring this curious Anglo-Saxon notion called "fair play," reproduced without translation—for there was no translation.

Now the element which is so difficult to translate in the idea of "fair play" is not the fact that there are rules. Rules are an integral part of German life, rules for behavior of inferior to superior, for persons of every status, for every formal situation. Rules for the hunter, who is ashamed if he does not hit his quarry in the appointed, difficult and honorable spot; rules for the man of honor who must know when to be insulted or be forever disgraced. Rules are common enough. The point that was incomprehensible was the inclusion of the other person's weakness inside the rules so that "fair play" included in it a statement of relative strength of the opponents and it ceased to be fair to beat a weak opponent. Something had to be done about a weak opponent so that he became a strong opponent, and, if possible, a slightly stronger opponent, else there could be no fairness, and hence no honor in winning. The crude idea that the point of strength is to triumph over weakness simply doesn't fit in. The rules of the game always include at least two players. When one's opponent is stronger than oneself, maximum effort is called forth; when one's opponent is weaker, maximum effort is no longer compatible with fair play. The Anglo-Saxon fear that a boy will be a coward contains in it the fear that he will also be a bully—for bullying is seen as a sign of responding to the same wrong stimulus—a difference in strength. The "fair play" character always finds the greater strength of his opponent a stimulus.[2] When the other is stronger, he puts out more effort, is "braver," and when the other is weaker, he reduces his effort, is "gentle." The coward, however, doesn't see the situation that way at all—another person's greater strength is a signal to him to cringe; and such an attitude finds its counterpart in bullying whenever the chance occurs.

But in the Anglo-Saxon version of bravery and proper displays of aggression, there is a far greater emphasis on the rules than there is in America. In England, aggression is taken more for granted. Boys are regarded by adults as tough little devils without any sense of the fitness of things, ready to kick and bite until taught that "hitting below the belt isn't done." The job of civilizing them is the job of teaching them a set of rules which have been devised to make men behave decently to each other. Boys are expected to fight; and while it is the job of schoolmasters to see they fight as little as possible, it is the job of the older boys to see that they become the right kind of boys, that when they do fight, they play fair. The attention of each boy is focused on the rules rather than on the opponent, for the opponent has already been included in the rules. The relative strengths of two who can fight a battle has been laid down, and if the battle is allowed, then the rules which disallow "blows beneath the belt"—or tacitly allow a given tackle because both are strong enough to carry it off—are sufficient to keep the fighters decent.

In America, a new twist has been given to this Anglo-Saxon position. Our attitude towards bullies and cowards, towards hitting below the belt and hitting a man when he is down, is the same as the English attitude. Our notion of fair play, like theirs, includes the opponent, but it includes him far more personally. Where a count of English admonitions would show a larger emphasis on "Play fair," the American is more likely to bristle with "Pick on someone your own size," "Cradle robber!", etc. The American child is taught to think about each situation as it comes up, rather than to relax into an implicit acceptance of a set of rules which all those whom he meets will play by. And for a very good reason. Practically every American boy who is not tied to his mother's apron strings is going to encounter other boys whose ideas of fighting are very different from his own; perhaps Negroes, whose view of what is fair is dangerously skewed by the circumstances that they themselves have been too long "fair game" for white people; or perhaps Puerto Rican and Mexican children, whose romanticism takes a direction other than fair play. He may meet Irish children whose valuation of fighting is simple and absolute, to whom fighting is something that one does, like eating, rather than part of an elaborate game; or he may meet first-generation Sicilian children, whose fathers still go about in fear of a stiletto in their backs.

It's all very well to talk about "fair play," but when one ten-year-old American boy—especially in a large city —meets another bigger than he is, he can never be sure that the other boy knows the rules. He has to be tough, gauge the situation on its merits, shift his expectation one way or another in quick response to the look in the other boy's eye. He is growing up and going out into a world that is not orderly and dependable—as was the world of English boys before the war where the toughest public house had its established code—but into a world which is too mixed and too unpredictable to allow him to rely on a code. It is not an accident that our cliché for the Englishman who carries his code about with him puts him on a desert island—dressing for dinner in an uninhabited waste where there is no one who doesn't know the code to throw a spear or a beer bottle or a rotten tomato at him.

So the American mother, watching her three-year-old learn to make his way among other children, is faced with a very real dilemma. She shares the Anglo-Saxon attitude towards relative strengths, towards bullies and cowards, and hitting a man when he is down. She also shares the Anglo-Saxon belief that fighting should be curbed. The type of legislation which outlawed dueling and the attitude which has never wanted a standing army are parts of American culture as they are of English culture. Fighting is crude and uncivilized, especially if the weapons are efficient. Guns and knives are the weapons of foreigners and criminals; fists, if you must fight, for the Englishman and the American.

The English mother or the English nurse has a simpler job. She must teach her charge to start as few fights as possible and that there are rules. That is enough. The men, his father, his schoolmaster, and the older boys will teach him quite enough of fighting later, taking him to boxing matches and all that. So women insist on the curbing of aggression, and men—as parents and educators—stress the rules which govern its permitted expression. But in America, mothers and nurses are more impressed with the dangers which little boys will encounter in a world full of tough, strange, foreign characters, of mixed breeds and manners, than they are with the little boys' potential aggressiveness. "He has to learn to look after himself" means something different on the edge of an American slum even from what it means in the East End of London. Will he be tough enough? That is the question which lurks in the American mother's eyes as she watches her two-year-old stand passive while another child yanks his toy out of his hand. In her eyes, the situation is the reverse of that which faces the English mother. Where the English mother is anxiously inspecting her bit of human material to see if he will, in a manner of speaking, shape up well, take a bit of polish and turn out as a man, the

American mother sees the external dangers which her child will have to confront. Will they be too much for him—first physically, and later in business, in politics? To take it, he *must* learn to dish it out. "Don't let him take that shovel, Billy. Hit him back!" She wants to teach him not to fight; she doesn't approve of fighting. But he has to have some practice in standing up for himself, or other people will walk all over him. Where the English mother can see—in her mind's eye—generations of schoolmasters and policemen umpiring the roughest games, assuring that 99 per cent of the children of the land will play by the same rules, the American mother sees instead a crude melee of frontier battles, gangster battles, tong wars, feuds, Indian attacks, and hijacking. American history mixes with the front pages of the tabloids; G-men and gangsters stride through her imagination. Her baby boy is going out to face this world of violence—and she looks across at her husband, belt unbuttoned, slumped comfortably, reading the sports news. He hardly ever gets angry, doesn't half stand up for his rights, could have had a raise years ago, but didn't like to start a row about it. If her small Jimmy, standing with toes turned in, looking very small in his new overalls, is going to get along in this world and be more successful than his dad—and for what else did she bear him?—he'll have to be a good deal tougher than his dad, who lets himself be pushed around. Which means that if she thought in theoretical terms, she would say, "His inheritance of aggression isn't enough. If he follows his father, he won't be strong enough."

Thus several circumstances conspire together: the rules of the game and the emphasis on opponents being equal and effort being permissible only against the strong, which we share with England; the confused, turbulent unpatterned quality of American life, part of it real and due to the mixture of different standards of handling aggression, part of it symbolic, so that all those groups against which one is discriminating, Negroes, Puerto Ricans, Foreigners, Orientals, become invested with that hostility which we have shown them and seem dangerous and threatening; and finally, the American insistence that the child shall surpass his father, be more successful than his father, which being translated means tougher than his father. All of these circumstances are given a special tone by the fact that it is women, the mother and the nurse and the sister, who exhort the baby boy to be tough.

When a man is teaching his son to double up his fist or throw a spear, he is teaching him something that he has learned the way of, a skill, a way of doing things. He is not merely teaching the child to be aggressive or even to be assertive, but how to behave once his aggression is aroused, how to defend himself, and how to attack. He is able to concentrate on the way of doing it and need not emphasize either the aggression necessary, nor the situations under which aggression is appropriate. For the mother's paradoxical, "Don't hit that little boy, Jimmy," and, "Stand up for *yourself*, can't you?" the father can substitute, "Here, not like that, son. Plant your feet now, plant your feet." Fighting behavior which is taught by males to males has inevitably a different quality from fighting behavior which is taught to males by females. American women, ambivalent towards fighting, considering it at once wrong and necessary, succeed in teaching their children that fighting must always be done in self-defense, and yet that you have to practice getting angry. Where a male mentor could emphasize practicing a technique of throwing spears or shooting arrows among savages, or of boxing, fencing, or wrestling among ourselves, it is not appropriate for women in our culture to stand about on street corners and give instructions in the techniques of uppercuts. They must confine themselves to vague exhortations about "standing up for yourself" without giving any detailed advice. So the American boy learns a series of lessons: aggression and fighting are wrong and are to be avoided as low, liable to arouse his mother's and often his father's disapproval; but aggression and fighting are also necessary, and, in fact, compulsory whenever anyone tries to "pick on you," "push you around," "take things away from you." "You have to be tough to get along in this world, and you, Billy, probably aren't tough enough. Your dad isn't."

The chip on the shoulder, which is not, as many Americans imagine, just a figure of speech, is the folk expression of this set of attitudes. In many parts of America small boys deliberately put chips on their shoulders and walk about daring anyone to knock the chip off. By putting a chip on his shoulder and then waiting to have it knocked off, a boy can epitomize all the contradictory orders which have been given. He isn't being aggressive, going about knocking nice little boys down. No, indeed. He doesn't hit anybody. But he has to get some practice in fighting; he must have a few fights to his credit just to be sure he can fight. And he has to reassure himself that he is tough enough to take it. So he sets the chip on his shoulder which defines the situation: here is a boy who knows he shouldn't start a fight, who wants to prove he's game, who defines the boy who knocks off the chip as strong enough to be a legitimate opponent, for it is always right to fight back. Meanwhile, the other boy, the boy who has to knock the chip off, can argue: "He started it, Mom. He was looking for a fight, or he wouldn't have put the chip on his shoulder. He was askin' for it, Mom. Honest he was. He'd 'a' thought I was a sissy if I'd pretended it wasn't there."

Out of a series of conflicting traditions, out of the confusion which can be built in the male mind when females are those who urge his maleness insistently upon him, there has emerged a special American form of aggressiveness; aggressiveness which can never be shown except when the other fellow starts it; aggressiveness which is so unsure of itself that it has to be proved. After all, it's all very well for Mom to say, "Go and stand up for yourself." She doesn't know how he can hit. She's a woman and she can't know. Yet she insists, and her son tries to live up to her insistence, until aggressiveness becomes labeled as something that women expect of a man, and potency itself becomes a symbol of aggression, rather than, as in the classical European form, aggressiveness serving as a substitute for potency.[3]

When will the American fight? When the game is fair; when he can't be told that he started the fight, nor that he is pushing around someone smaller than he is? Yes. And with his back to the wall, as the English fight best? No. The back to the wall position depends on the English basic assurance that they have more aggression than they need. When your back is against the wall, then, by the rules of the game, every ounce of aggression that is in you must come out. And, if you keep the rules and hit hard, you always win. That is the English conviction. But the American is a little different. His gaze has been concentrated, not on the rules, but upon his strength in the face of variable and unpredictable circumstances. He doesn't know whether he has enough aggressiveness, and he doesn't need the same absolute license to display it. Back to the wall positions are therefore not best for him. His best position is in a fight which somebody else started, for which he cannot blame himself and for which no one else can blame him, getting in good hard punches and surprising himself at how well he is doing. And despite his characteristic boasting, his "We won the last war, and we'll win this one," the American is always surprised when he does do anything like as well as he says he is going to, if his aggressiveness is at stake.

Boasting, for an American, has a special quality

which goes back to a style set up in childhood. This quality has been discussed by Gregory Bateson [4] as it contrasts with English behavior, and he has dramatized both patterns in terms of the breakfast table. At the English breakfast table, the father performs, hems and haws over his paper, expresses his opinion of the Prime Minister and the Irish question and other people's letters to the *Times*, and the children listen, quietly. Whether they admire or try not to pay attention, their view of exhibitionism versus spectatorship is based on father hurrumping to a juvenile audience. At the American breakfast table, the children perform and father is the spectator, listening to their outpourings of successful games, jokes, achievements. Into their exhibitionism before this grown-up, apparently sympathetic but also probably secretly amused audience, there comes inevitably an over-compensatory note; they paint the episode in brighter colors to be sure to catch and keep the parental attention, to be sure in fact that they have a right to the attention they are getting. The English exhibitionist father has occasionally to frown at a fidget to be sure his audience is not secretly slipping away from him; the American exhibitionist child has to shout and over-emphasize his exploits to be sure his audience will not be contemptuous of such small events. So the pattern is set; and later from the lecture platform, the Englishman adopts a style of behavior based on father at the breakfast table, and to an American audience he seems irritatingly arrogant, self-assured, glancing about with Olympian disapproval if there is a slight scuffle of feet in a corner of the lecture hall. The American, faced with an audience, patterns his behavior on his childhood, on his boasts at the family table, on the recitations he stumbled through in Sunday School. His audience is a group of parents to be impressed, legitimately, if possible, but otherwise with glorious strutting over-statements. To an Englishman, this style appears boastful.

Europeans often speak of Americans as childish and make elaborate analogues between a young country and people who behave like children or, at the best, like adolescents. This is, of course, nonsense. To assign maturity to the members of one society and immaturity to the members of another is merely to weight one kind of behavior as more approved and therefore more mature than another. Any society which reproduces itself can be spoken of as mature. Only if men and women so retained the adjustments of childhood that they were unable to assume adult responsibilities for the next generation sufficiently well to rear that next generation, would we have any right to speak of the typical adult of that society—which would not survive very long—as immature. (It is possible that extreme social dependency of adults, as in slavery, might be characterized as immature.) Nevertheless, it is possible to characterize a people in terms of what experiences of their maturation are used as a matrix, as a pattern for adult behavior. If English children learn about exhibitionism only from watching adults—because little exhibitionism is permitted to children—later their exhibitionism will have a peculiarly adult, heavy-father flavor. Similarly, American children learn their exhibitionism in childhood, and it retains the characteristic style of a child who is trying to put himself across in an adult world. The American lecturer is no more childish than the English lecturer—but the behavior of each is patterned on a different childhood experience.

This boasting goes with the whole American character in which the child is expected to outdistance the parent, to be brighter, stronger, more aggressive, more successful; and it is for the American child a sort of whistling in the dark, a necessary precautionary measure, as he tries to live up to an unknown demand upon his unknown strength. In wartime, great and unknown demands are made upon young men who had learned to settle down into the friendly human relations which men, as opposed to women, expect from men in this society. They must suddenly display again the aggressiveness which their mothers enjoined upon them and in which they are relatively unskilled. Boasting is very necessary. When Mersa Matruh fell to Rommel, in June 1942, the headlines splashed it for an hour, but later editions of the evening papers came out with: "American Planes Bomb Wake Island." Were we escaping from reality, smuggling away into small print the news that OUR SIDE had taken a terrible defeat? Or were we merely indulging in the extra touch of boasting which was necessary if, in the face of defeat, we were to go on fighting? I think the latter.

Speakers, editors, and propagandists—consciously and

unconsciously—are dealing every day with this two-edged problem of how to phrase the world so as to bring out our full fighting strength. We must see the enemy as stronger—either in men or resources or wickedness—or we cannot fight at all. That "must" we share with the English; it is part of the rules of the game. We may, of course, interfere unendingly in the affairs of very small countries under the heading of "keeping order," but that we rationalize as a policeman's job, not as a real fight. If the fight is to be real, the enemy must be as strong or, preferably, quite a little stronger. There must be a strong chance that we may lose. But at the same time, as our pattern of aggressiveness is based on the undefined, excessive demands made by mothers who articulately disapproved of all the techniques of aggression in small boys—who told them at one and the same time to "stand up for yourself" and "not to keep getting into fights"—there is an unsureness in our approach to a battle which has to be compensated for by boasting and over-confidence in our side. The taxi-driver in Detroit who said to me on the day MacArthur's arrival in Australia was announced: "It just makes me feel good, it makes me want to go and enlist. I was in the last one, and I think I'll get into this one. Makes you want to fight to hear about a man like that," expressed this position. What exactly had MacArthur done at that moment—merely reached Australia. But he was the symbol of OUR SIDE, and he had come through to fight again. Everybody felt good; everybody could go on now.

Pearl Harbor has been compared to Dunkirk—to

Dunkirk which woke the English up. But the Pearl Harbor which woke the Americans up was not the defeat we suffered there—because we didn't know about that for quite a while afterwards and we reacted to the later details negatively and poorly. The Pearl Harbor which woke America up was just the fact that Japan came along and pushed the chip off our shoulder and left us free to fight where our hands had been tied before. For two years we had been engaged in "National Defense"; unwilling to start anything, watching our enemies strengthen their lines about us, hog-tied by our own phrasing of life which forbade our starting a war—a phrasing which we share with the other democracies and which will some day be the basis of a better world. But right at the moment it was a handicap. And then Japan pushed the chip off, and we could fight; fight with a clear conscience, because we didn't start this fight. Japan did. And then Germany came along and ganged up with her and did the starting, too. Axis propagandists have tried to make a good deal of the fact that we presented Japan with impossible terms, of the fact that we put the chip on our shoulder. And so we did. It's an old American custom, and, when followed, has behind it that part of the American character which fights best when other people start pushing us around.

CHAPTER X

Fighting the War American Style

★

THERE ARE two ways of looking at the American Character and the year 1942. We can regard the course of the war, the shape of the world, as a sort of rigid and fixed scheme into which we, also rigid and fixed, fit. All the soldiers lined up on the other side are of a given strength, with a given caliber of arms; all the ships in the sea have a known tonnage; all our bombers a known cruising range. There will therefore be a given number of defeats and a given number of victories. The Office of War Information will handle this news in a given way, concealing just enough defeats just long enough to make us miserably worried and depressed; the Office of Price Administration will do a given amount of shilly-shallying about prices; the Senate will make a specified number of moves against Labor; the President will sometimes pull his punches very quietly and at a given moment let us have it, for all it's worth, etc. We could construct such an ironclad future and then add up our capacity to take it and go on fighting. That would be the Balinese way of looking at the future, all fixed but "not yet clear." A great many Americans appear to be thinking just like that today, acting as if the whole course of the war—which of course *may* go right in the end!—were out of our hands, just lunging along by itself, like an engine with the engineer asleep at the throttle. Whether disaster follows inevitably becomes just a question of how straight the tracks are, how much steam has been got up, and what the train meets. If the enemy is able to turn the switch so that the train goes into the river, it goes in.

This is an essentially passive attitude towards the world; an attitude completely out of key with American history, out of key with our picture of ourselves as a people who, virtually singlehanded—each man alone with an ax and a rifle—conquered a wilderness. It is an attitude born of riding on subways, working in office buildings, and poring helplessly over ticker tape—the attitude of men who wouldn't know what to do with an ax or a rifle, of women who have never in their lives seen a pump or a wood stove or a chicken which had to be cleaned before it was eaten. When our journalists get angry and say that Americans are soft because they have too many gadgets about, this is fundamentally what they mean; not that Americans can't run their three miles or swim a goodly distance or go without their dinners on a mountain side, but that they have lost their sense of being able to control their own destiny by their own inventiveness and toughness and determination.

The other way to look at the year 1942 is that it will

be, in part at least, what we make it. On the military front, our generals will pick the scene of battle, not Mr. Hitler. We may not win the battle—that will depend on transport and on material and number of men —but we can take the initiative, bomb Tokio rather than wait for the Jap to bomb San Francisco. On the home front, every good-sized community, every city, can tackle its own problems, get its own civilian defense going, organize its own housing and settle its own feeding problems without waiting for Washington like so many helpless and spineless invalids waiting to be lifted from one deck chair into another. The city that waits for Washington to tell them when to call a meeting of air-raid wardens, instead of setting up such a good system that Washington will send field workers out to observe what they have done on their own, is being passive, waiting to see whether "we can take it" instead of showing that "we have got what it takes."

But no matter how much we are able to push the passive gadget-born attitudes out of our minds and feel that the future is partly in our own hands and partly in the hands of the enemy but not at all in the hands of some vague force which is pushing both us and the enemy around—something called "History" or "The Decay of Civilization" or "Economic Determinism" or "The World Revolution" or any other mythological substitute for taking responsibility for our lives—it is still important to take stock of ourselves. The essence of the Puritan character, the character which has reached its most complete development in America, is the

mixture of practicality and faith in the power of God—
or moral purpose. "Trust in God, my boys, and keep
your powder dry," said Cromwell, a Puritan, emerging
from the Anglo-Saxon tradition which has nurtured all
of us. "Get your distaff ready and God will send the
flax" is the sort of motto on which the American
pioneer woman did her spinning for nine tall sons and
daughters on the edge of the wilderness. She didn't ask
God to send her a distaff any more than Cromwell
exhorted his men just to let their powder horns dangle
in the stream and God would look after them. The
combination of hard work, good sense, and recognition
of physical forces which had to be tamed and controlled;
with a faith that "All things work together for good to
them that love God" is the American faith which, if it
isn't silly enough to try to move mountains, is strong
enough to tunnel them or build them as the need arises.

In moments of crisis, in order to keep our powder dry
we must be accurately informed. What are our strengths
and what our weaknesses? If we have a weak flank let's
not leave it uncovered. If we have a shortage in materials needed for ship building, then let's not put our
faith in ships. Take stock, and take stock accurately;
don't fool yourself, don't overlook a single weakness
nor a single strength. Chalk it up on the door, so we
know where we stand. There are two parts to this cove-
nant which we as a people have made with a Moral
Universe: we must use every ounce of energy and inventiveness we have; and we must be moving in a direction

that we know is right. Then and only then can we feel that we are invincible.

During the last war a great lot of nonsense was talked about the folly of two sides who both prayed to the same God and who both felt that God was with them. We weren't both praying to the same God. The Germans saw God as on their side just because they were Germans, as preferring, for some reason which they found no difficulty in understanding, the color of their hair and the curve of distribution along which their long and round heads fell. They followed a tribal God whose preferences were determined by race. It wasn't necessary for him to scrutinize the rights and wrongs of battle; the only issue was who you were. If you were German, God, being a German God, was on your side. But what American could kneel and ask, "Please, God, help us to win just because we are us; never mind whether our cause is just or not"? The words would curdle in the mouths of the most fanatical. Nobody pays much attention to the words of the *Star-Spangled Banner,* but somewhere, in the dimly lit, seldom inspected corridors of our hearts, the phrases "Then triumph we must," "For our Cause it is Just," "And this be our motto, In God is our Trust" still echo and re-echo with an extra sonorousness. The only way to get God on one's side is to be on the right side—that has been the whole teaching of Puritanism; it lies back of the conditional love we give our children; it lies back of all the emphasis on work and disallowance of pleasure; and it lies back of our inability to fight on, if the battle goes against us continually and inexplicably, because we come to believe that we must have taken the wrong road after all.

For there is a fundamental weakness in the puritan position as well as a deep and abiding strength. The puritan is sustained in effort; sustained in his systematic attempt to turn one talent into many, to conquer the wilderness and build cities where forests stood before by his belief that he is right. As long the vineyards spring up and the walls of his city rise, his zeal does not slacken. Hardships do not faze him, and small setbacks only harden his resolve. He has idled, and God has warned him by a drought or a bank failure. So be it; he must work harder. But against great and overwhelming defeats, defeats whose moral relationship to his own behavior he cannot see, he is helpless. That is why the Depression was such a terrible blow to the American people. If there had been the necessary prophetic voices to come forward and say: "You have sinned, ye people of America, rich and proud and safe, you have left your brothers wounded and dying by the wayside, tossing them money when they needed your hands and your brains. The way was plain before you and you took it not, therefore are you punished," the Depression could have become a great moral experience. Americans might have realized ten years earlier, and far more vigorously, that the answer to the question "Am I my brother's keeper?" keeps getting more complicated—as communications narrow the world—but doesn't change. When we declared war on Germany in

1917, we recognized that we had a responsibility for Europe, and then we refused to carry it on.

This is not a theory of history that I am advancing; it is a theory of character structure. I am not suggesting that the Depression in America could have been averted if the United States had entered the League of Nations and the World Court. I am, however, suggesting that if we had seen the Depression as a penalty for our moral failure as a people, it would have had a very different effect upon our minds and hearts. For the essence of guilt is that it is relieved by punishment. The sequence: *I sinned, therefore am I punished, if I then endure the punishment, repent and turn towards new ways, then shall I be again blessed* is the essence of the puritan dogma. And always, to console the puritan for his extra sackcloth and ashes, there is the hope that like the Prodigal Son he'll get an extra fat calf—or, more charitably interpreted, that the fatted calf will taste especially tender because of the penitence in which it is consumed.

This war must be made to make sense to us, as a people, if we are to fight it and win it; and then work to keep all that we have gained. We must fight it like Americans from the start, taking care of our tools and our weapons and improvising new ones as we go, sure of our direction, and therefore sure of our ultimate victory.

American character is one of our principal assets, and we are adding up its strengths and its weaknesses. What then do we find in addition to this fundamental need to believe that we are right? We find a people who trust themselves more than their parents—and for parents read: leaders, officials, generals, etc. The whole emphasis of their education has taught Americans that they and their brothers and cousins are smarter than their fathers and uncles. Parents are all very well when one is a child, or when one is sick or a failure—otherwise, the grown-up American strikes out for himself, pushing his father aside and hardly noticing that he does so. This means two things: it means that we can only move forward as a whole people—not in terms of single leaders whom we passively follow—and that those heroes or leaders whom we do acclaim, we must acclaim as something like ourselves, not something different from ourselves. As long as MacArthur is the kind of man that every mother believes her newborn baby may be; as long as every little boy, posturing on the curbstone with a toy gun, feels that he is already MacArthur; as long as we feel that MacArthur is just the American spirit—large and reliable against the sky—we are strong. But if the war should ever come to seem a battle in which Roosevelt and MacArthur and Kaiser are supermen—father figures who do our fighting or our thinking for us while we simply watch the show—then there would be danger, for such an attitude would bring out not the strengths of the American character—but its weaknesses.

This means that we must never see THE GOVERNMENT as something other than ourselves, for then automatically we become children; and not real honest children, but adults dwarfed to childhood again in weakness and ineffectiveness. This is a danger that the NEW DEAL has never clearly envisaged and avoided. It has been government *for* the people, but often not government *by* the people. True, the poor and the downtrodden voted for the New Deal because the New Deal gave them bread; but they were not voting for something that was themselves, but for something that was other than themselves, good and kind—but other. Distinctly other. Democracy, the American brand, does not mean merely that all kinds of people participate in a program or that there are social measures directed towards the amelioration of the state of the poor. It is necessary that the people should have bread; but it is also necessary that the people should feel that it is *their* bread which they have earned. Under a modern economy, individuals cannot be held responsible for earning a living as they have been held responsible—never too fairly—in our immediate past; but no American is dignified by being fed by The Government, nor, sadly enough, by working for The Government.

A basic job during the war must be to close this gap, fostered by benevolent paternalism on the one hand and by the peculiar form of romanticism characteristic of the National Association of Manufacturers on the other. For if the New Deal was caught by the picture of Olympian social planners setting things right for men, the Republican Party and the N.A.M. were equally caught by the picture of an old-fashioned business man benevolently presiding over his own little factory, which he had virtually built with his own hands, manned by "his men" to whom he was bound by ties of benevolent affection. One side has fought for the right of a man to be fed by The Government when he is hungry; the other for the right of a man to starve until he voluntarily takes employment under a factory owner who knows what is good for him. Both sides have too often forgotten that this is a common venture; that benevolent factory owners have long since vanished in favor of corporations, monster impersonal mechanisms which moved of their own momentum, with public relations men to write their apologias; and that popular government was rapidly vanishing into a series of bureaucracies with public relations men to write their apologias; and with the people—as prime movers, not as passive beneficiaries—just exactly nowhere at all.

To win this war, we need the impassioned effort of every individual in the country; to get that effort it will be necessary to throw the ball to the people of the small towns and the large, of the farms and the mines and merchant marine. In the first shock after Pearl Harbor, the American people, like children afraid of the dark, wanted Washington to tell them what to do. But such an attitude is neither healthy nor dependable—if a government were foolish enough to want to build upon it. It will not be enough for each American to be told, individually, that the government wants him to buy so many bonds or grow so many pigs or so many acres of wheat or corn. Each of those individual Americans, with the people of his town or his township, his block or his union local or his ship, must become part of groups demanding the chance to do *more* than the government has asked, demanding the right to use their imagination and their devotion, and use it well. The War Department has done a fine job with its personalizing of the war effort so that each town and village can know when one of their boys has surpassed all expectations. But in every branch of the war effort the same thing must be done—each town, each village, each factory, must feel that they are doing more than was asked of them; more, in fact, than the government knew to ask. Out of their local brains and guts, out of their local hearts and purposes, they themselves are forging the weapons of war. The government must cease to be "they" and become "we."

For to win this war, we need our strengths, not our weaknesses; and our strength comes out when we feel that we are grown up and in control, but ebbs away from us when we feel a parent hand, no matter how kind a hand, on the wheel. Regimented, told what to do instead of told why something needs to be done, told to obey orders instead of demanding that orders be given, we will not be the stuff that victories are made of. This is the point which is forgotten by those who urge that we must streamline America to match a streamlined Germany. Streamlining peoples depends upon the stuff those people are made of. We would be as bad a version of a streamlined population as we would be bad at doing the goose step. It's not in our way of walking. Just as no horseman is foolish enough to curb a horse which runs better when given its head, so no American charged with the task of leadership—if he understands the American people—will risk trying to streamline them. For a risk it would be; round pegs in square holes, we'd rattle about in a hopelessly inefficient fashion.

We must be as hardheaded about this problem as Americans are traditionally hardheaded about machines. The American construction engineer, putting in a power line with a tremendous penalty clause in the contract, knows he's got a job on his hands. He mustn't make mistakes in his surveying; he mustn't choose his foremen wrong; he mustn't over-estimate; he must use just what he's got, with maximum efficiency. What we need at present is more of the engineering spirit in the conduct of the war on the human side. We aren't fighting the war with so many "hands" or so many "men"— just human ciphers, one 2,145,200,000th of the human beings on earth. We are fighting it with 130,000,000 Americans who are a very special kind of human material, with very definite qualities. These qualities take special handling. Dies made for aluminum won't work for stainless steel. When we say we have to fight and win the war the American way, we aren't making a vague moral statement about the superiority of democracy as a way of life over totalitarianism as a way of life. (Not that a lot of people who use the phrase aren't doing just that, of course.) We are saying something more. We are saying a war fought by a democracy has a certain style, certain definite handicaps, certain definite weaknesses, as over against the deadly concentration of a totalitarian state.[1] The only way to compensate for these weaknesses is to use the strengths you have got, and that to the full. There isn't much leeway. If a democracy gets under weigh slower, and can't get *further*, just exactly where are we? At every step, we must use what we have and use it wisely. Which means that Americans, in camps, in industry, in our towns and cities which must be disciplined to act as one if sabotage or bombing or invasion should come, must set up forms of organization which will evoke every strength and minimize every weakness. Are Americans bad at following orders literally? Then the answer is not to shout the order louder or shoot people who don't obey orders. The answer is to set up a form of organization which depends less on literal orders and more on whatever Americans are good at—taking responsibility, for instance. Are Americans quick to resent privilege—and start grumbling because "The big bosses don't have to subscribe part of their salaries"? The answer isn't to fire the agitators or even to try an abstruse and possibly quite accurate argument about income taxes, but for the big bosses to sign the same paper the employees do, publicly and quickly. Then the gun-carriages will roll over the assembly line. "We want to do it our own way, not the way the State tells us," says the Municipal Defense Council. The answer isn't to send out a tight-lipped executive order to throw out the vigorous municipal leadership and put in someone docile enough to take orders from the State office; the message is: "Go to it, but we're going to watch your record, my boys. You think you're good. Well, you'd better be."

We talk about "social engineering"—vaguely—as a way of describing making a few plans and possibly taking into account the system of transportation, the state of the land, water power, and distribution of population. Sometimes people even include the fact that social engineering is done with human material, usually only to say it is necessary to make allowances for its irrational and intractable qualities. If instead of "human material" we substitute "Americans in 1942" and study the qualities of those Americans, we find that social engineering—like other kinds of engineering —has some fundamental rules. What do you want to do? What do you have to do it with? How long have you got? Those are the questions, and the way in which the engineer uses his brains with the answers to all three questions in mind, determines the success or failure of the enterprise. There is a scientific logic about social engineering, just as with any other kind of engineering. Steel and aluminum must be handled differently. So must Americans and Englishmen, Australians and Irishmen and Poles. We are Americans. Are we using our strengths?

Perhaps one of the simplest and most dramatic instances of this relationship between a kind of political system, the kind of character which it fosters and upon which it is based, and a kind of wartime behavior is the question of telling the truth about the conduct of the war. It is not a simple matter of its being right to tell the truth and wrong to lie and that democracy and right go together, and, therefore, the whole truth must be told. This argument will be vigorously rejected by generals and admirals who say that this right, this duty, conflicts with another; it is right for a government to decide what is best for its people in wartime. "The people are in danger, only the Government can know, etc." An argument conducted on these terms may end in accusations of "autocracy" on the one hand and "democratic nonsense" on the other. It resolves nothing. But if we say instead: The people who are going to be told the truth or lied to are Americans. How do Americans take to being lied to? Very badly indeed. And who would have to do the lying? Dr. Goebbels, with every newspaper a helpless and compliant instrument of his will; with every radio just another mouthpiece; with all power highly centralized and controlled? Oh, no, certainly not; just the President, just the Chairmen of Senate Committees and the Chairmen of House Committees; just the heads of permanent bureaus who don't like the emergency bureaus and the heads of war agencies who resent the permanent bureaus; just the Secretary of War and the Secretary of the Navy; just a foreign envoy hastily finishing his speech to the Senate five minutes before he delivers it; just half a hundred different people, all working together in a loose and lightly co-ordinated fashion. And is a policy, based on lies rather than truth and administered in such a fashion, likely to succeed? Or will all the lies be found out and blazoned in whichever newspapers happen to dislike the politics of the person who uttered them? If this happens, won't it lower the morale of the American people? When we answer yes, we are not making mystical statements about Democracy; we have merely tackled a simple engineering problem. People who are willing to have their governments decide what they should and should not know, aren't the stuff of which democratic countries are made. Democratic governments *can't lie* efficiently. They will get found out; and when they are found out, the people will be angry. If, however, we insist that every spokesman who commands the respect of the people should attempt to tell the truth and then lambaste him if he fails to do so, we have some chance of succeeding at it. Ten people out of communication with each other have some hope of telling the same story about an event upon which they are all well informed. They have no hope at all of telling a consistent lie.

Which doesn't mean that military news shouldn't be thought about and placed in a context before it is given to the people. (This quite aside from the obvious necessity of withholding military secrets, which is not up for discussion.) As Americans we know what we can take and what we can't take. We think it's the business of the government to handle the news in a way that will make us stronger, not weaker, in fighting this war. Crushing defeats are hard to take. "They make us feel as if the bottom had dropped out of things. They make us feel like helpless kids. If you can tell us at the same time that you tell us about a defeat about some guy like Kelly it helps—something done by an American, just a guy like us. Let the wise guys tell us the loss of Matruh can't be evened up by bombing Wake Island. Sure, we know that. It's not that we need victories; but we gotta feel we have victories in us. It's not that we're asking for this war to be a pushover. We don't think much of the kind of guys that like pushovers. We know it's going to be tough. And when we lick something tough, we know we're good.

"But remember this, big boys who don't tell when things are going badly. We won't believe—as you want us to—that you didn't tell us for *our* good, for our 'morale'! We have an all-fired strong suspicion that our 'morale' is just another name for your skins. You think we'll blame you if we find out there was a slip-up, and that if you wait to spill the bad news until some nice little victory comes along, it will give you an out. Well, it won't.

"But one of the things that gets us down is uncertainty. We are fighting; maybe we won; maybe we lost; impossible to say; maybe a great loss . . . not knowing about Pearl Harbor. Having all those ships lost in the Java Sea sprung on us so much later. We can face a defeat. We're grown up. We can take it—straight. But all this muddy uncertainty, this fog in the Aleutian Islands, that gets us down. It's like something in the dark that Mom used to say would get us if we were bad. It hasn't any name. We can't talk about it and say So What? and square our shoulders and spit on our hands. Three hundred ships lost. Okay, we'll build three thousand.

But 'Things are going very badly.' . . . 'No announcement can yet be made.' . . . 'It is impossible at this time to estimate clearly.' . . . That stuff gets us down, specially when it's followed two weeks later by a great string of losses. Tell us the bad news, all of it, as quick as you can. Don't hold it up because you think it will make us feel better. It doesn't; it just makes us wonder what else you have up your sleeve. When we don't know what's happening, but just that something awful is happening, we feel like bad kids who are going to catch Something, we don't know what.

"So remember, dish out the bad news and put in as much good as you can. Don't soft-pedal our boasting. We're tired of these sourpusses who point out that what the hell does it matter whether our guys were heroes or not at Corregidor, if we lost Corregidor. But it does matter. For they are guys like us. If they could do it, we can do it. Give us time. We'll get there. And show a little sense in who you pick to do the crape-hanging too. Pick a guy that knows that what one American can do, another American can do a little bit better."

CHAPTER XI

Are Democracy and Social Science Compatible
Each with Each?

★

WINNING THE WAR is a job of social engineering, we have
said. We must understand and use American character
in the process. We must develop the insights of social
science to a point where we can say how this is to be
done. And at this point in the argument objectors raise
their heads. How, they ask, does such a course differ
from fascism and its ruthless control of human beings?
Dr. Goebbels' methods of manipulating humanity are
based upon what he believes to be an accurate analysis
of what human beings are like; how they will behave in
crowds; how weariness and certain kinds of light and
noise, reiteration and reduplication of lies of sufficient
magnitude, will affect them.[1] Nazi propaganda is based
on very careful calculations—on just how much hate
and hostility is available in human beings. After the
calculations are made, the propaganda lie or truth—
whichever seems likely to be most effective—is put
across. Wherein lies the difference between the stream-

lined Nazi state and a state in which we, as Americans, analyze and use the strengths and weaknesses of the American character? Whether we call it democracy or not, is it not the very negation of democracy to employ intelligently the potentialities of human beings?

Is not science, itself the child of democracy, the child of freedom to think and inquire, a monster child that must inevitably destroy its permissive parent? Once the habit of mind, which has given control over nature and over sub-human things, is extended to man, have we not made the discovery which will liquidate democracy for all time? If democracy is based upon spontaneous initiative from the people, can we ever find a recipe that will produce spontaneity; will not any recipe ultimately destroy spontaneity? This problem is basic to this whole inquiry; and upon how we answer it depends the fate of the twentieth century and of many centuries thereafter. A negative answer; a conviction that understanding and control cannot lead towards freedom and that there is a contradiction of terms here which can never be reconciled, leads to fascism, although not always by the same road. Thus, one may argue that control is necessary; that if one large and powerful nation has learned to shape its population into a tool, a composite of sub-human items who work together into a perfectly articulated machine, then if other nations are to survive, they must do the same. However pleasant or spiritually gratifying freedom may be, it cannot survive in a world where our enemies have discovered how to destroy it and to make capital of its destruction. The world cannot live half slave and half free, they argue, because slavery, properly administered, is more powerful. Therefore, with a regretful little sigh and a bow to self-preservation and a wreath on the tombs of the ancestors they capitulate and surrender the fort.

But there are other routes to the same surrender. One of them lies through the repudiation of scientific control of human beings. It is horrible—so those who take this point of view claim—to think of people as mere aggregations of neurons behaving in accordance with laws, no matter how complicated. This is a reduction of human beings to a level of the beasts; this is the final indignity against which human beings have struggled for many thousands of years. If this is the result of science, let us scrap it all and go back, back to the supremacy of the human spirit and any hierarchical form of society which is necessary to stamp out science, replace it by faith, and reconstitute man in the dignity of innocence again. And strangely enough, this route too leads to fascism, because it repudiates democracy as the mother of science and insists on turning back to an age when men were innocent because they were ignorant—on turning back to a pretense of ignorance [2] which is no longer real. It permits the destruction of democracy and the substitution of an authoritative state. Some of the men whose hearts were broken when Madrid fell and who turned back to Mediaevalism for an answer did so in this spirit, not realizing that the pages of history can no more be turned back in this way than a man, grown to man's full estate, can again become a child—wide-eyed in his confusion of himself and the universe, his parents and God—and still keep his dignity. When we yearn for the beautiful simplicity and homogeneity of other periods, we are yearning for something which it is salutary to appreciate but fatal to covet—as fatal as it is for man to seek to be cradled again as in infancy and find himself not become a saint, but a schizophrenic. It does not avail us anything to say that in the Middle Ages he would have been a saint and that the role of saints who light other men's paths to heaven is more noble than that of the inmate of an asylum given insulin treatment every week. We can't honor him as a saint, but we may study him and cure him and learn to prevent schizophrenia. No matter how poignantly we recognize the values and the rewards of other ages and other cultures, they are not for us; for cultures live not in a mere rearrangement of government or philosophy, a verbal and political sleight of hand to be conjured up overnight, but in every disciplined nervous fiber of men's beings. To the extent that any line in the ground plan for a new world is conceived as a return to a lost innocence, it becomes fatuous and regressive, a spiritual liability leading to a morass.

A third group, of whom the Communists are the most articulate but which also includes much socialist thinking, embraces a controlled world, not as a *pis aller*, because our enemies have done so; not from the primary fascist motivation of a will to power for their own group; but as a good way of life. They contrast the order which would result from man's scientific control of natural and human resources, his careful planning so that there would be food and shelter and clothing, knowledge and the arts for all, with the present chaotic state of the world. They say that no price is too high to pay for such order, order designed to benefit the masses of mankind rather than some power-drive group of self-elected masters. Let us use science, they say, to build such an ORDER. And what, one asks them, if in the course of the free scientific inquiry principles are discovered which are incompatible with those principles upon which your Order was stabilized? What, if to build your Order, you have had to erect the passing hypotheses of a just-emerging science into articles of political dogma? This has been the case with the discussion of the role of the environment in Russia and the accompanying emphasis upon a Pavlovian view of humanity in which human beings are seen as mechanisms which lend themselves readily to conditioning. When some scientist within that Order challenges one of these premises—as he must if he is honest—what will you, who have committed yourselves to a fixed and controlled order as preferable to uncontrolled freedom, do? Is not exile or execution your only recourse? Can science—even the genetics of wheat culture—flourish in a society which has accepted control based on science and rejected the insurgency of freedom?

So we find ourselves caught in a most curious and challenging dilemma. Whether the argument comes from the Right or from the Left or looks backwards to

Greece or the Middle Ages; whether it is proposed to use part of science, all of existing science, or none of it —we come out at the same place: in rejecting democracy we are rejecting the growth of science. One may consent to use what we have got, to work with crowd-hypnotic techniques which reduce man to sub-human terms if one is of Hitler's way of thinking; to educate children by conditioned reflex techniques if one plans a socialist state; continue to install plumbing and electric lighting even in monasteries which ape the Middle Ages; but on none of these uses of science can free inquiry, which is necessary to the development of science, flourish. The science that lives upon a narrow set of permitted premises sharply demarcated on either side by verboten signs may produce more and more deadly weapons of war, more *ersatz,* more synthetic substitute materials. It may feed people from wood pulp and dress them in spun glass. But it becomes a closed system, feeding upon its own innards; it has lost its possibilities of growth.[3] (It was thus, in fact, that Spengler, who found fascist philosophy so congenial, saw the development of knowledge as proceeding in cycles, each one of which contained within it the seeds of its own destruction.)

It is possible, however, that with the development of social science, with the application of real scientific inquiry to the ways of man, with techniques for freeing ourselves from the limitations imposed by our own culture, with techniques for including and allowing for the psychology of the investigator himself,[4] the world has entered a new era; an era as different from the past as the machine age is different in its utilization of energy from the ages which were based on human labor alone. It is possible that this type of social science, which is not a mere lifeless aping of the mannerisms of the natural sciences but which shapes its hypotheses [5] to its materials and includes the repercussions of a hypothesis inside its equations, can give us premises by which we can set men free; release in them energies which can be trusted to develop towards more freedom instead of towards a machine model of slavery or Utopian totalitarianism.

But it is necessary to ask the right question if we are to get the right answers. "We know the answers, all the answers, it is the question that we do not know," wrote Archibald MacLeish in 1928. There is a question we might pose: Can science set in motion forces which will implement human freedom? We have not been seriously asking any such question. We have talked about the "meaning" of freedom, the philosophical "basis" for freedom, whether freedom is compatible with order, etc. Then on the basis of that sort of discussion, we have taken various back cracks at "deterministic" science. We have not been seriously asking a HOW question, and not until we do will we get a scientific answer. The social sciences as a body, always lagging behind and imitating the fifty-year-old professor's memory of a high school physics which was twenty years out of date when he grappled with it, are still asking WHY questions. Why do cultures change? Not: How do they change? Why do prices rise? Why do people go to war? We should ask instead: How can we organize a society in which war will have no place? And as the scientific question most germane to freedom: What are the conditions in a culture, in its system of education, in its system of inter-personal relationships, which promote a sense of free will?

If we turn our attention then to the problem of how to use social science to promote a degree of human freedom which will itself provide the ground within which more science and more freedom will grow, we see at once that we have shifted our discussion from a question of simple linear causation to an organismic type of thinking. The totalitarian asks: How can I establish the kind of state which I want—either for my sake, or for other people? He plans to build a machine which will then stay the way it is, subject either to his will—if he is fascist, fascinated by power—or maintained forever in one kind of balance by the people whom he conditioned as children to the right responses. The plan comes first, and the people are to be fitted into it; educated from birth to be the right sort of material to maintain the Order which he has dreamed. Where the fascist builds for himself, from the souls and bodies of those whom he manipulates, a tool or a weapon, the socialist wishes to build a self-winding clock which will always tell the same time. He will, of course, not phrase it that way; he will speak of more and more discoveries of how man can conquer nature and develop artistic skill in the breast of every child, but if one examines the implications of planning an order and then fitting people, child by child, even adult by adult, on its Procrustean although perhaps sumptuous bed, one finds that this is the implication. It is the implication for one very simple reason: the socialist state is not a self-winding clock, but has to be wound, to be set in motion, by men who live now in a non-socialist world in which they were reared, though they dream of a socialist world.

These dreamers, these planners, are the instruments by whose mediation the new equilibrium is to be brought into being. They accept the dream as primary: that an order in which everyone was happy and secure and well fed is a dream of such urgency and validity that no sacrifice—of themselves or others—is too great. They then proceed to try to bring the new order about, to use any means—for is not any means justified in the effort to produce a Utopia in place of this confused tumbled milling of peoples that we call the modern world? But once they have accepted the premise—that the new order justifies any means which is necessary to bring it about—they have doomed that new order at the start. For the decisions which are to doom groups in the population to starvation, to exile, or to death, cannot be written by some impersonal machine, faithfully and innocently conveying the human race towards happiness. They must be written by human hands. The men who are to become the leaders of a world dedicated to humanity must violate that humanity, day in and day out, as they drive towards their goal. Every act of ruthlessness, no matter how logical and how necessary, leaves its mark upon the responsible person who gave the order. Any new order built upon a flouting of human rights in the name of humanity enters upon its existence hopelessly encumbered by leaders whose behavior has shaped their minds and souls so that they are completely unfit to lead in the world they have worked to create. The destructiveness, the righteous fury which knows no pity to stay the hand, either for self or for those blind members of one's own society who would hold back unborn generations from a better life, is the necessary stuff of revolution; but it is not the stuff of which the new perfect equilibrium can be built.

There has been much discussion of the paradox of American history—that Americans, whose national life began in revolution, should be so intolerant of revolutionary ideas, so committed to the slow processes of democratic change. Those who argue so should reread the opening lines of the Declaration of Independence: "When, in the course of human events, it becomes necessary for one people to dissolve the political bands which have connected them with another, and to assume among the powers of the earth, the separate and equal station to which the laws of nature and of nature's God entitle them, a decent respect to the opinions of mankind requires that they should declare the causes which impel them to the separation."

A less revolutionary document it would be hard to find. Here was no anger against harsh rulers, no pent-up anger against those who held the driving reins and oppressed the poor, no patricidal rage. "Two peoples," the document says, "dissolve the bands which have connected them;" two groups, each with its own rights and purposes, whose association is no longer seen as valuable. The men who wrote that document could go on to do the most self-conscious and constructive piece of political thinking of which we have any record. They were free. Their hands were not stained with the blood of the parents; they had not fought and killed part of themselves; they had not tortured and executed that part of their own group which did not agree. They remained fit leaders for a new society, because they themselves had not become hopelessly, heartbreakingly distorted in building it.

We must recognize that one of the principal tasks in building a better world is to develop and conserve the leaders who must shape it—and here I speak of no simple moral preference, but of what is, in the light of what we now know of the effects of experience upon human beings, a scientifically demonstrable fact. We cannot afford to let those leaders commit acts incompatible with the world towards which they are working. We cannot afford to let them say, even once, that the end justifies the means. This is a simple engineering principle, as simple as the requirements for tempering steel. And we must find a way, a scientific way, of protecting them from such a course. If social science warns that the corruption of the leaders by the use of means unworthy of the ends towards which they are directed is fatal, it must also provide the principles by which we may avoid such corruption and still move forward. Can it do so?

The releasing formula has, however, a misleading

simplicity. It seems so simple that the listener either admits it too easily to recognize its importance or dismisses it as lacking the paraphernalia of true scientific dicta. If I could express it in mathematical terms, or even in pseudo-mathematical terms, in a verbal fraction, then it would command respect. But how to clothe a recommendation—in itself quite simple and direct, yet developed upon the basis of most careful research and examination and re-examination of data—in words which will command the respect which we have learned to give only to that which is incomprehensible, I do not know. The statement must conform to the principles which it is expounding. I have said no end can justify discrepant means, because the means so used will compromise the end. To dress up what is a very simple statement, difficult only because we are culturally untrained for the appreciation of the simple, in a fanfare of pseudo-science, would be an example of that against which I am arguing. The warning that this suggestion will seem too simple is, however, I think, justified.

If we are to work towards a world in which those who work will be able to lead without damaging all they work for, we must see the job to be done as directed towards *processes and not towards identified persons or identified groups,*[6] towards creating instead conditions within which unidentified individuals may act of their own free will. Suppose, for instance, that the government decides that we will need to quadruple our crop of soy beans in 1943. The totalitarian system would be to tell individual farmers, perhaps all the individual farmers resident in one area where the soil is suitable for growing soy beans, to grow so many acres of soy beans under penalty of fines, imprisonment, or death. The democratic way will be to make the growing of soy beans more profitable, either in straight money terms, or in terms of exemptions from taxation, or extra facilities for farm labor, or better credit conditions. No farmer in the soy bean country is forced to grow the soy beans, but with these conditions a great number will do so. Each, however, feels that he has choice; that he can take advantage of an opportunity; not that he, individually, is being pushed around. The men in the government agricultural bureau which makes the plans need not see themselves as ruthlessly pushing individual men around into activities in which they do not wish to take part.

Or suppose that in a well-organized society it is recognized that ten years from now more doctors will be needed. It would be possible for a totalitarian to select arbitrarily the boys who, on the basis of their school records, will make the best doctors and simply order them to become doctors, the state footing the bill. The democratic state would offer specially good scholarship conditions for boys with the right abilities and advertise these widely. Either course can produce the desired result—more doctors; but by the first method, identified boys—James Smith and John Brown—who wanted perhaps to be lawyers or engineers are forced to be doctors. By the second method, unidentified boys who want to be doctors have the way opened to them.

We may identify different varieties of social control here, the system in which you select a group of identified people and tell them they must follow a given course of action for which they will be rewarded and for failure to follow which they will be punished. The socialist tendency is towards reward, with punishment as a less desirable alternative; the fascist towards straight punishment without the rigmarole of a reward. Both systems insist that identified persons, or members of identified groups—merchants or Poles, who are given no choice, except the choice of whether they will comply or undergo punishment—should fit into a plan.

In the democratic system we may again work either with reward or punishment, but we reward or punish an identified course of action which will be followed by *unidentified* persons. The administrator never carries the burden of making identified human beings conform to his plan.* Our whole concept of law with its final expression in the Supreme Court is based on this necessary impersonality of those who mete it out. This means that we can have no clear vision of a final form which we want society to take; for the minute that we have such a vision we begin to educate, cajole, force people, identified living human beings, to fit into the pattern which we have conceived as good for them. It wouldn't

* In wartime, of course, a democratic society of its own choice temporarily delegates power over persons to the constituted authorities, and by so doing abrogates the sort of freedom of which I have been talking. But we are concerned in this chapter with the problem of whether social science and democracy can be compatible, not merely with the problem of wartime surrender of democratic political powers.

be enough to teach children to think for themselves. They might think the wrong things. So the socialist, like the fascist, is forced to control the children's thinking—and they cease to think for themselves and he ceases to be fit for leadership in a free world. Freedom in fact has gone out of the window. If we are content to set up an educational system which leaves the mind free, a political system which leads to more and more possible initiative from the bottom, to more and more contributions from more and more people without decreeing that when the contribution comes it shall take such and such form—then we can work and direct the course of the world without compromising it by inappropriate methods. But one identified child starved in the name of feeding all children can wreck forever the leader who planned to build a world in which all children were to be fed. One mind coerced so that there will be freedom of speech, one paper lawlessly suppressed in the name of freedom to write the right things—is fatal.

If we turn our attention towards processes, towards directions, and away from fixed plans into which we attempt to fit living human beings, we deal immediately with an open-ended system, a system in which we cannot know what the outcome will be. We have inevitably accorded to human beings, the human beings of the future, the right to a destiny which lies in their hands, not in ours. What we do will, of course, have its sequent effects with which those who come later must cope, but this does not compromise their freedom. We have not laid down their future for them; we have only said: "We think that in this direction lies a freer life, a life in which more of the energies of human beings can be used than have ever been used before. We have set your footsteps on this path, we have equipped you to think well and to feel sensitively—what you make of your future lies in your hands." In doing this, we strip ourselves of that one nightmare of science which is incompatible with any idea of a free and democratic way of life—the element of absolute control.

It is probable that social science can also give us the premises, the knowledge by which we could—if we would—fit men to a fixed mold, beat them and bend them until they were unable either to escape from it or to rear children other than themselves. Therein lies the terrible danger of fascism. While the socialist who wishes to build a free and self-developing world is stymied by his own participation if he uses revolutionary means and forces human beings to do his will, no such inexorable disability dogs the footsteps of the fascist. He can incorporate himself and his lust for control into a system as deadly in its controls as he wishes and thereby incorporate no automatically discrepant elements. As long as there is a free country on this earth, strong enough to nourish in men's breasts a habit of freedom, fascist states may be in danger, are in danger, from without. But once let the light of freedom be put out all over the world, and there is no guarantee that it would ever spontaneously burst into lovely light again. Democracy is an invention, like fire and language and marriage. We have no record of the thousand small, unnoted circumstances and usages which fathered it; we have no proof that it would necessarily ever appear on the face of the earth again.

So we may say that power *directed towards persons,* power given either by the possession of office and a police force adequate to enforce one's will, or power given by knowledge of the springs of human conduct, can fit a man only for control within a fascist state. In suggesting that we must devise a form of social planning in which we never draw a final plan, in which we work to change social processes, not to coerce living persons, in which we determine the direction but not the end of the road, we are, in fact, using science to free us from the one circumstance, itself born of science, which might hinder us and enslave us in the end. On the basis of a scientific knowledge of culture and human behavior we can say that the power to control individual human behavior and the exercise of such power are incompatible with human freedom. By recognizing that circumstance, by voluntarily tying our own hands and laying a solemn injunction upon our ardent imaginations, we become able to use the control that science has given us to set future generations free.

CHAPTER XII

If We Are to Go On

★

WE HAVE a certain kind of character, the American character, which has developed in the New World and taken a shape all its own; a character that is geared to success and to movement, invigorated by obstacles and difficulties, but plunged into guilt and despair by catastrophic failure or a wholesale alteration in the upward and onward pace; a character in which aggressiveness is uncertain and undefined, to which readiness to fight anyone who starts a fight and unreadiness to engage in violence have both been held up as virtues; a character which measures its successes and failures only against near contemporaries and engages in various quantitative devices for reducing every contemporary to its own stature; a character which sees success as the reward of virtue and failure as the stigma for not being good enough; a character which is uninterested in the past, except when ancestry can be used to make points against other people in the success game; a character oriented towards an unknown future, ambivalent towards other cultures, which are regarded with a sense of inferiority as more coherent than our own and with a sense of superiority because newcomers in America display the strongest mark of other cultural membership in the form of foreignness. What is the possible role for such a character structure—after winning the war—in working towards building the world anew?

We may ask first whether such a character has a future; whether it was not specially suited to pioneer conditions when success could be regarded as the reward for industry and abstinence; and whether the chief reason why puritanism flowered in America while withering in England was not just this favorable condition. It takes very special circumstances to back up a belief in the close connection between virtue and success. Most other cultures have had to construct their ethical systems on a less exacting model. The peoples have suffered for the sins of their kings; one evil deed has corrupted the land. Theories of reincarnation have permitted the notion that the luck fluctuates from one incarnation to another, or the whole problem of success was shelved altogether and each man took the fortune which a blindfold fate meted out to him. Christianity traditionally dealt with the problem in terms of heaven and hell, and those whose lot in no sense matched their effort or their deserts might flourish or suffer on earth; but all these inequalities were righted in heaven. The belief in the after-life was a particularly flexible method of reconciling a man who was exhorted to goodness, to a life without earthly rewards. But the essence of puritanism, although it retained all the color and terror of hell fire, was a belief that there was a relationship here on earth between good behavior and good deserts. God prospered the good man and withdrew from the evil man, and success could be taken as an immediate outward and visible sign that one had so lived as to find favor in the sight of God. Very few peoples have ever trafficked long with such an unmanageable moral code, but the peculiar conditions of American life promoted this attitude rather than diminished it. In Europe if one were born one of ten sons, and one's neighbor was an only son, and the inheritance consisted of farms of the same size, nine of the ten, if it were entailed—all of the ten, if it were not—were desperately unlucky. But in America, the nine could go somewhere else and often prosper more than the brother who remained at home. The favors conferred by birth were obscured by the opportunity to wrest favors by hard work and enterprise.

The American version of luck, best exemplified in the press stories of Hollywood success which have been analyzed by Rosten,[1] point up our essential puritanism by insisting that when sudden, undreamed-of, unheard-of success and fame befalls some unknown movie star, she should have no birthright claim to it. She was not, the careful press stories explain, even pretty—they had to alter the molding of her nose. She is not the right height—when she plays with the star she prefers she has to stand on a box. Her success, her luck, is an artifact pure and simple, synthetic from start to finish. It might have happened to anybody. It might have happened to you and me. This is an excellent example of what the anthropologist means by the regularity of culture: that an apparent contradiction, like these tales of great and absolutely undeserved good fortune, when it is analyzed more closely nevertheless fits in with other ideas in the culture which it appears to contradict. The American logic is: Be intelligently good and you will be successful. As for those who cannot in any sense be shown to have been specially good, who have not worked or saved or slaved or supported their widowed mothers while they burnt the midnight oil and finished night school—when they succeed, we represent their great good fortune as due to a capricious turn of a wheel rather than tolerate the notion that those who benefited so greatly had some single initial advantage. The assumption that men were created equal, with an equal ability to make an effort and win an earthly reward, although denied every day by experience is maintained every day by our folklore and our daydreams.

Running through this emphasis that work brings its own rewards and that failure is squarely the fault of him who fails is another thread for which the sanction is not guilt, but shame. Shame is felt perhaps most strongly over the failures of other people, especially one's parents,[2] who have not been successful, have not worked hard enough to have an inside bathroom or an automobile or to send one to a private school, to live on the right street, or go to the right church. As class is an expression of economic success, then it follows that to belong as a child or adolescent in a class below others is a statement that one's parents have failed, that they did not make good. This is bad enough when they have not risen, unbearable if they have started to fall even lower. Deeper than our disapproval of any breaking of the ten commandments lies our conviction that low economic estate is something dreadful and that a failure to keep moving upward is an unforgivable sin. If one analyzes the novels of American life and the case histories of adolescents which have been collected by American sociologists, this terrible shame of children over their parents' failure—a failure which the parents themselves may well handle in terms of guilt rather than shame—comes out very strongly. Success and conformity—outward conformity made possible by economic success—these are the marks that one is a good American. So the boy or girl who is held back by the idiosyncrasies of rich parents from conformity to the standards of the adolescent group may suffer almost as much as if he were held back by poverty. Whatever the cause, the lack of conformity attests to the difference and so to the inferiority of his parents, those parents whose status in the world defines his—until he has made his own.

The only non-European people of whom we have any record who have ever tried to build a society on such a close relationship between sin and wordly success are the Manus, where endemic malaria makes it possible for illness to be regarded as punishment for sin and the recovery from malaria—which almost always follows in a day or so—as the reward for atonement. But the

Manus do not include in their decalogue that one should honor his father and his mother. As soon as they begin to fail, to drop out of the race for success, their children can turn upon them and heap abuse upon their heads, thus saving themselves from involvement in their moral failures. But for Americans to whom honoring parents has been insisted upon just to the degree that immigration which sets a premium on Americanization and a premium upon rise in economic level has rendered it almost impossible to carry it out—this easy way out is not there. "Blood is thicker than water," and we are not permitted to disown our poor relations —who carry the taint of failure in all their doings—but must continue to recognize them. The simple directness with which an English family disowns those on whom breeding has not taken, who have not learned to behave according to the family standard, is not for us. Our obscure desire to escape from our origins, which is present in all but those few families whose status is a function of their ability to trace genealogies where no one else can, carries with it its own sanctions. To deny one's origins is wrong and, by extension, to fail to face the failure—the ultimate moral turpitude of one's kin—is also wrong. And for handling these shames over the sins of others we have no formula except bitterness and misery. After all, you can repent of your own sinfulness and work harder or you can accept your own sinfulness and go to the devil with a certain grim pride in your own temerity; but you cannot gracefully accept other people's sins for which you can take no responsibility and yet in whose consequences you share. Thus class membership, for all but the upper upper, becomes a possible source of shame to Americans; it is the outward and visible sign of how far our particular parents did not get. While pride is possible in terms of the distance that they came, the distance has to be almost the whole mythological gamut from log cabin to the White House before it can be really satisfying. One's own position is continually compromised by the things that one's ancestors did not do, such as not coming to Boston earlier, not making better deals with the Indians, not going West in '49, not buying the right land. In a hundred ways present conditions show that other people's ancestors were, not more fortunate, for that one could bear with a good grace, but more enterprising than ours.

This is our character; this our need for success. That need has been terribly frustrated since 1929. A whole generation of fathers have faced their growing children with bowed heads because they had somehow failed; a whole generation of children have grown up under the shadow of that failure, believing in many cases that someone—the Federal Government, or somebody—should do something about it, anxious for a panacea which would assuage the guilty unhappiness of their parents or anxious for some scapegoat on which to vent their resentment. Fortunately, the desire for the panacea has been stronger than the desire for a scapegoat. While the men at well-covered dining tables, to which the only repercussions of disaster came dimly in discussions of the sale of a yacht or a country estate, have found a scapegoat necessary to absorb their sense of defeat, those parents whose apparent failure to find jobs has meant no bread for their children have, touchingly enough, felt far less hostility. They have for the most part continued to believe in the American dream that those who are good shall be happy, that all who are willing to work can work and buy a little home of their own. But neither among the angry men who rage about That Man in the White House nor among the Okies wandering over the country has there developed, as yet, any final questioning of the assumption upon which Americans have lived for generations—that the world is a wide, wide place with room for all who come to it with willing hands, good hearts, and hard heads.

When we talk about saving America from the fate that menaces her now, we can mean many different things. We can mean that we wish to protect our foreign markets and so protect the present economic system. Men may be quite willing to send other men to die for this great cause; but they will not go themselves. Dying for foreign markets has always been someone else's, and a helpless someone's, job. Or we may mean saving our soil from foreign conquest, from the actual print of tank treads on our soil. This Americans will to some extent die for, but not with the same fervor that an Englishman or a Norwegian will. For after all, the soil of the United States is not laced tightly with the bones of a thousand of our ancestors nor built securely and firmly into our whole picture of life. The soil of America as it enters our picture of the world is empty and open, uncut forests and unplowed plains. It does not matter that such forests and plains don't exist any more, they are part of our picture, just as secure hedgerows are part of the English picture. Invasion by foreigners—aren't we, in fact, always being invaded by foreigners, not always armed with guns—but still, you know, every Italian carries a stiletto, and certainly the Californians' treatment of the Okies did not differ greatly from an attitude towards an invading army. Always invaded, always outraged, with the best families' names always disappearing from the news columns and the names of new people, names you can't spell, cropping up. Our feeling about invasion, although it is there, cannot inspire a holy crusade. We will fight and fight hard if invaded, but we will find nothing to boast of or sustain us afterwards, as we tell over the tale—and pride in our own good behavior is essential to our picture of ourselves.

We talk about saving the American way of life—and this stands for a number of vague things such as refrigerators and automobiles and marrying whom you like and working for whom you like and not having to be regimented and wrapped up in yards of governmental red tape. Or it may mean something more; it may mean saving that dynamic principle which associates success and goodness. Our character structure is based upon having a job to do which can be done, just as the Manus savage's goodness was based upon associating his failure to work with a disease from which he got well. If we cannot again work and move in a world where there is some relationship between our success and our effort and willingness to work, this American character is doomed to disappear with the physical frontier which fostered it. This insistence upon a relationship between what we do and what we get is one of our most distinguishing characteristics. On it is based our acceptance of men for what they have become rather than for what they were born. On it is based our faith that simple people, people like ourselves, are worthy of a hearing in the halls of the great. On it is based our special brand of democracy. Americans who are once convinced that it's all a matter of pull, of who you know, that working hard doesn't get you anywhere nowadays, that it's all a racket anyhow—which is the cynical obverse of believing that effort and success are linked—are not a desirable breed. No one who was interested in building the world anew would conceive of asking such people to help. Once we lose our moral keystone to an orderly world, the whole structure comes crashing down about our heads, leaving us with a type of American who has neither vision nor humility, who lacks the will and the purpose which have helped us shape a great country from an untouched wilderness, who lacks even the constructive fire which might come from bitterness and a genuine hatred of those who have brought him to such a pass. That there are already many such Americans it is impossible to deny, just as it is impossible to ignore those scattered areas in American life in which all ideals have been sacrificed to a limbo of cynical grabbing—politics being the most notable example; business ethics often being another. In whole areas of life, Americans have ceased to see any element of moral responsibility, and they have nothing else, no valuation of style or breeding or of sheer virtuosity to put in the place of moral purpose. Traditionally we have disallowed these European valuations and insisted on our own; if we discard or discredit our own, we have nothing.

It is this cynicism which could well form the basis of an American fascism, a fascism bowing down before any character strong enough and amoral enough to get away with it, to get his. This note is found running through the admiration for Hitler which runs like a muddy sewer underneath so much outwardly patriotic conversation. There are very few Americans who can identify with Hitler in his cold destructiveness, but they can identify with his success in getting away with it, in the way in which he has made monkeys of his opponents. The belief that all life is a racket and the strongest racketeer gets the biggest pile of loot is the bastard brother of the belief that life is real and life is earnest. Its presence in this country, in the tone of our music, in the flavor of our jokes, in the wisecracks which are on every lip, cannot be dismissed lightly. It stands as a terrible warning of what may come from any concerted attack upon our success creed as sentimental, unreal, and outdated. Those who see a worship of success as the worship of seven devils should ponder deeply the story of the worse devils who entered the room so swept and garnished. A puritan who goes to the devil, who sells his soul and knows it and is ready to burn in hell and keep his word, has a certain grim and terrible dignity. But a puritan who has lost his puritanism has nothing left but a cynicism that clatters like invisible handcuffs tying his hands forever from any deep commitment or great purpose.

Yet this American character which has done great things, which built cities faster than cities had ever been built before, which created a civilization in which men were more nearly equal than they had ever been before, which created a civilization which could dream of freeing the whole world—does depend upon valuing success. Shall we say that the day of these crude equations between personal morality and enterprise and a million dollars or at least a Ford car is over, and over for good; that when the American dream, which was nourished on a historical accident and lies sick upon a despoiled continent, is played out, we now have nowhere to go, except back to our origins, accepting some political system made in Europe? Shall we accept this verdict, bow our heads and let the winds of the old world mow us down? Or will Americans fight to continue to be themselves and for the right to define themselves as the champions of the good life?

If we are to keep it, we must do two things: we must redefine success without, however, breaking the thread which ties success to effort; and we must find a place which, like the great plains of the New World, gives us a wide stage on which to act out our parts. In the past when there were no new lands and no new gold mines, there were new inventions. The automobile brought us a tide of prosperity as surely as did the building of the railroads. For a little while men believed, some men still believe, that we have within us on this continent the power through making new inventions to open up more and more frontiers, new stages for industriousness and enterprise. But the closing in of the world, until all the peoples of the earth must rise or fall together, has changed that frontier and given us, instead of new inventions—to be built on American soil and sold to ourselves and perhaps the world—the chance to become devoted entrepreneurs of a whole world that must be built new, according to a new plan. Those who read Henry Luce's *American Century* with approval think that was what he was trying to say. Those who reject his phrasing reject it because they think that he is preaching a new imperialism in which Americans, tall and well fed and mechanically trained, will go about the world building dams and factories, lending money and sending armies to collect the interest or protect our investments. They think that he is replacing the old imperialism, which rested upon a sense of responsibility or divine right, by a new imperialism which will rest upon nothing but the lust for wealth, power, and conquest. That intelligent people can read *The American Century* two ways—that some read it and see the mark of what someone has euphemistically called "the clean fascists," while others can read it and fail to find this mark—represents the dilemma in which we stand today. Many who feel the strength and vigor of America still stirring are forced to phrase their faith in the ruthless terms of American big business, while many who have faith in a world where other values rule look with no faith at the ideals of Americans around them. The second group think they know the goal but can find no one to work towards it; they feel that the others trust Americans so exuberantly and crudely that the goal seems inevitably compromised.

Can we not take this sense of moral purpose—so intolerable when it sets itself above the world, but so indomitable when it sets itself to a hard job—and shape from it a tool with which the building of a new world can be done? Granting that Americans have a genius for seeing themselves on the side of the good and right, can we not use that genius and the energy which comes from a gleaming and almost intolerable self-approval when things are going well? Can we not tackle the job of post-war planning as we once tackled the wilderness, given energy by a belief that we are right, and given canniness and a willingness to work on new inventions by the belief that we must succeed in order to prove that we are right? Get the distaff ready and God will send the flax . . . if it is a good enough distaff.

For our willingness to work on inventions, our belief that problems are to be solved by purposeful thought and experimentation, is another aspect of this type of character structure. In most of the civilizations of which we have record, man had an alibi for not using his mind; the world was as God had made it and willed it to be; balances were righted in heaven; Fate or Chance or the order of the universe were responsible; and man's job was to fit in rather than to seek to change that which was there, to cultivate various virtues like dignity or resignation rather than to seek to reshape the world. Only in those societies which shifted success from heaven to earth, and so put the whole impact of religion back of efficiency, could we have a type of character in which it became a virtue to do the kind of thinking which lies back of invention, a virtue to set problems and solve them. For the puritan did not believe that man was saved either by faith or good works, but that he was saved by *intelligent* works. Much of the energy which has made man the constructive inventor of the last two centuries was generated by fear of the guilt he would feel if failure should prove to him and his neighbors that he had somehow done wrong. There are those who are so disgruntled with most of our inventions and with the violence to other human values which is implicit in this American cult of success that they would gladly scrap the whole show, return to a fixed status society, in which one's happiness came from being rather than from doing and food was guaranteed because of what one was born, a human being of a given age and sex.

But before we fling aside this peculiar drive towards efficiency and success which has been developed by the middle-class, success habit of mind, it is worth while asking whether this is not just the mechanism that we need to build a new world. The very impetus under which our reformers work, the moral passion with which they denounce social iniquity, are all fathered by this puritan tradition. As it has provided energy to conquer time and space and bind the whole world together as a physical unit—never to be split apart again— may it not also provide the energy to make the inventions which will bind the world together as a social unit? Is not this character structure, this driving will to prove that one is good by being successful, a tool made ready to forge a new world?

If we can once harness American shrewdness, that mixture of mysticism and a knowledge of machinery which has been so falsely dubbed "practicality," to the problem of making social inventions, we will be going a long way towards starting on a new road. The American who is asked to devise a way of handling synthetic rubber does not talk about human nature, man's right to natural rubber, the religious incompatibility of synthetic rubber and an ethical ideal, the racial dynamism of rubber, or the meaning of rubber for freeing the proletariat. He thinks first and foremost about his problem. Rubber has such and such qualities. He wishes to make a substance which has such and such qualities. From what materials, with what machines, using what processes will he work?

Our social thinking has been hampered by our lack of recognition that social organization is also a matter of invention. The use of fire is not inherent in humanity, although human beings functioning on this earth would have been very limited had the use of fire not been discovered. Language is not inherent in humanity, but the discovery and elaboration of languages has enormously enhanced our dignity and scope as human beings. War is not inherent in humanity. Warfare was an invention [3] which accompanied the development of group solidarity, itself also an invention in living together. Just as we would not expect people to eat their food raw or stop talking merely because someone told them that fire and language were wrong or "unnatural," we cannot expect that warfare, which is the most adequate invention to date for protecting one's own group against the purposeful depredations of other groups, will be given up because it is branded as ethically unacceptable. It will not be given up until we invent something better. The old *lex talionis*, the eye for an eye and tooth for a tooth, was not given up until courts of law and justice were invented. Barter was not abandoned merely because someone sat on a local molehill and described it as clumsy and inefficient. It was abandoned when money, which was more efficient, was invented.

There are those who will object that warfare is inefficient, that it involves an expenditure of human life in a way which no one can condone and everyone must condemn. But that is just from our own point of view. The efficiency of any invention must be judged in terms of the goals for which one is working. Dive bombing is inefficient if you care more about the lives of your airmen than about the destruction of enemy battleships; it is terrifically efficient if you do not. As long as nations care more for the preservation of their political entity and autonomy than about anything else, then warfare is efficient. We have now reached a point where a great body of people have ceased to believe that nationalism is a goal or value by which one can judge the efficiency of social techniques. We want a world without war more than we want to be merely a strong nation. That is a simple clear issue. Our enemies want a world with strong nations, built and perpetuated by wars. For them life is a continuous war, punctuated by armistices. For us, life has come to be seen as a peaceful orderly existence, punctuated by wars. What is efficient for them is not efficient for us. But, in a very terrible sense, our enemies still have the choice of weapons, for the very simple reason that the weapons, the tools we need to build a peaceful world, have not yet been invented. It is not merely that they, warring states, attacked us and so forced us to fight. It is also that in the intervals when they were sharpening up their weapons and refurbishing their arms, we had no alternative to offer that was good enough. The world is so constructed today that if one army marches against another, the other army must obey the rules of war, must fight or surrender. Not until we develop a comparable strategy of peace, a plan of social organization which is so all-embracing that all who encounter it have no choice except to begin to play by that set of rules, will we have made the necessary inventions which will supersede war.

We have made such inventions inside our national states. If one man hit another five hundred years ago, the other man had no choice except to hit back or be dishonored. He was trapped in the rules of personal, hand-to-hand fighting whether he fought or not. To-day, he need neither fight nor be dishonored; he can merely hand the drunk or disorderly or insane person over to the nearest policeman. He is as firmly embraced by rules of orderly procedure as his ancestor was em-braced by rules of disorderly procedure. It is not so much that people today think brawls on the street are wrong, and shrink with a fine ethical fury from indulg-ing in them, and call up conscientious scruples and sanctions against violence. A man may be a believer in violence or a Quaker; but on Fifth Avenue at ten o'clock in the morning, if he encounters violence he will call a policeman. A new invention has superseded an old. But it will, of course, only supersede the old as long as the ideals of the society are congruent with it. It is significant how civil law, which was compatible with steadily widening areas of social order, disappears as the glorification of warfare comes back under fascism. When I insist that the only way to get rid of an accepted social invention which we no longer wish to use is to make a new invention, I can give no guaran-tee that that new invention will of itself, unsupported by the whole direction of the culture, win out. But equally certain is it that without the inventions with which to implement order, we cannot hope to have any order in a world which contains such a full panoply of inventions for implementing disorder.

There is no necessary connection between warfare

and human nature. Human nature is potentially aggressive and destructive and potentially orderly and constructive. Possibly some individuals are born with a slight preference for one type of behavior over the other, but this has never been demonstrated. But whether the bulk of a community will delight in violence, murder and rapine, or in a quiet pursuit of agriculture, of trade or knowledge, is wholly dependent upon the cultural tradition within which each generation of children is reared. Warfare is simply a sanctioned form of social behavior into which the most diverse character structures will fit if they are convinced that the use of this form is congruent with the aims which they hold most dear. Nor have we any absolute proof that those who believe in war fight better than those who believe in peace. Those who believe in war as a way of life carry with them certain liabilities which those who believe in order do not. The man whose male honor depends upon war can be wholly wrecked by defeat. The man who takes up his rifle to defend his home, convinced that he has no other choice but repudiating the trappings of militarism, has no such vulnerability. He is not proving he is a man by fighting. He has already proved that by living in an orderly world for which he is now willing to fight, and die, if necessary. Upon the faith that such a citizen soldier, who has no personal impulse to power or destructiveness and whose investment in battle is simply all that he believes worth fighting for, is stronger than the professional soldier of a warrior state, depends our greatest hope of victory. Our enemy is fighting for the right to keep on fighting indefinitely; we are fighting for the right to stop and build a stable world. The method we are using is his method. He has chosen the weapons; he has chosen his seconds; he has chosen the place and the hour. Unless we can pit against him an abiding determination to make an invention which will outlaw his, he is stronger than we. Unless we can say, yes, we are playing your game now and we intend to beat you at it, too, but afterwards, we will invent a better game and never again are we going to be caught playing yours, we have no hope. Proposals in Congress for a great standing army after the war are confessions of defeat, confessions that we cannot make the necessary inventions, that we are going to accept the enemy's definition of the world. Every proposal for a permanent army—which is called an army and phrased in the old jargon of war—is a step which weakens us as a people. We will not fight for the love of fighting; we will not fight because we are afraid not to fight lest we be dubbed cowards; we will not fight for mere survival. And when I say this I am not making ethical remarks or commencement speeches. I am not preaching pacifism; I am merely describing, scientifically, a condition which exists and which the captains and the kings must take into account.

Erich Fromm suggested in his *Escape from Freedom* [4] that nc people, once having tasted freedom and turning back towards slavery, could escape a terrible penalty in maladjustment and neurosis. It is probable that the same statement can be made about people who have tasted and loved order based on peace. They can be annihilated by those who love war; but they themselves cannot be made to love it. If our generals and our admirals will hold before their troops the chance of remaking the world, they will fight with every energy that is in them. To the extent that our generals and admirals want victory, want to go down in history as the winners of a world conflict, they must do this. If they are trapped instead in defense of a profession which they think of as immortal instead of belonging to one great phase of history, they will defend the permanent necessity of war.

Yet, to attack our professional soldiers because they practice their art well is again a suicidal act. To disarm when you have no technique for keeping your adversary disarmed is a form of silly wishful dreaming *within the framework of war,* characteristic of so much pacifist thinking. Most pacifists take their clues from war itself and think that by sinking battleships or insulting generals we need have no more of it. Not until we tackle this problem as calmly as we would tackle a problem of inventing a new synthetic to replace an old, not until we see it as calling, not for heroics or sermons, but for inventive thinking, will we get anywhere at all.

If the American people are told that they are fighting to get peace they feel trapped in contradictory nonsense, for, of course, it is nonsense. You don't get peace by war; you only get armistices. To pause between wars makes good sense to a warlike people. That is why it is the Nazis and their sympathizers among the United

Nations who keep talking about a negotiated peace. The point of a negotiated peace is so that everybody can stop, have a breathing spell, and fight more efficiently in the future. War to the finish is never the slogan of people who like war. Like the head-hunters of New Guinea, war-mongering leaders realize that if you kill all the people whom you habitually head-hunt, there will later be no one for your young men to prove their manhood on. Head-hunters' victims, like game, must be preserved. Unless we say frankly that we are fighting in order to get the chance to set the world in the kind of order that we want, a kind that the military nations do not want, and fighting for that chance alone, Americans will smile cynically at our oratory. But if we are to say this, we must mean it. We must see the job ahead as a job, not a matter of capital ships and power politics, but a challenging, practical job, a problem in organization which can be solved just as Americans have solved the problems of mass production. And we must see it as our duty—if we are to call ourselves good—to fight for the right to do this next big job uninterrupted. When the Indians and other European nations interfered with the job which we had decided to do on this continent, we pushed them aside without scruples. It lies within the American character to see a job as so important, and so pre-eminently our own, that, to the extent that we work hard enough, think intelligently enough, and pay enough attention, we have the right to tell other people to keep off the grass or only come on it if they mean to work at the same job as hard as we.

To say we are fighting this war so as to have a chance to make the next, the needed, inventions, makes sense in American terms; and we can only win the war if we fight it in terms that do make sense—to Americans.

CHAPTER XIII

Building the World New

★

IF WE ARE to draw upon the dynamics of American culture to fight the war on an all-out basis because we
believe in the possibilities of a post-war world which is
worth fighting for, what must we do? If that post-war
world is to be built in accordance with the dictates of
democracy, then we cannot make a finished blueprint
into which we will force other people to fit. We must
work in terms of a sense of direction, not a finished
plan. If we are to trust to future generations the details
of how it will develop, we must educate a next generation fit to carry on the job. If the post-war world is to
catch our American imaginations, then we must see it
in American terms and must see our role in that building. And what are American terms? Briefly, we must see
the emerging world as a world of plenty, of great expansion, of room for everybody to make a contribution and
succeed. We must see a world in which every human
being has a right to develop what he has in him—a right
to succeed, a right to the rewards of success. We must
see a world built with a moral purpose, built because

we think that we are right in so building. Above all, we must see ourselves tackling a job which we believe can be done practically, like any other big job. We must be confident that if we put our minds to it, if we invoke every bit of science and every bit of inventiveness that is in us, we, the people of the world of 1942, can find the answers. We must believe that we can make war and tariff walls and passports, uneven distribution of the world's goods, and restriction of individuals to the special human inventions of his own society—to one language, one art style, one form of personal relations —as out of date as the cannibal feast, the barter market, the trial by fire, and the sign language of the Plains Indians.

As we must draw upon our American strengths to the utmost, so also we must as consciously guard against American weaknesses, and there are certain things which this job must not mean to us. I have purposely called this chapter "Building the world new" instead of "Building a new world" because building a new world is a phrase which brings out certain defects in American character too keenly. We are too eager to believe that the answer is to scrap everything that is old, to turn in all the ways of life which other peoples have developed, and make everything new and "made in America." We are too eager to believe that if we can just tear down the old building, right down, rip it up with a demolition machine, and start from the bottom with new materials, new plans and the latest ideas, we can produce fine results. We are insensitive to the im-

portance of those patterns and designs which take centuries to develop, too willing to listen to the calculating
machine, unwilling to listen to the cultivated human
heart. We have been used to doing things too quickly
and not taking human factors into account. When we
built our great factories for production in this war, we
could have decentralized them, set them in pleasant
places where men already lived decent lives. Instead,
because it was quicker and more impressive, we built
terrible and out-of-date monster plants far from any
form of housing, monster plants which gorged themselves on workers traveling incalculable miles over inadequate roads. Year in and year out, we do cost-
accounting on materials and refuse to consider costs in
terms of human lives. We grudge the school lunch even
when it cuts down the cost of schooling per child, because to think in terms of human beings has never been
one of our measures of efficiency. It would be too easy
to make a plan which disregarded all the values of all
the other peoples of the world and lay down a physical
plan which, like a monstrous Willow Run bomber
plant, was to provide food and clothing for all the
peoples of the world and at the same time condemn
them to lives of utter meaninglessness and vacuity.

To build the world new, it is necessary to recognize
that we have a world worth keeping—a world in need
of repair, a world in need of much redesigning, a world
which is not organized on a world scale, but a world
which contains many irreplaceable values, which once
destroyed might never again be rediscovered. Each

people in this existing world has something to contribute to the whole—not merely rights to demand, as small countries or minorities, but values to add, points of view and ways of behaving, skills and insights and abilities which no other culture has. It is in keeping with our American belief—that each people should have the right to its own religion, its own way of life—to recognize the *rights* of other peoples. But we must add to this sheer negative willingness to tolerate other peoples a sound engineering recognition of the positive contributions they can make, a recognition that in this reorganized world which we want to live in, we need what they have and need it badly. From our conscience as a people, our whole tradition of political and religious freedom, we can draw the motivation for not attacking other cultures, but we also need a motive for relying—in a positive sense—on what they have to give.

If we want to cast our post-war planning in terms which will use every value which has been developed on this planet, every value which is not incompatible with living on a world scale, are there American precedents to which we can turn so that the conservation of these values will make sense to us? What were the steps by which America moved away from the old craftsmanship and specialized hereditary skills of Europe through the pioneer stage when each man was his own smith, carpenter, ironmonger and architect, soil chemist and experimental geneticist, to our present age of machine tools and assembly lines? Is there a parallel here, a parallel in those parts of American history of which we can most uniformly be proud, in which manufacturer and skilled laborer and unskilled laborer, in which statesman and postman can agree that Americans have done a good job? If there is, we are the more fortunate; for to the extent that we can find in work that all have counted good a model for the work to do, we move the faster. Two Americans may argue over the relative beauties of the natural Niagara Falls or the Old World charm of Chartres, but both can take a distinctive pride in Radio City. How did we set about this conquest of a continent?

First, and this is very important, we broke the fetters of crafts and custom and discarded the habitual behavior which had been the Middle Ages'. We changed our expectation of men's abilities. The man who had done only one thing in Europe had to do a hundred in the New World. In pioneer times, he did all of them at once; today, he does a number of them in turn, shifting from occupation to occupation, but either way a new flexibility enters in, very alien to the old patterns by which even rural labor was differentiated so that a man was a shepherd or a hedger but not a farmer; he was not ready, as American farm laborers are, to turn his hand to a hundred tasks. This necessity, to alternate or combine skills which had been thought of as exclusive one of another, carried with it a new expansiveness, a new belief in the self. If one job failed there was another. Jobs and status no longer were bound together. During the last years, Europeans who watched the terrible reinforcement of fascism which came with the necessity for the lower middle class to do factory work in Germany, have prophesied that the same thing would happen here. They do not realize that to Americans, the fact that work is well paid and the thing to do is more important than what it is—that overnight, school-teachers would leave their white-collar jobs and crowd into the bomber plants, that overnight we would have trailer camps in which members of the American Association of University Women coped with the difficulties of living in one room.

So we can put down as one characteristic of Americans a flexibility,[1] a willingness to tackle any task, learn any new skill, quickly, easily, without deep involvement. This willingness combines a sublime and optimistic confidence in one's own ability with a definite lack of appreciation of the difficulty of any job. The man who has shifted, easily and unworried so long as the pay was good, from one job to another, has no deep respect for himself as a virtuoso or for the mysteries of the skill of which he so lately knew nothing and for exercising which he now commands good pay. His faith lies not in the long years that go to train the eye and hand until they are fitted to do one thing supremely well and other things not at all—as are those of a European craftsman—but in himself as a responsible and intelligent being, able to adapt himself quickly to new circumstances. He has slight respect for conventions. He recognizes none of the barriers that come from a frozen and fixed order of society.

We might, if we were to make a quick superficial

judgment, simply say we have developed a people who are Jack-of-all-trades and therefore ought to be very good at learning new and unheard-of skills quickly enough to make use of them—not a terribly precise and accurate and perfect use, but still a use. But there is one element in the history of the transformation of American pioneer economy into streamlined American industry which we must not neglect. In the course of this development, we did need skills, the precise and beautifully perfect skills which can come only from old and stable civilizations in which men specialized as we had never specialized. We had the energy, the adaptability, the will to succeed; but we lacked these special abilities which we had had to strip off when we rolled up our sleeves in the wilderness. So we imported our skills from Europe; we imported our weavers and our rug makers; our blacksmiths were Basques; our spinners came from England. We made the framework, but they filled in the details. We built, in fact, a framework in which more diverse and special delicate skills could be used more quickly than ever before. These skills we showed no disposition to copy. We took the children of the trained spinners and weavers, the children of the mechanics and the watchmakers, and turned them into Americans, energetic Jacks-of-all-trades, masters of none. And when the supply failed—when immigration cut off our sources of skilled labor—we still did not learn those skills which we had depended upon in those nurtured in old and tight traditions. Instead we set about studying the operations in which their skills consisted, and we made machines to do what they had done. American inventiveness mediated the break between European hand skill and the machine and, significantly, we did this without ever learning the skill which was being mediated. We substituted an ability to analyze and build for the ability to feel and to be something different from ourselves. The wary, inarticulate knowledge passed from father to son in some remote Basque village, where the low lights of the forge and the tone in which the smith's wife sang her child to sleep were all part of the training, was translated by American engineers into machines, automatic machines which would do the same job perhaps a little less perfectly but well enough to serve millions where hundreds had been served before. We did not have the skill, we do not have it now; but we have been able to identify it, to analyze it, and to get the job done.

Every step in this process must be scrutinized carefully. How did we make the inventions which have placed our assembly lines ahead of any in the world? Did we simply say: "We want to weave beautiful cloth, let's consider how to do it"? No. First we brought from another culture human beings who carried in their every posture and gesture, in their whole way of life, an attitude which we did not have towards making cloth. They came in hundreds, lit by their desire for a freer world, but carrying with them an infinitely precious load, their special skills. We put them to work in our factories, often with little enough recognition of why they had come here or the freedom which we had offered them. They gave us the clues, the clues on which our machine-tooled machines were finally built. Skills and knowledge which it had taken many centuries to develop, which we did not have and could not have developed if we would, we were able to find and to study, to analyze, to rationalize and to re-create in a different form. Today we have learned how to handle so many of these processes on a purely mechanical basis that we tend to forget this indebtedness for clues. We are unaware that much that is built into American industry was provided by the skills of other civilizations brought to our shores by living human beings who demonstrated their abilities on our doorstep.

This has been our distinctive contribution—the contribution of a people without the type of culture which creates the narrow virtuoso, deeply committed to one skill alone. It has not always been a contribution. Because we lacked the kind of cultural perspective which gives depth to life, we often used this special assembling skill of ours cheaply. We learned to build in a way that man had never built before; but we often built something which was not worth building, furniture and houses which lacked beauty or dignity. The very energy with which we can take over and reconstitute the painfully acquired skill of others comes from our lack of discrimination; our interest in quantity rather than quality; our emphasis upon the degree of success, not upon the kind of success. While we meticulously reduced to a machine pattern the vanishing skills of a craft world, we were engaged in no such delicate and searching analyses of the other gifts which these patient immigrants brought with them. They who had left their old ways scorned them, and we borrowed the scorn of their newly Americanized children and scorned them too. Their skills we could use, they brought us money; but their values we threw aside like empty husks. We did not realize that values, like the ability to weave or to forge, cannot be reproduced without a pattern; that just as we depended upon long generations to give us the model skill on which we could make a machine, so also, in art and in music, in inter-personal relations, in making love as surely as in making cakes, patterns were necessary, and that we, working hastily to put up a tent in a wilderness, had scrapped most of the patterns that we had.

In our search for the arts which has lain back of our great museums filled with the spoils of Europe, we did not follow the same course which we had followed with the weavers and the blacksmiths, watching the human beings, analyzing, often unconsciously, what they did, and inventing another way of doing it. Instead we brought over the objects, the end results, hung them on our walls and put little electric lights under them or over them. But when we wanted to produce cloth, we did not bring over English cloth; we brought over English weavers or we went and watched English weavers at work. When we needed iron-work, we brought the blacksmith, not the forged tool. We brought a way of behavior, and we learned from that, not from the mere product of that behavior. Art and music we tried to buy, but we were humble before the mechanical and workaday skills—and practical enough to learn. We orchestrated—in our great mechanized factories—skills nourished in a thousand villages where human beings speaking a hundred different tongues had chattered and sung at their work. We have apparently built a new world overnight, but only by learning quickly and efficiently from those whose skills took hundreds, even thousands, of years to develop.

We now stand on the threshold of another great period in history, a period which will be as different from all that has gone before as the machine age is from the stone age. Today, we can learn nothing in the realm of production from the stone age Eskimo. There is no principle which lies behind his harpoon, there is no principle in a kayak or the arched ceiling of his snow hut which we have not rationalized and incorporated as the background of our inventiveness. Inventions which he made by accident, through long, cold centuries of trial and error, once seized upon by an articulate generation, become principles upon which to make more and more inventions. The lever and the wheel, product of untold generations of early civilization, are the mere ABC's of our mechanics. We have gone beyond stone age man, beyond the realm of random experimentation, beyond the level where the genius was the man who saw the importance of what some other man had probably done by accident. A modern aeroplane factory may not be usefully compared with a group of Australian aborigines laboriously shaping their spears. Conscious invention, articulately implemented by systematic knowledge, has introduced a qualitative difference between the Eskimo or the Australian aborigine and ourselves, between the age of random trial and error and the age of purposeful invention.

A second hiatus, a break which also makes the past and the present not comparable, came with the substitution of power-driven machines for human and animal labor, a shift in the distribution of energy. The whole problem of population, of natural resources, of food supply, has been altered when vitamin B_1 can be manufactured cheaply by the pound, and a crew of four men can transport thousands of men along railways or across oceans. This break, not yet fully accomplished, which shifted the whole problem of man's relationship to nature from one of crafty dependence to one of conscious and effective utilization, has not yet been fully realized. Our statesmen and our politicians still talk in terms of natural resources and access to natural resources as if this were—as it once was—a problem of survival in peace and not merely a problem in war. We still talk as if the problem were to get the food to feed people instead of merely the problem of organizing the distribution of the food so that all may eat. Our slowness in grasping that our whole position vis-à-vis nature has been reversed by machine power is partly responsible for the continuation of wars. Wars in turn tend to perpetuate the illusion that we still live in dark ages restricted by a scarcity of raw materials and man power and beasts of burden and dependent upon the natural fertility of our fields. In war, when we are destroying more than we produce and are artificially confined to one part of the earth's surface, the old position in which man had to live by what he had and perished if his enemy happened to have a better supply, is reinstated. Yet we are not short of steel or rubber or alcohol or sugar—as such. We are short of them, in a given context, in the middle of a war, when we are racing against time. It is important that this should be kept well in mind, so that after the war, people will begin to realize as rapidly as possible that we know too much about production for the amount we know about consumption, and that it is in the field of consumption—the field of living, rather than producing in order to live— that the new inventions are needed.

For if we turn our eyes away from our power to produce and look at our skill in consuming, in dividing up the products so that every human being's life is progressively dignified by freedom from unnecessary or soul-destroying labor, by freedom from want and insecurity and preventable disease, then we find that the hiatuses which separate us from the Eskimo in the field of production suddenly vanish. In the field of social organization we are still in the trial and error period, although we have used well, as was the case with the savage and his boomerang, many accidental inventions. We have learned of course a great many things: how to keep larger and larger groups of people in smaller and smaller spaces, peacefully. Where headhunters only dare to live in small scattered villages, because in a village of more than a few hundred, some men's hands will again be raised in the hope of taking their neighbors' heads, we dare to put millions in a few square miles, with a negligible amount of resulting violence. We have learned how to communicate with many millions of people in the same tongue, where our savage ancestors communicated with hundreds and our medieval ancestors with thousands. We have learned how to pickle the past in written records, so that we can return to it and learn from it, and we have thus given another dimension to "historical civilization." For savage culture was flat and contemporaneous. That which has no continued relevance is soon forgotten when there is no repository for learning except the fragile memories of a few individuals. We have learned to systematize the transmission of knowledge, to take the children of illiterate parents and make them literate, to take the children of Japanese parents and make them Americans without a gesture or a thought to show their cultural origin, though still pitifully trapped in the fascist-defined prison of their physical appearance. We have learned to take one beautiful face or beautiful painting and reproduce it a million times, to confine a rare and lovely singing voice upon a wax record, to multiply one definitive gesture on a thousand feet of film.

The human race, looking backwards over its hundreds of thousands of years of slow and fumbling civilization, may well feel deeply proud. But greater than any of these achievements, and they are not mean ones, is that invention which has already given us control of the natural world and should now give us control of the social world. This is the invention of invention itself. As long as man, intelligent, curious, and questing, manipulated and investigated the world around him, inventions were made once in a while; but they were often made where they were not needed or were out of step and out of touch with the pace of the culture. So the Chinese discovered vaccination centuries ago, but had no use for the saving of life in a culture where life as such was not yet valued. It took Christian emphasis upon the value of the individual human life coinciding with the discovery of vaccination, before that discovery could be turned to the service of men. For countless centuries man has been the sport of his own inventiveness, just as he has been at the mercy of the elements, the uncertain seasons, the distribution of minerals in the earth, the presence of mountain barriers, and the impassability of rough seas. He could not decide that he needed a new piece of knowledge, a new skill, a new material, now, at once, in order to attain his goals within his lifetime or in the lifetime of his children. His dignity was the dignity that goes with making much of little, with bearing nobly the slings and arrows of outrageous fortune, with wearing quietly or passively not only the garments of mortality but the garments of ignorance and weakness. For metaphors with which to sing his praises, the poets had to go to battered oaks or lonely pines. As he constructed a view of life which gave him courage to mature and marry and bear children, to toil and suffer and finally to die—so the poets could acclaim him. He was at the mercy of his own brain, of its power to invent for evil, of its capriciousness and undependability in making inventions which were good.

For some fifty thousand years man's pride has lain in making up good answers to the riddle of human life, good explanations of why the crops failed, why hurricanes came, why people died of the plague or of starvation. It has only been very recently that we have turned from making up answers to asking questions, asking careful, purposeful, properly phrased questions, setting ourselves problems instead of reconciling ourselves to disaster or finding new ways to reconcile ourselves to old disasters.

So far we have confined ourselves to setting technological problems, how to fly, how to communicate without wires, how to bottle up a voice or transmit a photograph through the ether. When a new problem of this sort presented itself we did not sit with bowed heads, shame in our hearts, and say, "We do not know how to fly. We are worms, we deserve to be wiped off the face of the earth. Surely, we must be a degenerate, a soft, an effeminate generation, not to be able to fly. Or perhaps we have sinned greatly and the Lord has punished us. Our blood has been corrupted by intermarriage with people who speak a different language. Our wills have rotted from sitting in over-stuffed chairs. We are not the men our ancestors were who learned to span the seas." No doubt quite a little of that sort of philosophizing had been going on in one form or another for thousands of years—and it served very little purpose until men who wished to fly began to ask the relevant questions about which aspects of a bird were worth borrowing and put together such existing inventions as the propeller and the internal combustion engine. Then we had aeroplanes.

Yet in the field of social organization where we have just begun to ask questions, instead of really concentrating on the right ones we continue to bow our heads in impotence and shame that the human race, half of which now despises war, should still be fighting; that half the human race, in spite of its cities and its granaries and its ships, should be starving to death. We have prostrated ourselves before our failure to make inventions of which men have only begun to dream, instead of standing up and tackling the problem of making them. Why should we be so ashamed that we have not yet solved a problem which we have not tried to solve? Instead of being ashamed that we have not got the right answer, we should be ashamed that we have not yet asked the right questions, and this shifts our shame at once from a cause of impotence and despair to a cause of activity. The question: How can we look ourselves in the face, when civilized men in the twentieth century are fighting each other as if they were in the stone age? leads us exactly nowhere. The question: How can we analyze the problems of man's relations to man as we have analyzed the problems of man's relationship to nature? is one which sets us free. We stand on the threshold of another great period, of another step forward in which nothing that comes after can be compared with what came before. For the chance to take that step, we can fight with all the dignity of our great inheritance. If we had held in our hands the power to go forward to the machine age or back to man's weakness when he depended always on his own hands, what American would have gone back or would have failed to put all his energy into going forward? Now we face a comparable great choice.

But if we are to fight, to win the war and win the chance to tackle this next great question, the organization of the whole human family into one orderly unit in which no human gift that has existed on earth will be lost and new gifts, now undreamt of, shall be developed we must feel not only that this course is possible to man, but that we, Americans in 1942, are specially fitted to take part in the enterprise. When we build a great factory, we are untroubled with doubts as to our fitness for the task. When we recommended America to the millions who came to our shores, we were again untroubled by doubts about whether it was worth their while to come—in the steerage and as peons —to this glowing new world. When we saw our troops off in 1917, neither they nor we had any doubt that democracy was worth fighting for. If we are to give of our utmost effort and skill and enthusiasm, we must believe in ourselves, which means believing in our past and in our future, in our parents and in our children, in that peculiar blend of moral purpose and practical inventiveness which is the American character.

Can we hark back to the way in which we learned from the skills of other cultures when we first made our machines? We did not invent *de novo;* we did not try to spin techniques from our empty brains; we studied existing techniques and learned from them. If we wish to build a world which will use all men's diverse gifts, we must go to school to other cultures, analyze them and rationalize our findings. We must find models and patterns which, orchestrated together on a world scale, will make a world as different from the old as the machine world was from the craft industries of the Middle Ages.

Each culture cultivates some potentialities of mankind and disallows others,[2] develops the sailor and denies the farmer, permits the salesman and scorns the artist, encourages the mechanic but has no time for the poet, or rewards the poet and disallows the practical man. We cannot, by mere hospitality to different gifts in our own children, hope to build a world in which all of these gifts will be given play, even though we intelligently solve the problems of distribution and consumption and order. It is that recognition that Americans might be able to produce an ordered world, replete with mechanical conveniences but empty of many of the other values which older civilizations have cultivated, which makes so many of our leaders (and European leaders also) pause—reluctant for America to take leadership at all. But if we could once sense the parallel between the way in which we learned from the weaver and not from the cloth and so realize that we must learn from every existing civilization, from China and England, from France and Albania, from Siam and Brazil and Java, from Russia and Norway and Roumania, from Germany and Italy and Japan . . . then the way would look far clearer. If we are to learn from all these peoples, it is necessary that they should continue to maintain their own way of life. We cannot learn from their dead products any more than we can learn the weaver's art from the cloth cut from the loom. To learn from them, we must develop techniques for analyzing the delicate processes of inter-personal relations, of forms and ceremonies, of ways of bringing up children and burying the dead, which taken altogether make a unique culture, a unique contribution to human life.

But we must not bring to this job of helping preserve and develop all these contrasting historical ways of life a mere bent back, mere humility before all that is different from ourselves. Just as it is the crassest kind of stupidity to refuse to recognize values in other cultures which we lack ourselves—hobbling our imaginations and depriving ourselves of models and patterns which we desperately need and without which we could not go on in the direction we wish to go—so also it is equally stupid to give uncritical acclaim to the achievements of other cultures. If we enter a pact with the peoples of the world, if we say: "We will try to build a world together to which all of us contribute each from our peculiar knowledge, contribute by having people who embody our different values work together to plan the new world," we can also say: "Our special job is going to be analysis. We aren't an old culture, as you are. We have not had centuries of continuous tradition which have developed ears that catch the faintest rhythm of experience to turn it into poetry, or bodies so graceful and so economical in their movements that they virtually do not know fatigue. What we have got is a very practical skill in using old clues in a new way. We are going to approach this task of learning from you, from every old and coherent way of life which survives on the face of this earth, with the full realization of what the job may require."

Every culture known to science has developed certain human gifts and neglected others, developed certain keenness of sight or hearing, certain sounds in the language, certain cadences of musical notes, certain combinations of food, certain categories of meaning, certain methods of regulating human relations. Each culture has done this at tremendous trial and error cost, over hundreds, sometimes thousands, of years. And such experiments cannot be made quickly. It would take a whole lifetime or many lifetimes to find out whether rearing babies in a given way is going to result in individuals who die gallantly or cravenly; it takes a generation or many generations to find out what kind of lovers and husbands, thinkers or workers, artists or actors or politicians, they will make. And we cannot make these experiments if we would. Suppose we wanted to be sure which elements in Chinese education produced some element in Chinese character which we like: we cannot start American mothers practicing—fifty practicing one part of Chinese education and fifty practicing another—in order to find out. And if we did, we, the experimenters, would probably all be dead before the babies who had been the guinea pigs had grown up. Nor would the experiment be worth anything, because every other condition of life in America would be different. Only by going to each people, now, while they are living their own lives in their traditional way, can we find out these accidentally discovered, these inarticulate and priceless secrets of how to draw out of each generation of children unguessed potentialities. Once we have learned this, the task of devising ways of picking which children should be so trained as to show a given trait, now restricted to some other culture than our own, will be reasonably simple. If we use the clues which other great cultures give us, and if we work with members of those cultures in building the world new, we will have ways of tapping human energies as startling, as exciting, as the ways of tapping natural resources which so dazzle our eyes today.

It is necessary to learn how cultures hang together, what are the rules of coherence, unity and emphasis, as our grammar books used to say about our sentences. What kind of child care goes with what kind of marriage? Can you bring boys up by sneering at them for behaving like girls and then expect them to tolerate women who copy—and outdistance—men? Can you bring up children to believe they must stand up for themselves and yet never hit anyone, and not expect them to be confused? Can you teach the executives in monster corporations the romanticism of the days of the single mill owner and expect them to engage in responsible public negotiations? Our own culture contains many of these hybridizations, these discrepancies. We wish to correct these and to provide against similar discrepancies in any plans which we help make for the world. We do not wish to set up goals of understanding and tolerance and the dignity of man and yet leave institutions flourishing which are incompatible with such goals. So, as we look at the different cultures, the different ways of living which man has developed, accidentally, through long ages of inarticulate trial and error, we will look for principles. What are the rules of cultural organizations? Which types of culture give the minimum recognition of human dignity which we must demand of all? And which inevitably contravene it?

For to be culturally tolerant of precious inventions which, if they perish before we have understood them, may elude us altogether for centuries or for ever, does not mean that we must have no standards of our own, that all ways of life are equal. Slavery is not noble because it is the way of life of another people any more than it was noble as an element in American culture. The democratic assumption is to say: all cultures are equal in that each is a complete whole, a social invention within which man has lived with man and has found life in some way good. There is no hierarchy of values by which one culture has the right to insist on all its own values and deny those of another—that is the essence of the old German theme of Kultur superiority. But though all cultures have the dignity of wholes, some of them may be utterly incompatible with living on a world scale. Some of them may depend upon war to preserve themselves or upon slavery or upon the monopoly exploitation of natural resources which in turn leads to war. If we set ourselves the task of treating the world as a whole, of organizing human social life on it so that threats of war—appropriate enough to the random accidental strivings after integration of an earlier age, but now out of date—shall disappear, then we must accept the responsibility of trying to eliminate in other cultures and in our own those particular habits and institutions which lead to war, to separatism, and to a desire to dominate or exploit.

The precept about the beam and the mote needs to be reinterpreted. Only by taking out the beam from our own eye *and* the mote from our neighbor's, both at once, can we hope to get anywhere. If New York had one hundred cases of smallpox and Boston one thousand, we would not argue that we should first wipe out the cases in Boston and then turn our attention to New York. We know that smallpox in Boston and smallpox in New York are interrelated, and that only speedy isolation of cases and vaccination of everyone else, in both cities, will save the United States of America from epidemic. The useless circular argument by which we have no right to work for freedom in India because of the way we treat our own Negroes gets us nowhere just as fast. As long as there is anywhere in the world a center of infectious intolerance, intolerance for a race or a sex, an age group or an occupation, a caste or a class, or for those who profess one religion rather than another, all of us are endangered, every day, every hour. Europe was saved from plague only when the carriers were isolated and confined, everywhere, in the small countries as well as the large, in the villages as well as the cities. Now the rapidity of modern communications has made this interdependence a world condition. We have only to look at the new laws for medical inspections and vaccination which the aeroplane has brought in, for the parallel which modern communications have brought in in social organization. Smallpox on an East Indian island did not threaten Scotland in the sixteenth century, nor did slavery in ancient Hawaii have any implications for Norway. Today, the obscure intolerances of German minorities, bottling themselves up in the Sudetenland, in Austria, in Hungary, in Roumania, in South America, have nurtured a social virus which endangers the whole world.

So, while we respect and conserve and study the ways of life of other peoples, we must be at the same time critical, as clear in our purposeful refusal to foster, or help them foster, values which are incompatible with order and the dignity of man, as we are in our determination to foster our and their respect and interest in values different from our own or their own. The kind of relativism which says there are no ethics because one people has found good what another has found bad is not meaningful when you are trying to build a world new. We must ask: "Good for what?" and "Bad for what?" We must realize that ways of life which were meaningful in one context, which made sense at one historical level of ignorance and provincialism, simply do not make sense at another.

There is an apparent contradiction here. We are to study and conserve the cultures of France and Albania, and Roumania and India, that we may learn from them, that there shall not perish from the earth discoveries so basic that we may never make them again. At the same time, we are to make demands on all of these cultures that they eliminate certain elements which are incompatible with world order as we see it. We are to cherish tolerance as a basis, not only of democracy, but of learning, as an essential if we are to keep for our future and our children all of good that now survives on earth, all that men have learned about themselves and their varied potentialities. Yet, we are also to be intolerant. We are to be the instruments to shape a creative order, based on respect for difference, and the scalpels which are to hew away that which does not fit our particular dream. Is not this nonsense? Is not this the very problem which has defeated those who would bring in a socialist state by revolution?

Yes, it is the same problem, and to solve it, we must make new inventions, inventions in the phrasing of relationships between peoples which we now lack. When we brand a given element in a given culture as unacceptable, as dangerous to us and to the whole world, we have several choices. We can say: "This element is linked with the race of those who practice it: the practice of superordination is inextricably bound up with the German race; an inability to see either themselves or Negroes as simply human beings is an instinct of the American Southern white race; a tendency to cringe and invite sadism is an instinct of the Hindu race." If we say this we become fascists quickly, even though we started out with the best intentions. This phrasing of the problem is unsuitable to the end we have in view.

Alternatively we can say: "All the members of a given nationality share in a certain dangerous and undesirable trait. We do not say it is racial; we realize that it is the result of their upbringing, that if they had been moved as babies somewhere else, they would have been different, but still—there they are, some forty or sixty or eighty millions of them. They are all hopelessly indoctrinated, and the only thing to do is to annihilate them, wipe them out, scatter them to the four winds, so that this evil thing which their civilization has bred can never function again. We must liquidate them as French revolutionists liquidated the aristocrats, as the Communists liquidated the kulak, as the Germans liquidate the Aryan intellectuals whose education has unfitted them to appreciate fascism." This course, which is being seriously preached in many places, would again unfit us to be what we aim to be, instruments in building a better world. The annihilation of peoples, innocent victims of a way of life into which they were born, will not do. Once we had carried out such a program we would have compromised the future because there would be no one left spiritually fit to build the new world in whose name we had committed mass murder.

Is there then an answer, or do we have to foster and tolerate German culture and Japanese culture until it grows strong enough to threaten us again? Are we caught in a ridiculous treadmill in which we must go round and round, fostering our enemy because it will wreck our characters if we don't? In the days of St. Francis it was a Christian duty to wash the feet of the sick. To have feared infection would have incapacitated the Christian soul for canonization. Yet Christians today do not wash the feet of those who are sick with an infectious disease; they build hospitals and laboratories of research; they finance the manufacture of vaccines and the dissemination of knowledge about disease. When we quarantine a man with smallpox and vaccinate his children, we are committing a Christian act as Christian as St. Francis', but implemented by knowledge. Those who are sick with infectious diseases, we place in good hospitals and attempt to cure. Only if they are incurable do we continue to segregate them, and then we do what we can to make them comfortable. Far from carrying hatred in our hearts, we have only the deepest compassion for those who have become infected with diseases which cut them off from normal human intercourse. Curing them is not only protecting others from them, but protecting them also from the consequences of that which they helplessly carry in their bodies. We can do these things and remain fit to administer a world to which we hope to restore these sick and diseased and insane people, whom we have had to temporarily remove.

If, however, we do not combine with the segregation of those who suffer from infectious diseases, a determined and unending attempt to discover the cause and cure of the disease from which they suffer, and if we do not use every means in our power to protect others from their fate, then again we become morally culpable, unfit guardians of our own ideals. If we hit a man when he is down, we become bullies, damned in our own eyes, committed to further bullying to wipe out the memory of the act, or to appeasement, binding up the wounds of those whom we weakened until they become strong and dangerous again. That is what we did to Germany in the last war. It is what we are in danger of doing in this war. The Germans are articulately skilled in exploiting our guilt, and a new cycle of appeasement would start again.

We must devise a phrasing of the post-war reconstruction, in which we handle those institutions which breed men committed to warfare and dominance and ruthless cruelty as if they were dangerous viruses and treat those individuals who are deeply infected with them as carriers of fatal social diseases. We must analyze the social organization of Prussia and Japan, especially, and attempt scientifically to strike out those elements which produce the convinced fascist. We know something of what these elements are—in Japan [3] the way in which the male child is allowed dominance over women and taught subservience to men, and the way in which whenever he slips or wavers the outside world and his own family *both* turn upon him at once in a cruelty which cannot fail to breed a comparable cruelty when he holds power himself. We know something of the way in which a mixture of dominance and inferiority is bred in German children by a family system in which the father is a tyrant in the home but must cringe before his immediate superiors outside the home.[4] We know something of the way in which insistence on status and association of status with personality promote a lack of imagination in human relationships and breed personalities ever vulnerable and ever fiercely defensive. If we set to work to revise those elements in the cultures which have nourished fascism and in those cultures which have just failed to nourish fascism—the United Nations—and systematically not only try to alter the forms but isolate those intractable individuals who carry the forms, we can work with clean hands and clean hearts. If we fix our eyes on the disease—for a disease it is, this systematized hatred which is attempting to creep over the face of the whole world—and not on those who carry it, if we fight the disease, and, only if we must, segregate those who are most virulently infected, if we are as stern and inflexible with ourselves as with our enemies—we shall escape corrupting ourselves as instruments for a new order. The quarantine official who neglects to isolate his own children loses all the moral authority which public education and laws made to protect all the people of the community have given him. The judge who takes a bribe endangers irretrievably the law he is set to represent. "Judge not, that ye be not judged" has only limited implications, but "Judge your neighbor *and* yourself"—both at once and both in the interests of someone else, of the community, or of the children, or of the whole world—is a broader dogma.

The logic of this position is made clear if we look at the question of treatment of prisoners of war. Those who do not surrender but simply stand and die if necessary are also morally free to take no prisoners. Those who train their officers to surrender and so save their men from slaughter must also take prisoners rather than kill, and treat their prisoners well. Either position is clear and does not compromise those who follow it. But a mixture is fatal. We cannot demand anything from those whom we have conquered which we are not willing to demand from ourselves. This does not mean that we should disarm because we must disarm our enemies, as many might lightly interpret it to mean. But we must set out to remove—inside our own culture—all those tendencies which would lead us to misuse the arms which we keep, and with equal vigor we must set about developing within the culture of our enemies those tendencies which will enable them to use well the freedom which they have never had. If we fail in either job, if we let those fascist tendencies flourish at home which we have disarmed abroad, we, of course, win nothing. We shall have spilled a great deal of human blood to reach an ignominy which we could have bought more cheaply. And if we fail to make every effort to cure all the curables in the other culture, then it is clear that what we glossed over as hospitalization was really after all only a prison designed to punish, not to cure. We shall ourselves develop the unlovely countenances and manners of international jailers, stalking about inside the walls of a world turned jail, the keys of our calling rattling at our belts.

The lesson that the world is now one, that we and our enemies are caught in the same net, that we cannot hew a way out for one or eliminate one side without also compromising the future for the other, must be held clearly before us. What we decide to do with them, with their culture, with the living representatives of that culture, with the repercussions of that culture inside our culture, all are crucial—for us. When we talk of policing the world, this is meant to be a transition from armies to police, from seeing the world as a set of warring national entities to seeing it as one civic unity. Yet it would be well to inspect very carefully the character structure which is developed among police, whose principal occupation is stopping other people from doing things, guarding the *status quo,* walking beats, keeping order, but unconcerned with what that order is. In order to give ourselves the moral authority of an order which does not yet exist, we would dub ourselves police instead of setting about the job of inventing an order worth policing. To call ourselves police of a non-existent, unplanned order is as idle as to dream that we, by ourselves, or with any one ally, can build the best world form which could be built. We can contribute much of the energy, much of the dynamic will to work at a gigantic job in the faith that it can be done. We can insist upon the moral framework of basic human rights within which the new structure is to rise; and we can insist on the extirpation of existing institutions which deny those rights and make disorder possible. We can contribute the practicality, the insistence that the job be done scientifically, on an engineering basis, insisting that we must know what the materials are—human beings of diverse cultures, human cultures of different designs, human societies of different constitution—out of which we plan to build. We can insist that no one ever made a transmission belt run by prayer or ideology alone and that to faith in the rightness of the job must be added knowledge of the materials, the mechanisms, and the processes with which we are going to work. This much we can offer—and then we can turn to the other peoples of the earth who are to be our partners and ask them to lay their cards down. What have they got which we haven't got to contribute to the job? What skills at organizing human beings, at preserving human values, can they offer? The platform which America can offer is a skeleton, a minimum platform—the four freedoms, moral purpose, engineering methods. What have the English and the Australians, the French and the Greeks and the Abyssinians and the

Chinese, the Russians and the Brazilians, AND the Germans, the Japanese, the Italians and the Hungarians to contribute. It's like a game of permutations and combinations or a game of anagrams. The more letters you have the more words you can make. Americans and Englishmen thinking together can only think up a few good ideas, but for every group of people that we add, we have not added another single set of ideas but have increased geometrically the number of possible ideas. It's not only decent—in terms of our American ethics—to give every other country a chance at the game, but—the reliable old puritan ethic again—it is also efficient to do so. We want the job well done, and we can do it better the more we insist that every other country does its own particular stuff. If we drop the old idea of only giving to each nation its minimum rights and substitute the idea of demanding from each people their maximum contribution—that should make enough sense to Americans to enlist their enthusiasm. Instead of asking each country—or ourselves—what we want, let's ask each country—including ourselves—"What can you do? What have you got? Put up or shut up and come into this game of remaking the world, to use everything we've got, to start building something which combines with all we have learned through the ages, a way of life of which no man has even dreamed."

CHAPTER XIV

These Things We Can Do

★

WE CAN, if we will, lay the foundations for this new world, a world that is different and far better than any that has come before, a world which is not American or English or Russian or Chinese, that is not German or Italian or Japanese, that does not represent the triumph of the white race over the black race, or the triumph of the yellow over either. Is this something for which Americans will fight? Will they fight better for the chance to build something that has never been than they will to defend something which happens to exist at the moment? If not, then it would be folly to be discussing it, because at the moment there is no issue more pressing than the winning of the war. Even though we run a terrible risk of winning it in the wrong way, of winning with hate and fascism entrenched in our own society as well as in that of the enemy, still as long as we are not sure that this is so—we must fight, because if we lose it is certain that hate and fascism will be sitting high in the saddle. We must fight for the right to go on building, and, above all, we must not waste overmuch time arguing about the details.

But in urging that we now have the necessary tools for developing a world order within which men might live secure and orderly lives and realize untold potentialities, I do so because I believe that it is essential—if we are to fight to our utmost—that we should have this faith in ourselves and in our civilization. Without it, Americans will not fight hard enough, and unless Americans—on the battle front and the home front, in Congress and on Main Street, in the factories and on the farms—take this war seriously, not all the tenacity and suffering of the English, the reckless daring of the Australians, the incredible patience and resourcefulness of the Chinese, nor the passionate singlehearted fighting of the Russians, can save us. If we feel that this is just another war, that there will be another Versailles, another Manchukuo and another Spain, leading on inevitably to another Munich, we will fight but not well. If we feel that the war will lead, inevitably, as did the last war, to a temporary boom and then a terrible worldwide Depression robbing men of their security and their bread, we will march with lagging steps. If we feel that the war will end in American domination of the world, in making this the American Century, we may sputter and boast and talk big, but our hands will lie flaccid, half grasping the tools and weapons of war. We have been too proud of our non-imperial record, too proud of our fulfilled pledge to the Philippines and their loyal recognition of that pledge during these last months, to get up much enthusiasm for imperialism, even made in America. If we feel that after the war we will refashion the world into an American image—not imperialistically, but just because somebody will have to take up the white man's burden, and democracy after all is the political form we are fighting for—again I say we will not fight well enough. Too many of the proud hardheaded youngsters whose energy is essential know that merely forcing democratic forms and prepared breakfast foods on alien peoples is not the answer, that it was not the answer in Germany in 1919 and will not be the answer now. Nor will we fight to bring peace— for that is a contradiction in terms. Unless we can sweep aside all these partial commitments to ends which are not good enough, and all our fears and reservations about our power to cope with what will come after— we shall not enlist our full strength.

But do we need our full strength? That question may be answered in two ways: by military events—the tide of battle—and by the logic of our American character. Even should the tide of battle be with us so consistently that we would never need to draw on the last ounces of our reserve—as England has had to do—still it will be better for us and for the world if we have given ourselves wholeheartedly to a task which we mean to keep on working at—this time—not to desert half finished as we did before. Americans will not fight merely for power, not merely to protect their property; they will not fight for honor alone, nor yet for the love of fighting. They will fight only if they believe, with every fiber in their being, that their cause is just—and new—that they are fighting for a new and better world, not for the perpetuation of an old, indifferent one.

So the sober recognition of this aspect of our morale must carry with it some sober planning. If we are to help build this new world, we must be made aware of just what our special abilities are which fit us to do so. We must assess at their true value the places where we can depend upon ourselves and the places where we must depend upon our American ability to analyze and use the qualities of others. This means that by the end of the war we should have as a part of our equipment to go on with the job a scientific knowledge of ourselves, of our allies, and of our enemies. What can each country do better than any other in the construction of order? What age-old values has each developed which it is important to conserve in a world which is neither East nor West, white nor black nor yellow, but a world which has become as small as an island, where every life touches every other life? Such a world must be built by human beings who themselves carry in every casual gesture the skills which are needed. We cannot manufacture robots for this gigantic job of creation. Like those American inventors who took their clues from Old World skills, we must find our clues in the actual behavior of living human beings of different cultures. We will have to work with what we have, and we cannot afford to ignore or neglect a single skill which has been developed through the centuries that have gone before.

Those social behaviors which automatically preclude the building of a democratic world must go—every social limitation of human beings in terms of heredity, whether it be of race, or sex, or class. Every social institution which teaches human beings to cringe to those above and step on those below must be replaced by institutions which teach people to look each other straight in the face—and that whether the institution in question is the German family or the New York public school system. But no institution is to be rejected in hate; each is to be examined to see what values there are in it and what other valuable institutions it supports. Each is to be considered not as a mere law or formal practice, but as something which is deeply imbedded in the habits of living human beings. To kill these human beings would make us, as we have seen, unfit to inaugurate a new world. Gradually to eliminate the institutions which crippled them will be more arduous, but it will grant us immunity from the corruption which comes from playing God in a human world.

We can freely realize that all this will not be done in a day, that there will be a job to do for several generations, perhaps for many generations to come, and we can present this as a challenge to Americans. We must eliminate forever the childish belief that one peace treaty should have been able to solve all the problems of Europe. That childish belief and our equal childish disappointment were partly responsible for its doing the opposite so completely. We can prepare for a job which is big enough to deserve all of our attention and effort. It will be fatal to make the job look easy; it is fatal also to make it look impossible.

It is also fatal to do nothing about it but talk. When someone makes a speech and says we need ten thousand planes in six months, the American public asks: "Have the plans been drawn up, the land surveyed, the best engineers engaged, the workmen chosen?" IS THE JOB UNDER WAY? So it is with this task of building, from a hundred cultures, one culture which does what no culture has ever done before—gives a place to every human gift. It will be encouraging to men to believe it can be done. But once they believe that it can be done, then Americans, with their belief in a moral universe where success crowns the efforts of the efficiently good, have a special role to play in doing it. People will begin to ask: Are we getting ready? What sort of efforts are being made to prepare the people of America to co-operate with their allies after the war instead of relapsing into snarling isolationism? What sort of efforts are being made to train a legion of men and women who will understand the highly technical job of analyzing civilizations, of using institutions and sets of habits to build with, as well-trained engineers use torques and stresses and tensions?

If it's a technical job, an American job, an engineering job with a purpose that we are being given a chance to do, will we be trained for it? There are some dozen training courses going on here and there—two-week dibbits for young career diplomats, six-week smatterings of foreign languages for those who may have to assume administrative posts in countries which we may "occupy or liberate." Who is teaching these courses, and what are these men being taught? They are the merest drop in the bucket of what is needed; but they are significant. Are these students being taught to analyze and use the gifts of other cultures or merely to evade or exploit them? Are they getting ready to orchestrate many cultural gifts [1]—a possible route to a real new order—or to drown out every voice but ours beneath the bass of the big drum? It is important to know. Are we really getting ready to do a job of world-shaking proportions, a job which, as it unfolds, could dazzle the imagination of every participant—or not?

For think what it would mean. Not only a world in which man is no longer subservient to climate and season for his food and his comfort—for man has conquered that; not only a world in which no man need go hungry and insecure—for man has conquered that problem, although he does not fully realize it yet; not only a world in which no group owes its continued existence and cohesion to its willingness to bully and oppress other groups or its willingness to be oppressed and bullied by other groups—for only so will those peoples who, like ourselves, wish neither to oppress nor to appease be left free from war. But more than these, a world in which we no longer need to buy one value by the destruction of another which does not fit in. Since the dawn of history, primitive cultures and modern civilizations have muddled along, by rule of thumb, the sports of accident and helpless to use nine-tenths of the human gifts born into them generation after generation.

We look back now with pity and horror on all of those who died because they lacked the knowledge of how to plant and harvest and so perished when there was a dearth of wild roots. We pity the Australian natives who walk thirty miles to a pool where they expect to find lily roots and, finding none, must bear the sight of their old people—whom they cannot carry because they have neither wheel nor draft animal—falling down exhausted to starve to death. We can look back on the deaths of a few years ago before insulin or sulfanilamide was discovered—and at the gap which separates the power of someone who loved hopelessly in 1910 from that of someone able to save his love in 1942. Competence and helplessness are separated by hairbreadth lines; by knowledge that a seed might be purposely placed in the ground and later its fruit harvested; by knowledge that animals need not be hunted with weariness and frequent failure in the forests, but can be domesticated and brought into camp; by knowledge that man could scratch a few symbols on bark or stone and so leave word for those who were following after, and who before the invention of writing might have become hopelessly lost. Hairbreadth lines divide men with control over some aspect of their humanity from men without it, but these lines make the difference between dependence and weakness and pitiful petitioning before some fetish of straw or wood, and purposeful and dignified control of our own destiny. Some day, if we win the war and really put our minds to the job of using science for social ends, as we have used it for building bridges and curing diseases, we shall look back with equal horror and pity on the unused human gifts which every culture spills year by year as lavishly as Nazi Germany spills human blood. As long as we build each culture to a single theme, whether the theme be success or power, or resignation, or maintenance of a fixed caste universe, we live in the dark ages—in the age of an unclothed people crawling across an empty desert, sustained by a few lily roots which we may, or may not, find at the next waterhole. We can leave this pitiful impotence far behind us. By using our minds, by setting problems and solving them, we can leave this present period behind us forever if we will to do so.

But it must be done now. Once a steamroller of any conquering state, either our enemies' or our own, has rolled over the cultures of the world eliminating clues which it has taken a thousand years to develop, we will be as helpless as those Americans who attempted to develop good painters by hanging Old Masters on the walls. We must work with the living stuff; we must know what the Chinese mothers say to their babies and how they hold them, to develop their special virtues; and what the Russian mothers say to their babies and how they hold them, to develop theirs. We must understand what gives the Englishman his serene belief that he cannot lose, just as we must understand what gives the American his dedication to success. From the living stuff that these cultures are made of, from the way in which they fight and make love, discipline their children, organize a meeting, administer a town, or lose a battle, we may get the clues we need. The methods are ready. We are like a people who have engineers ready to throw a bridge over a roaring torrent, from an arid and uncertain land to a land of promise—whose promise we are not even wise enough to be able to guess in full. We have the engineers, the torrent roars before us, men die in battle and children die of starvation in this land where we live. Yet no bridge is built, no one has said to the engineers: "Get to work; muster your skill; train thousands; train millions; but build, men, build—and that quickly." We are Americans, we have made unnumbered dreams come true, in steel and concrete and wide fields sown where there was only forest—we can provide the energy for this dream also.

This book may seem to have harped on a single note, what we as Americans are and what we must do if we are to fight with all our hearts and with all our strengths, and what anthropology as a science can offer to implement that fight, to say to every American, "Here is a tool you can use, to feel strong, not weak, to feel certain and proud and secure of the future." Because I am an American, because I am an anthropologist, I have stressed these things which I know. I have outlined American character as it looks against the background of seven other cultures which I have studied with as microscopic an attention as my canvas here has been broad and rough. I have stressed the strengths and the weaknesses of Americans and the importance for winning the war, of using our democratic character structure in a fashion which will use its strengths and discount its weaknesses. I have stressed letting the sense of initiative come from the bottom, letting competition with near equals provide the energy for achievement, recognizing our need for success by permitting us to boast of victories, recognizing our willingness to tackle any obstacle—no matter how great —as long as we believe it within our own strength. I have emphasized that we are a moral people; a people who believe that there is direct connection between effort and efficiency and rewards on this earth; and that we, therefore, need success, because as failures we must also brand ourselves as evil in the sight of God and Man. This special need for success is suited only to an expanding world, and if we would keep this emphasis, this driving energy to prove by our own works that we are worthy, then we must work in an expanding world. We must see this war as a prelude to a greater job—the restructuring of the culture of the world—which we will want to do, and for which, because we are also a practical people, we must realize there are already tools half forged.

But when one speaks, from inside one culture, about all cultures, from one period in history about other periods, past and to come, from inside one science, about the contribution of science to the world—despite the special training which the anthropologist is given for stepping outside his culture and his century—one speaks a limited language. To build this world in which the orchestration of existing ways of life will produce, by interaction, a way of life which we are not even able to outline now, we need anthropologists from all countries and social scientists from all disciplines. It is the essence of the argument that, to the extent that each one sees sharply, he also sees with blinkers on, paying for his clarity with narrowness. This is not a job for one nation alone; nor for one science. Yet, because one may never treat human beings mechanistically, but must work always through the purposes which have been developed within them, although this is not a job for Americans alone we must see it as America's. Americans will not do it—being what we are—unless we feel that for some aspect of it we are better fitted than any people on earth today. We are proud but not sure, anxious to succeed but never certain that we will, willing to go ahead and tackle any job—but it must be our job. If we are to fight, if we are to win, if we are to hold before us as we fight a goal we will count worth fighting for, that goal must be phrased in American terms, in that mixture of faith in the right and faith in the power of science: Trust God—and keep your powder dry.

CHAPTER XV

The Years Between: 1943–1965

★

So the world looked to me in 1943.

The United States was on the verge of becoming a great power. Yet the country remained uncertain of its strength. Throughout the last years of the war Americans struggled with the problem of how to revise the traditional picture of the country as young, weak, and always in the right, standing up to an old, wicked, and decadent Europe in the face of whose authority we boasted about our accomplishments and virtues. By the end of the war responsible American newspaper editors, speaking from a position of great national strength, began to discuss the necessity of learning the art of compromise. But most Americans still felt that the concessions necessary to compromise endangered the best interests of both parties; we had not learned—as we have not yet learned—how to settle for a place where our path crosses the path of another nation that is bound explicitly for some other destination. And the indubitable, terrifying position of power we attained through possession of the atomic bomb was an extraordinarily difficult one for a people who prided themselves on never starting a war, on waiting for a provoked opponent to take the initiative.

Our original commitment to nationhood, when we severed the ties that bound us as a people to the mother country without replacing the monarch from whose kingdom we departed, left us essentially a nation without a head. Unity of government depended on the balance of power. What we devised, in fact, was a pact of brothers, none of whom succeeded to the power of a strong father and each of whom could view himself as *primus inter pares*. From the beginning, the country was held together by the pitting of group against group in competition that was sometimes healthy and sometimes unhealthy as city was pitted against city, city against state, state against state, the states against the federal government, North against South, East against West, the Congress against the Executive, the House against the Senate, the Army against the Navy, Harvard against Yale. The president of the United States, who in wartime assumed leadership as commander-in-chief of the armed forces, was too often in peacetime little more than the leader of one political party against whom members of the other party were free to launch their barbed attacks. By 1945, we had learned to make war with a fair degree of unity and purpose, but our knowledge of waging peace still was limited to our long national experience of balancing internal rivalries.

At the war's end it was therefore natural for us to transfer the familiar pattern of working through rivalry

—rather than adjustment and compromise—to the world scene and to interpret the problems facing us in terms of rivalrous struggle. The obvious rival in the struggles ahead was the Soviet Union, the only nation to come out of the war strong enough to constitute, as our vis-à-vis, the "other team." In our eyes competition had narrowed down to that between two countries. Even Britain, the country against which we had for so long measured our progress, was exhausted by the war and out of the running. The liquidation of the British Empire had begun and Churchill, whose voice had rallied and led a people who fought best with their backs against a wall, declined to preside over the process of dismemberment. Our new position was a disconcerting one. In the past we had visualized our relationship to Europe as that of a child exhibiting its growing strength to parental figures. Now we were unavoidably placed in the position of the succoring parent in relation to a devastated Western Europe. This role was the more disconcerting because in our experience children inevitably chafe against parental authority, even when it is expressed in largesse. Nor was it less disconcerting for the British who expect parents to chafe against the demands made by children.

Our intense preoccupation with the Soviet Union—a preoccupation that is losing some of its intensity only now as we are reluctantly forced to take into account the growing strength of the People's Republic of China—had many consequences. Matched athletic teams in the United States model their behavior on each other, keep careful track of each other's gains and losses, and are constantly on the alert for each other's shifts in style. As we regarded the Soviet Union as the "other team" against which all our efforts should be organized, our national behavior in those years was in certain ways a true reflection—or was regarded as a reflection—of Soviet initiative. But as the "other team" also was viewed as a deadly enemy, our taboo against taking the initiative in any kind of fighting also came into play. So our various acts—building the hydrogen bomb, arming SAC, building our radar screen, deploying bases around the world, building missiles and anti-missile missiles, tightening our security measures against internal subversion, launching larger satellites that carried increasingly heavy payloads, working toward a landing on the moon, and even stepping up our school programs at every level of education—have been placed in a competitive context of matching in defense of freedom Soviet initiative in the Communist attempt to dominate the world.

Furthermore, by localizing the whole enemy initiative within the Soviet Union, although as yet we understood only in part the need to match Russian aggression with firmness, we were committed to treating the rest of the accessible world as a battleground of arms, ideas, and technical assistance that was given for the stated political purpose of fighting Communism. This interpretation of the world situation and the fact that we have defined so many other activities in terms of defense (including the maintenance of a huge peacetime draft, the provision of Federal funds for the bulk of research work in the country, and the introduction of necessary reforms in our school systems and universities) have helped us to retain our wartime sense of ourselves as a nation.

The necessity of holding on to a sense of national purpose abroad had the effect, indirectly, of opening ways of thinking on a national scale at home. Today students compete for national merit scholarships, adolescents plan for college with the resources of the whole country in mind, local mental health activities are financed with federal funds, and television networks bind the country together through programs that make possible the simultaneous viewing of events across the whole continent. The Kennedy-Nixon debates, the astronauts' activities, particularly John Glenn's first globe-encircling flight, the shared mourning at the time of President Kennedy's assassination, the detailed coverage of both parties throughout the 1964 presidential campaign, the funeral of Winston Churchill, President Johnson's inauguration and the nationwide coverage given to his key speeches on new programs at home and abroad, and the successive events—some of them localized in single small towns—in the Civil Rights struggle, all, as viewed on television, have the quality of shared national participation. "Did you see what happened when . . . ?" is a question Americans from any part of the country can ask each other today. And a nation which in the past owed to the press a continuing grasp of state and local issues has now become one in which newspapers under the same ownership can take different political positions and major networks can arrive at parallel plans for the handling of some major event (as they did immediately after the death of President Kennedy) without specific consultation about those plans. With television, a whole generation has grown up convinced that seeing is believing. But the older generation of intellectuals, for whom reading was—and still is—the key to understanding the world, find themselves increasingly disoriented and alienated in a world that has in a certain sense shrunk to the size of a village green, where all is in plain view and nothing that can be seen or heard need be imagined.

During the years in which the United States enlarged its commitments as we worked to rehabilitate our former enemies and to help our allies get back on their feet, took a hand in the building of new nations, became involved in the activities of United Nations agencies around the world, and attempted to contain the Soviet Union, it became increasingly clear to Americans that our nation is both strong and rich, that it may be, indeed, the richest nation the world has ever known. From the viewpoint of the energy resources alone, made available to the ordinary home through electricity, no other nation as yet has had such widespread wealth.

But our recognition of our comparative wealth and its wide distribution throughout the nation was tempered by the anxious memories of the middle-aged and the elderly who had experienced two World Wars and the Great Depression and felt that a period of prosperity might be interrupted at any moment. This very diffuse sense of unease and the general distrust of affluence combined with an increasing awareness of the dangers inherent in scientific warfare to produce a postwar generation that was determined to live a lifetime within a few short years. And for more than a decade young people withdrew into a private search for the whole of life now, at once, before the world changes again or blows up altogether.

This younger generation, the children of depression marriages, lived under the shadow of old parental anxieties. A few of its members, particularly young men, made a virtue of owning nothing and of assuming no obligations or responsibilities. But by far the majority responded to affluence by reaching out for everything immediately—jobs, marriage, parenthood, and houses such as their parents could only have dreamed of and saved for over long years. In the beginning of the 1950's older anxieties were given new poignancy by the Korean War, which broke out so unexpectedly soon after the end of World War II. And new anxieties also developed as people began to grasp, without yet assimilating, the vastness of the problems that confronted a newly inter-communicating world. In this context, the generation of the 1950's was politically silent and chiefly bent on having its share of private life—now.

Jobs were plentiful and relatively well paid. Adolescents could earn unheard of amounts of money and parents could give financial help to their children whom society contrived to put into positions in which they "had to get married." In these years the individuals who in the past had assumed leadership in pointing out new

directions for growth and new aspirations for the idealistic lapsed into silence or used their energy to inveigh
against McCarthyism as the silencer of the young. Lacking any kind of leadership, young people had another
date, found a new job, got married, and concentrated
on having babies, one after another, who were as much
the delight of their young fathers as of their young
mothers. Ambition dwindled and the family, long the
burden bearer for other American institutions, became
the center of American concern. For this generation the
good life was the private life of good human relations.

At the same time the nuclear stockpiles grew and
anxiety mounted that the world might be shattered by
some nuclear accident, if not by a nuclear war. The rest
of the world pressed in upon us, also. Events in Sumatra
and Borneo, Kuwait, Yemen, Saudi Arabia, Argentina,
Guatemala, and Cuba came uncomfortably and unin-
telligibly close. Africa was racked by the struggles of
new, tumultuous nations. The United Nations changed
its form before our eyes.

An era of moral slackness set in, the outgrowth in
part of earlier, misplaced attempts to legislate good behavior through, for example, the Eighteenth Amend-
ment and the Volstead Act. Corruption and bribery
were suspected and from time to time uncovered in
state and local governments, in Washington, in gover-
nors' mansions and city halls, in management and in
labor unions, in universities and in schools, in ongoing
social programs, in professional sports and in inter-
collegiate athletics, in churches and in voluntary organi-

zations. An atmosphere of profound distrust and cynicism was created, on the one hand, by those who gave and received favors, bribes, and graft, those who entered into and those who tacitly countenanced deals, those who sought to subvert and those who were, for whatever reason, subverted, and, on the other hand, by those who sought to expose graft, bribery, and deals, those who sought to expose the breakdown of older standards of morality, particularly sexual morality, and those who sought for evidence of subversion within our most respected institutions, not excluding the Presidency, the Supreme Court, the armed services, and the churches. Confusion about public morality was matched by a kind of moral permissiveness, a situationalism and an indeterminacy, that developed after World War I in a generation of parents who were unsure of their right to impose their own or any other standards of behavior on their children. Middle class Americans, who set the tone for the country, had abandoned threats of hellfire and eternal punishment; yet there was little clarity of thinking about new problems of private and public morality. Responding to the loss of older standards, the generation that came to adulthood at the beginning of World War II could ask: "*Ought* one have a conscience?" After the war, in the 1950's, those who were moving toward adulthood solved their ethical problems by evading the issues—by standing aside or by entering into premature parenthood without taking time to look into their own hearts and minds or facing the world around them.

The decade rolled on. The bomb did not fall. But

suburbs sprawled farther across a bulldozed countryside while the centers of cities rotted and decayed. Then, very slowly, the families enclosed within their four walls became restive, and still more slowly the recognition grew that we soon would live in a different world. Significantly, we began to question our own image of ourselves as a people who were rich, overgenerous, and careless, a people who were being played for a sucker by the rest of the world, a people who had "never had it so good" and who (as in our picture of the upper class) had no place to go but down.

By 1960 the children who were babies when I wrote this book were finishing college. The children who were then in grade school were now junior executives, officers in the armed services, established writers, poets, architects, engineers, and scientists, experienced politicians and civil servants. The discomforts and disappointments of the 1950's were giving way to a restless and determined questioning. In that fateful summer of 1945, when the world changed forever, some of us estimated that if the world could survive the next twenty years without a holocaust, there was hope for a future. That time is now upon us.

In the 1960's children are growing up who were born and have been reared in the new world. They are bound together by worldwide communications and by a sense of common danger. They can share one another's joys and sorrows half a world away and they are seeing the most remote and savage peoples preparing themselves for nationhood. They take computers for granted and see automation as part of the future. They are old enough now to ask questions that stimulate their elders who still wield the power associated with wealth and experience, however estranged they may be from this, their children's world.

These children have never known an America that was not acting as a nation among nations nor have they known a world in which nationhood was not as much a reality as statehood is. They do not believe we can ban the bomb and thereby achieve peace on earth. They know we must learn to live with the bomb, stockpiled or not, as a dread possibility. They know that insecticides and pesticides, used indiscriminately, can bring about a "silent spring." They expect to learn other languages and communicate with other peoples. They know man will go to the moon. When they look up, they know they may catch a flashing glimpse of some satellite orbiting the earth. In contrast, those of us who grew up with only the moon, the planets, and the stars overhead in our night sky can remember only part of the time that man has moved into space.

But these children of the solar system, whose dreams cut across the new fears that man may after all be a prisoner of one small part of the universe, are still very young. They do not yet sit in the seats of the mighty. The exaggeration of President Kennedy's youth—the picture of him formed by college students who felt that somehow he was "our age"—was a spontaneous attempt by this new generation to push forward their effective participation in a world they never made but which they understand as the natives of a country region understand its seasons and the portents of its storms. Because they do have a new understanding and are still very young, their chief contribution to the country—and so to the world of which we are so powerful and significant a part—must be to ask the right questions.

A high-school boy turns to me thoughtfully. "You talk about our taking the lead in solving the population explosion. But do we have to win all the time?"

I pause before the unfamiliar phrasing. Win? Win what? Then I see. He moves from lead to lead time— lead time in the missile race—and from lead time to winning, always winning, in the race to the moon, in the size of our stockpiles, in the number of our trained scientists, in the success of our programs. . . . The old motivations driving individuals toward success and making good are still there. Children still writhe beneath their parents' real or imagined disappointment at failure. It is inconceivable that the United States should lose, should not be first. Yet stated in absolute, uncooperative terms, stated as the unconditional victory of one nation that has less than one-sixth of the earth's population, we cannot "win." In this new guise the old insistence on winning provides fuel for the fires the extreme political Right is attempting to light all over the country.

But the essential practicality, the political wisdom of the old saw, "If you can't lick 'em, join 'em," is also there. It underlies the demand that we concentrate on making the kind of world in which Americans can maintain a sense of power and significance, not just as one team in competition with some other team but as a member of a league, all of whose members are both mutually supportive and vigorously competitive.

The new generation just growing up must meet and deal with a whole set of interrelated problems. They must find a new way of countering the compulsive search for marriage through premature sex and premature parenthood that has laid an incredibly heavy burden of responsibility on young adults. But this is not all. They must also come to terms with our new knowledge about the state of our country and its people as a whole.

For in a period of affluence the poor and the disowned become strangely visible. In the midst of the strident growth of new cities and new suburbs, the engineering of vast freeways, the production of new gadgets, and the promised marvels of a computerized industry, some 35 million Americans, whose only share in their country's success is the bitter knowledge that they are somehow cut off from a chance to succeed, suddenly stand out. Gradually, as the country's needs changed in the postwar years, the spate of jobs-for-everyone slackened. The new job seekers pouring out of high schools found no jobs waiting for them. Those whose darker skin or foreign speech marked them as different from the idealized white majority were the first to feel the further handicaps of their lack of skills and they were the first to lose their precarious hold on jobs. But the movement for integration and for the establishment of a situation of more equal opportunity for all, which began in the colleges—particularly in the colleges where students knew the limits of the opportunities open to them—in the 1950's, has been fiercely opposed by those who see in any attempt to change or improve our system a maneuver of the enemy.

In this form of response there are parallels between the situation in the United States and the Soviet Union. In the Soviet Union those who rigidly uphold the old Stalinist line have fiercely opposed those who have inclined toward policies of accommodation with the West. Change is made difficult by the intransigence of the Communist dichotomy: Whoever does not completely subscribe to a given position is an enemy to be destroyed absolutely. And the theory that men work by conspiracy (as, indeed, those who take power by means of a military or a political coup must do) rouses the counterfear that where a very few have succeeded before, a very few may succeed again. In these terms, in spite of the relaxation that has accompanied a growing prosperity, the Soviet government periodically clamps down hard on its writers and poets or on some other group with demands for a firmer line. This intransigence has its parallels—perhaps its echo—in the United States, where periodically individuals and groups are gripped by the phobias that temporarily were very successfully exploited for political purposes by McCarthy in his play on fears of corruption, sexual deviance, and subversion. In the 1950's, McCarthy's activities were brought to a halt by his political peers.

Yet we are giving young people few directives toward a different course on which this country, with their help, might steer. President Kennedy asked every American to be prepared to make some sacrifice for his country. The words of his inaugural address were deeply stirring when he spoke them and again when they were read over his dead body. But no sacrifice has been spelled out for those who ask what they can give to their country. The actual sacrifice that is made is seldom the glad devotion of those who, acting out of strength and a knowledge of their affluence, give time to an enterprise like the Peace Corps. Instead, it is too often the sacrifice made by those who have nothing, the underachieving and dispossessed children of the poor. Undereducated, unaspiring, shut out, standing on street corners, seldom knowing money that is legitimately theirs, never going forth from a home of which they can legitimately feel proud, they are themselves a sacrifice. This unworthy sacrifice of the dispossessed contrasts bitterly with the sacrifices demanded of a whole people in wartime, when the rich and the poor, the clever and the stupid, the fortunate and the unfortunate temporarily are joined together in work and sacrifice for a cause that is meaningful to all of them.

One of the major problems facing us is that of creating peacetime contexts within which an equal and a sufficient call will be made on all young people and, periodically, on every member of our highy diversified society. Whatever forms this may take, they must have some national significance and add to the dignity of every individual. Today, instead, we are making a conspicuous sacrifice of those older adolescents who are out of school and have no work; of the poorly educated men and women in middle life who have already been counted out and who may never, under present conditions, get a worthwhile job again; of all those who because of skin color or ethnic origin lack the opportunity to acquire or exercise skills; and of the women who, having given over their early adult years to rearing children, now find themselves with half-empty hands in a world that appears to be asking for much less than they have to give.

At the same time a large part of our society is working too hard. College students are trying to put themselves through school, support a family, and meet the unexpectedly high postsputnik standards of education for which nothing in their earlier schooling prepared them. Young fathers and mothers, caught up in the belief that they must provide their children with everything advertised and discussed in resourceful magazines, are moonlighting and sunlighting, working nights and Sundays, too strained and harried to find time for joy or sorrow. The laments of those who are worrying about the effects of the new leisure on people who are unprepared to use it constructively ring strangely on the ears of too many Americans. Committed to working fifteen hours a day in their efforts to keep up with the needs of three or four children for whom they have ambitious plans, they do not know the meaning of leisure time.

Inadvertently we have created a trichotomy of those

who are working too hard but enjoy what they are doing, those who are working—some of them too hard and some only lackadaisically—because they must if they are to live as well as exist, and those who are cut off from the chance to earn a decent living. This is a dangerous division for a country like ours, far more dangerous than a division into social classes. In a society with fixed social classes, out of any one of which it is difficult for individuals to move, the working class may have few aspirations beyond the comforts to which its members seldom have had access—adequate food, clothes, housing, beer, and a little spare money for the football pools. Americans, however, have always pictured their country as a land of high aspirations, and we lower those aspirations at our peril.

One side of the coin may be keeping up with the Joneses. But the other side is a perennial ability to conceive of something different and better—a game in which the product engineer and the resourceful advertiser can always devise new moves. The telephone provides a good example. To begin with, think what having one's own telephone will mean. Then think what having an extension will mean. Think how convenient it would be to have *two* telephones, so that in spite of endless teen-age conversations father could get a message through that he had missed the 5:15 train. Think of the convenience of having a telephone in the bathroom while you are bathing the baby, beside your bed in the middle of the night, in the kitchen while you are cooking dinner, in the laundry while you are putting clothes in the washing machine, in the garage while you are working on the car. Think of the convenience of having a telephone brought out to your car while you are stopping for gas. Think of the pleasure of having one brought to your table while you are sitting at dinner in a restaurant. Beginning with the fact of a telephone there is no end to the ingenuity exercised by the telephone company and the individual telephoner. Telephones can be installed almost anywhere. They can be styled to match every color scheme. Hitched up to a recording device, they take messages in your absence. And now, you think, every possibility has been exploited. But not at all. Two new moves bring the teleconference and the telelecture. Today I can sit comfortably at home holding a fragile white instrument in my hand and give a lecture to assembled students in seven different colleges in a midwestern state. I can hear their questions and they, in turn, can all hear my answers.

One of the principal delights of this game is the sense it gives of escalation, a peculiar feature of the openness of American society. Keyed to a rising standard of living that makes possible the continual transformation of new ideas into new objects, it is sufficiently pervasive to give a large part of the population a feeling of participation in movement that is satisfying, even intoxicating. And the possibilities, it would seem, are unbounded. Not only simple things, such as telephones and cars, lend themselves to endless elaboration, but also books or pictures that may be mass-produced by new color processes or circulated as originals rented from a picture-of-the-month club, or, at a different level, versions of adult education that bring teaching into the home or, on the contrary, take the student on extended tours.

Surely a people with this zest and enjoyment also has the energy necessary for establishing the kind of country we would like to have. But to release this energy for new purposes we must take stock of ourselves. Do we still have the character structure we had twenty years ago? Or have changing conditions also affected who and what we are?

Americans still are a people to whom the idea of success is tremendously important. But today far more Americans than in the past turn aside from the search for success. Feeling themselves demeaned as men when the jobs on which they have built their lives have been abolished, some men have turned aside in despair. Others, young men who look forward to comfortable, private lives with their wives and children, have decided that the price of personal success is too high. Condemnation of the cost of success is stronger and more widespread than it was a generation ago. Mere success, mere accomplishment, whatever form it may take, offers fewer rewards. The assumption that money should be easy to come by is also widespread; many people meet a lack of money not with intensified effort but with bitterness, cynicism, or a contemptuous disregard of the world in which having money is meaningful. Negation of this kind is found in very different groups. The unemployed street corner adolescent turns aside with a shrug when he is offered five dollars to shovel a snowy walk. What does five dollars matter one way or the other? Nagged at to start their careers with a record of high marks, students decide that a college degree is not worth the candle. The disgruntled research scientist who fails to get a $100,000 grant takes a cynical view of those who "said research was needed."

The problems we face are made more complex by confusion. Twenty years of asserting national goals and national purposes, as if we were at war when we are not at war, has added to the confusion. Twenty years of using the fight against Communism indiscriminately as a justification for everything from winning a local school board election to preventing the sale of surplus wheat to Communist countries has all but defeated efforts to achieve any clarity of thinking. In these circumstances, the demand of the resurgent Right that we return to the good old days of clear goals and announce our intention to maintain American honor, even if this means the destruction of the whole world in the name of freedom, has a strong appeal for some young people. For such statements have an apparent coherence and clarity. But equally, the battle for Civil Rights has a strong appeal for young people. For the goals of the fight for integration are concrete and clear. Allegiance here leads to action.

In 1943, Americans needed to achieve a clarity of moral purpose. Today the need for clarity is, if anything, still greater. But the clarity of purpose in World War II was somewhat deceptive. Hitler could be defined as a monster as well as an enemy and in the wartime atmosphere those who were willing to fight any and all enemies of the United States could join with those who saw the battle against Nazism as a crusade on behalf of mankind. Today the problem is much more complicated. Those who still cling to the old, simple definition of patriotism have not yet recognized that since Hiroshima there cannot be winners and losers in a war, but only losers. And they are vocal out of desperation about a world they do not understand. Joined to their voices are those of an earlier group of adherents to progress, democracy, and freedom—the trade unionists who do not realize that craft unionism is dying, the industrial trade unionists whose chief concern is not to build on existing foundations but to hold rigidly to the formulas of a different era, the old style liberals who take for granted that every picket line is in a worthy cause (a position as old-fashioned as that taken by William Jennings Bryan who, when he was asked which version of the Bible he believed was inspired in every word, replied: "All of them"), and the old style liberals who believe that the parliamentary methods of the pre-Communist world still suffice to protect individuals from the scarcely distinguishable slanders of the Right and the Left.

Where thought is difficult and its rewards very uncertain, there is a tendency to turn instead to action. Early marriage, large families, the Peace Corps, CORE, White Citizens Councils, riots, strikes, marches, and even the senseless, destructive student holiday outbursts of violence have one thing in common. Each is a form of action. Each gives to those involved a feeling of breaking a deadlock, a sense of escaping a trap, a belief, however illusory, that they are no longer fenced in, tied down, caught in a rut, buried in a hole in the ground. Action, almost any kind of action, is a counterthrust to the dread that sweeps over us when we look at the incomprehensible and unmanageable problems posed by nuclear war, the pollution of the natural world, the population explosion, the rise of new peoples of races other than our own, and the new reality of space.

It is not that Americans have changed so very much. What has changed is the world itself and our ability to comprehend and act on our comprehension of this changed world. In 1942, we still saw ourselves as a young, poorly established, uncertain, and striving nation. In spite of the part we played in World War I, we had yet to prove our capacity to turn probable worldwide defeat to decisive worldwide victory. Ours was the stance of the man whose forebears have worked to get ahead and who believes that work will take him where he wishes to go. We had not fully grasped our size and strength. We still believed that European men somehow had subtler minds than ours and that they might easily "pull the wool over our eyes" and "make suckers of us again." Ours was the stance of youth, weak, brash, and convinced of being in the right. Our sympathies were with the underdog, with all those defined as handicapped and weak and underprivileged anywhere—the occupied countries of Europe and Asia, the peoples of India and

China, and all the colonial peoples of the world. Whereas the British, visualizing themselves in the parental role of strength, differentiated between themselves and those they tried to help, we identified with those who, as we saw it, needed the help we could give by taking their part and fighting their battles. The position we took was essentially a congenial one—the position of an energetic, striving, morally justified people engaged in a fight for the right and prepared to go further than our fathers at home or in their fatherlands abroad had ever gone.

Our character has not changed. But it is less easy for us to fit our character to our new position in the world. Instead of seeing ourselves as a young nation, we now know that we are, in fact, one of the most stable, traditional minded peoples on earth. Instead of thinking of ourselves as relatively poor or still lacking in economic and political power and authority on the international scene, we know that we are a very rich people who can no longer fall back on the plea of new growth and change in explanation of the poverty in our midst. We cannot foresee a future in which we shall be relatively richer and more powerful than we are now or even a future in which we, acting alone, can do greater good for the world. True, the Marshall Plan may have saved Europe. But European nations are going ahead very fast now, strong competitors in our markets. True, we worked very hard on the rehabilitation of Japan and West Germany and even though the help we gave was predicated on the empty belly theory of Communism, it was constructive and generous. But look at these new friends, our former enemies, now. They are prosperous and self-confident, ready to go their own way even to the point of flirting with "the enemy." True, the whole world has benefited by our technical largesse. That the bounty of our giving has been less in fact than in popular belief is not what matters here; it is the picture of bounty. But look where this has got us. One country after another, large or small, smarting under the inequity of receiving where no return the recipients could make would have meaning to us, has turned against us. In our giving we have acted without real recognition of the importance of reciprocity. Or where we have seemed to demand the price of allegiance, we have seen the bread of help turn into a stone.

Over twenty years, while the various forms of assistance we have given and the expansion of American business have played a greater or a lesser part in reshaping large regions of the world, the rest of the world also has changed. The Communist world has expanded and the importance of new nations, whose peoples belong to many races, has grown speedily. Relatively and comparatively, our position cannot but diminish in importance. In the future, we shall not be able to maintain our unexpected and (as we ourselves see it) possibly ill-deserved superiority of riches and power. Our position does not allow us any ease and our sense of uneasiness grows heavier as we contemplate our own reckless waste of food and the world's limited store of natural resources.

Moreover, in the immediate present, there is a widening gap between the rich and the poor nations. And as once the feasting nobles feared the hungry mobs gathered in the streets and byways, so now the feasting nations look with a certain dread at the new nations' efforts to organize. And the new nations, poor and unindustrialized as they may be, fully share in the contemporary belief that all peoples have an equal right to the good things of the world. It is academic to ask now whether or not it was a good idea to construct a world of nations very disparate in size, wealth, population, and resources, each unit of which expects to act independently of the others. This is the shape of the world as it is. If, for any reason, a great power chooses to ignore the identity of the new nations, this lack of attention will be fully exploited by a rival power. In the earlier postwar period the United States and the Soviet Union were the principal rivals in the exploitation of emerging national ambition and anticolonial pride. But today the number of power centers has increased and other political doctrines are growing in importance on the worldwide scene. Over time new regional organizations may emerge that will be more congruent in resources and in the state of their technology. But whatever the direction of political and economic development, heavy demands will be made on the rich industrialized nations. Relatively, the position of the United States in the world may decline, but the definition of our country as extraordinarily wealthy will still be inescapable.

The question remains how Americans will interpret

the position of this nation in relation to the nations of the world. What we have to draw on is our own image of the wealthy, our own attitudes toward rich men and toward our own unstable upper class.

The traditional picture is perfectly clear. The self-made man, while he is rising from newsboy to multi-millionaire by his own efforts, is drivingly ambitious, loyal mainly to his own interests, and ready to ride roughshod over his employees and his rivals. But once he has acquired his millions, he begins to give his money away. Since the inauguration of the graduated income tax, of course, the government has facilitated this process.

Like everyone else connected with the self-made man, the multimillionaire's child is believed to suffer in one way or another. Born with a silver spoon in his mouth, overindulged in childhood and with nothing to strive for, the rich man's son is pictured as a playboy or as a man whose life is spent in a vain attempt to find a field in which he can maintain the luster of the family name. For the family name does not become generalized as a possession of the whole nation, but rather is treated as one of the prizes father or grandfather won in the race. Theoretically the great-grandson of a very rich man should find himself back at the point from which great-grandfather started. From shirtsleeves to shirtsleeves in four generations sums up this idea. But the young man is handicapped in any attempt to make a new start by possession of a name that adorns ivied halls and art museums or charitable institutions. The disparity between what has been attained and what he begins with saps his initiative. Although the facts belie the picture, this is what we expect. And the picture is unchanged even though in the past decade a number of men with great inherited fortunes have held high political office. Their great wealth helped them in their political campaigns, but nevertheless it has been a handicap. Americans do not really expect rich men to be good men or men who can came close to other people.

Complementary to these expectations are the fears of those who have inherited wealth and power and, in the case of the middle class, of those whose accumulated savings permit them to spend their later years living comfortably on their income. In a nation where the earning of a fortune should be its own reward and the wealthy should disperse or dissipate their wealth in order not to handicap their children with the weight of unearned riches, those who are enjoying accumulated wealth are bound to feel uneasy. Our expectation is that wealth should be returned to the mainstream of national life. It should be invested in new enterprises or it should be dispersed through charitable, educational, religious, or medical gifts. Furthermore, whoever lives on accumulated wealth, whether this takes the form of money, reputation, past effort, or a great name, loses the major motivation to action in American life—the drive toward progress, material or non-material. For Americans must somehow keep moving. Even among the elderly, the urge to travel and travel and travel—an occupation that turns the well-to-do retired into restless globe-trotters and the less well-to-do into the inhabitants of motels and trailer camps—expresses this feeling that to be part of American life one must, literally or figuratively, keep on the move. But the wealthy and those whose wealth has brought them upper class status have nowhere to go but down. How can they progress? And the fear of falling breeds other fears—the fear that excessive taxation will deprive them of their place; the fear that some group believed to be hostile to wealth and high status, such as labor unions or some minority group, will somehow deprive them of their security; the fear that a strong central government will weaken their hold on local sources of power; the fear that public programs requiring new, heavy taxation, such as federally financed medical care or education, will eat away what they have without benefiting them in any way.

Translating these expectations, we can readily see how Americans picture their world position. America is rich, but not because this generation of Americans have made fortunes. Fifteen years ago when Stringfellow Barr challenged Americans with his pamphlet, *Let's Join the Human Race*, it was possible to repudiate his suggestion that we, like European colonial nations, were living on the exploitation of millions of people overseas. Hadn't we made our wealth with our own hands? Hadn't our ancestors, most of them very poor, humble people, worked long and hard to build this country? Who could say that we were living on the sweated labor of the brown peoples of other lands?

Actually, however, these arguments miss the point. The uncomfortable simile is not based on a comparison between the United States and British or Dutch imperialism. It does not fit the first-generation self-made man whose riches represent profit on the toil of men and women working in factories. We are not imperialists in this sense. Nor are we getting richer by exploiting the new nations overseas. Nevertheless we are rich and we ourselves in this generation have not acquired our accumulated capital. Our wealth represents the initiative, the enterprise, the sweat and the hard work of the millions of men from Europe, Africa, and Asia who cleared the forests, mined the minerals, built the railroads, the ships, the factories, and the roads, and farmed the land, planted and harvested the grain. We are, in fact, the heritors of past labor, living like the children of the rich, indulged and perhaps spoiled, on the proceeds of other men's toil.

What then should we expect of ourselves as a nation? Like those for whom the price of wealth is increased responsibility, we should use our inheritance for the benefit of those who are in need of education, medical care, and social protection. In fact, since World War II, this is how we have, in part, used our wealth. But there is a difficulty. Where we can identify with the obligation of the very rich to dispose of wealth responsibly and to assume social and political responsibility, giving can add to our sense of security. But there are also the fears of those whose position is more precarious, who feel that their inherited capital can be wrenched away from them, that they can be stripped bare by forces beyond their control. In private life these are the people who arm themselves with heavy insurance policies, protect their homes with elaborate devices to outwit burglars and other intruders, and shudder away from taking on responsibilities that much poorer people assume gladly. They have not earned their security, and they would be incapable of recouping their losses. In public life, this is a group that feels insecure and exposed. Any change may be directed against them. The United States will be played for a sucker. Gold runs out of our veins. If we do not set up every kind of insurance, we will be robbed blind. For this group the world is filled with traps to catch the foolish and the unwary.

The solution proposed by these Americans is a simple one. Let us keep what we have. Let us withdraw from the fray, stop the fatal outflowing of vital resources. Let us stay at home and enjoy what we have. Let us take no chances of being mocked, robbed, tricked, or trapped into losing our position of superiority. This reaction is not restricted to the members of any one social group, any age group, any race, or to people living in any one part of the country. It is a viewpoint that is more congenial to those who have retired than to those who still feel they are on the move. But there are many men who know—or fear—that they have gone as far as they are likely to go. New opportunities opening up no longer are theirs to grasp. Like many of those who have retired on a fixed income, they feel they have nothing more to build on. The chief accountant who knows he will not now become a company executive, the state legislator who knows it is too late for him to move on to the national scene, the principal of the small high school who will not realize his dream of becoming a state superintendent of education, the craft union that will not open its doors to new categories of membership, the Negro college teacher who distrusts integration because he fears for his protected job, the physician who is unwilling to accept as patients those whom he is accustomed to treating out of charity—all these and many others belong to the group for whom change looms as a threat, who see in generosity a trap.

There are, in fact, many kinds of Americans who are frightened by the place of the United States in the world. Whatever is done internationally by this country activates their fears, not their hopes. But a program of active self-aggrandizement would in no way solve the problem. A program of conquest, in which we made use of every threat at our command and threatened the use of every weapon in our arsenal to extend our power and strengthen our position, would in all probability fail at home before it could be carried out abroad. For such a program would arouse in Americans not fear but guilt. Our traditional moral repudiation of imperialism would come into play as well as our fervent belief in the right of autonomy and self-determination for all peoples in the world.

But a policy of unashamed self-aggrandizement also would undeniably have the effect of involving all Americans in a series of practical decisions. Instead of struggling with diffuse fears and anxieties—fears that can only find expression in vague nightmare images of being

robbed, poisoned, or infiltrated—we would be forced
to face up to the unmistakable dangers to our population, our industrial plant, and the very land on which
we live. Instead of being plagued by vague worries
about being duped or tricked by our friends, we would
be forced to face up to the very real problems of who
would take our part and who would stand up to our
threats or our weapons.

In an earlier period of history we might well have
taken such a course as we saw ourselves as a nation
condemned to remain in a position in which, standing
alone, we could only lose, never gain, national power.
As Americans we could not, it is true, have initiated a
program of conquest. We could, however, have turned
to aggression as a form of defense. We could have threatened others with destruction in the name of some
idealistic principle.

In fact, today, such a course would be out of the
question. A program of outright aggression implies a
belief in the possibility of victory. And today, in the
context of scientific warfare in which any attack on or
by a major power carries with it the likelihood of the
destruction of the human race, the very illusion of victory is impossible. Consequently, the open transmuta-
tion of a sense of relatively diminishing power into active
aggressive behavior is denied even to those who would
set out on such a course with enthusiasm.

In the United States the problem is compounded by
our traditional attitudes toward initiative and provoca-
tion in war. The armed services, traditionally the

protectors of our safety and strength, are today cast in a role that more and more clearly approaches that of a national police force, modified by our participation in ever larger policing units within NATO, SEATO, the United Nations, and so on. The better their training, the higher their dedication to their traditional tasks, the more the present situation is likely to evoke in men in our armed services a desire for action where action must be denied. As the clear, simple logic of defense and offense no longer fits the modern world, there will inevitably be found in the armed services those for whom despair, the blind father of violence, replaces optimism and a belief in the country's solid strength, their traditional sources of morale. In these circumstances it takes only an extra degree of simplicity of mind or a heightening of individual, personal stress to translate the apparent irrationality of the present stance of the United States into a confused individual response. This is ironically represented in the fictionalized character of the general in *Dr. Strangelove* and possibilities for secret action are explored in the intrigue of an officer clique in *Seven Days in May*, two films that struggle toward a clarification of this issue.

Yet the closer men in the armed services come to the centers of the new scientific warfare, the more certainly they are exposed to the logic of the new position that all-out war is impossible and, at the same time, to the recognition that the danger of an all-out war occurring is very great. From this point it is too easy a step to the fear that the source of the danger lies not in one of their own trusted number but in some subversive action. Confronted with a fictional film in which a general, acting out of patriotism and desperation, moves toward the destruction of the world, there is an almost irresistible temptation to reinterpret the general's behavior as evidence that he has been turned into an agent of the enemy against whom he has been trained to defend his country. Not *our* madness but the enemy's perfidy—or at least the enemy's madness—is, on the face of it, the more reasonable solution, even where this means acceptance of the exceedingly dangerous idea of internal traitors. For Americans this choice among several intolerable solutions has apparent elements of reality. It is easier, in a sense, to turn against our own— against some group in our own country, for example, who only yesterday were Europeans, Asians, or Africans and today, imperfectly incorporated into American life, have become emissaries of some foreign power. As long as enemies are within the country, we can start a crusade to expose them, unmask them, or even march against them and wipe them out.

This is something much more complicated than the simple search for a solution through a scapegoat, and any attempt to reduce what happens to a scapegoat formula misses the point. For what is involved is not men's evil impulses that have got out of control, but the frustration of men's good impulses. It is a quite logical outcome of a national style that developed as Americans built this country. Here I am not discussing the logic of extreme Rightists, but the matrix out of which the ideas and the viewpoints of the Right develop. For we must come to grips not only with the problems presented by the extremist viewpoint but also with the problems arising from an apparently greater activity of extremist groups in contemporary American life. Central to both in this time of transition is the fact that our present national posture evokes fear and uncertainty in all Americans, responses that are heightened particularly among those groups in the population who individually or occupationally see no hope of progress ahead but only loss and deprivation.

This was our mood for a decade.

In the 1960's there have been many welcome signs of a changing climate of opinion. The key to the change lies in a renewed capacity for self-criticism and self-evaluation, a renewed ability to look within and not always to the enemy (including an enemy who has succeeded in penetrating within the gates) for an explanation. Young Americans in the present generation bear the marks of a different political sequence from that which marked the generation for whom this book was first written: instead of World War I, the Depression, and the New Deal, the critical events have been World War II and the bomb, Korea, and the dismal 1950's. But there are many resemblances. There is now, as then, a high valuation of action, movement, and purpose. Those who express doubt about the individual's ability to control his own destiny nevertheless believe that power over one's own destiny is a good thing. Those who question the future and recoil before a world that appears to have become too large, too omnipresent, and too complicated for comprehension nevertheless welcome the statement that the world can be made comprehensible and that it is possible to intervene in the course of history. Those who take a jaundiced view of misspent foreign aid and are made restive by reported foreign criticisms of American practices abroad nevertheless are moved by poverty and the difficulties of unindustrialized peoples. Essentially, what we need today is what we have needed in the past, that is, a stirring belief that there is a tremendous job to be done that Americans can do—if it can be done by anyone.

And there are signs that the tide is turning. Our statistics on unemployment, school dropouts, racial injustice, the waste of woman power, depressed areas, crumbling cities, crime and delinquency, illiteracy, and cultural deprivation are not taken only as signs of disorganization but are seen also as a challenge. The birthrate is beginning to fall. Educated married women are beginning to question the meaningfulness of a life that is based only on "togetherness." Old people are rebelling against the idea of living apart in Golden Age ghettos. The country is becoming responsibly alarmed about the actual pollution of land, water, and air. The Nuclear Test Ban of 1963 had, among other things, the effect of a signal as it led to renewed self-appraisal and a modified anxiety about external enemies. However, this relaxation has its own inherent dangers for, in the face of some new crisis, new national efforts may be made to focus our fears on a desire to dominate other nations.

Flaring up after a period of relaxation, our fears may loom even larger than in the past. But counterefforts also are growing in strength. There is a sense of movement, of something happening, in the country, a feeling that we are coming out of our suburban retreats with a greater readiness to do the work that needs to be done.

In part this may have come about almost through political accident. For where President Kennedy skipped a generation when he brought a new leadership group into action, President Johnson is placing reliance on a great many men who knew the excitement of the New Deal and who as young men carried into their political careers the combination of vigorous effort and hope for change that also motivated their activities during World War II. And these men, in their turn, are calling on others at the regional and local levels who have been standing aside but who now see the opportunity to put to work their long experience in such activities as TVA, REA, community reorganization, or adult education—with the added chance of training a new generation in new kinds of work. In part the change of mood is related to a renewed confidence in the value of disciplined effort growing out of the response to the needs—and even more the new possibilities—of the Space Age. In part it is a response to the very decisive insistence on immediate fulfillment of the hundred-year promise of full civil rights. In the 1960's this demand has been given a new urgency by the children of men who fought for equality during World War II and who see in the nation's and the world's situation a renewal of opportunity.

But most significantly, this new mood arises from a shift in emphasis away from what we have and may lose toward the job we must do in order to be ourselves in a new world. The revolutionary consequences of automation and an affluence that is divorced from man hours or the availability of working hands are beginning to make themselves felt. What we can and must do takes on significance not just from our past but from an open future as well. In some sense it is our curiosity about what we, the most industrialized country in the world, can make of a world with extraordinary new possibilities of mechanization and the development of unlimited sources of energy that has captured our imagination.

Essentially, the same values still appeal to us. There must be other nations, other peoples, with whom we can compare ourselves and our progress. The contest must be close. The stakes must be high, the outcome in doubt, but the chances for success good. What we do must matter to those who watch as well as to ourselves. We have the men and the resources. We have a delight in purposeful action. And we have something to work for.

Given this resurgence of hope, it is not surprising that the 1964 election campaign should have led to an open clash between those who were responsive to renewed hope and those who were caught up in the mood of distrust, fear, and hatred turned out on the world or in on some part of our own society. Nor is it surprising that voices on the Right were raised to a new pitch in the effort to meet the challenge of a national election.

In the months before a presidential election, there is a temporary merging of voices at all levels in each party's massive effort to catch and hold the attention of voters. And in the 1964 election American voters crossed party lines and disregarded local political loyalties not only in response to the arguments of the Right but also in overwhelming fashion to repudiate the premises underlying those arguments. The number of votes amassed by Mr. Goldwater seemed enormous to those European observers in particular whose political appraisals are based on conditions in countries where a mutiplicity of national parties usually precludes the massing of very large numbers of voters behind one candidate. But Americans, whose political reality is of a different kind, emphasize instead the strength of the affirmation in this election. When the votes of narrowly loyal Republicans and of voters in the South who switched parties in a frantic effort to hold on to a caste system are taken into account, it is clear that the vote for the Right was very small. The nation voted against the Right and had no interest in the Left.

In the 1930's, politicians on the Right and on the Left were able to convince a relatively large number of Americans that they had only a single choice— Right or Left. Advocates of a Left position attempted political coercion of this kind when they nominated a tired and troubled Wallace to run in the 1948 election. But the failure of this splinter group, taken together with the failure of the splinter group of States Rights Democrats, served only to point up the unexpected strength of the moderate views expressed in President Truman's victory. In 1964, President Johnson steered through the shoals of charges and countercharges to a success the dimensions of which must be measured in part by the failure of a coalition for which Right Extremists—among others—spoke.

In the 1964 election President Johnson was given what he asked for—a mandate for a great surge forward in national development. His picture of the great society is built on a sense of national responsibility toward all the nation's children, all its aged, and the whole of the working population. He urged the building of a society strong enough to heal the old wounds left by the Civil War, strong enough to rescue the pockets of people in Appalachia and elsewhere who have been left behind in the country's progress, strong enough to absorb into the national economy all those who by reason of their race, color, national origin, lack of education, or lack of opportunity have been denied their share in the general national prosperity, a country strong enough to develop a high level of achievement in arts and letters, science and social invention. This picture of a future that is dependent on a giant mobilization of men and resources had—and has—great appeal.

For this reason, above all, there is a sense that something is stirring in the country, a belief that Americans have a renewed feeling of purpose and a willingness to make commitments. Even the most modest plans that have so far been set forth for carrying on the War on Poverty programs, for the conservation of our natural resources of land, water, air, wild life, and green life, for improving medical care, for widening the scope of education, and for strengthening the existing foundations in the arts and the humanities can be regarded as new charters for action.

The country's most immediate need is for candidates to fill the new positions in the new programs and the new fields that are opening up. The able, the imaginative, the experienced, the highly skilled, and the highly trained in almost every field are under tremendous pressure to become participants—to go here, to study this, to lead that, to reorganize an old institution, to build a new institution, to start a new university, to plan programs for training the nation's unemployed dropouts, to draw up programs for giving a better start to all the nation's pre-school children, to design a new city, to redesign an old city, to design models for industries in which computers can do the work of many men and models for the daily lives of men who have been freed by harnessed energy and computerized skills, and to take part in the ecumenical movements that are sweeping the world in new religious hope. The mandate has been given and the invitations have gone out. But those who have accepted are as yet too few to turn the vision into reality.

Many of the men who came to maturity in the 1950's are too preoccupied to come to the feast. They have their pleasant positions, their comfortable homes, their growing children, their full lives. Why should they give up what they have to do more? This is not wartime when men are obliged to do the things demanded by a national emergency. This is not a depression period when men are willing to do what they must to keep their heads above water and hoards of eager, educated young people are ready to take on almost any load. On the contrary, we are in the midst of a period of unprecedented employment of the educated and the highly trained. True, there are new opportunities. But they entail responsibilities of a kind that a comfortable, somewhat cynical middle-aged group are less than eager to take on. The inability to fill the many posts that are there, waiting, is treated by some as evidence of doubt in President Johnson's leadership. In fact, it is a reflection of the mood of many successful men who are content to pursue their private aims.

Where then are we to find the responsible leadership necessary for implementing a design that is bold and good in itself but that must be given life by a great number of people who believe in its possibilities? We can go first to those to whom we would not ordinarily turn except in wartime or some other emergency—the women, the young, the retired, the social mavericks, the imperfectly trained, the restive, the eccentric, and, for the first time on a large scale, those whose talents have been overlooked because of their race or color. Instead of insisting as we ordinarily do on the maintenance of bureaucratic rigidity, so that half the people who want to do something are debarred because they do not have the formal qualifications, because they have not done a kind of job before, or because they have passed an arbitrary age limit, we can deliberately by-pass large numbers of disqualifying regulations. As an emergency measure this will help. Young people can be given a chance earlier. The elderly can be brought back from too early retirement. Married women can be given more flexible time schedules. Elder statesmen can be asked once more to advise a nation in the throes of reorganization. But all these are stopgap measures, good in themselves but not good enough. The realization of large-scale plans drawn up along new lines requires the involvement of the best of those who have the experience and the imagination to lead and to make decisions.

Americans have always been stimulated by the sheer size of a task. In World War II there was a motto that contained the boast: "The difficult we do at once. The impossible takes a little longer." To the extent that the great society represents only the "difficult"—that is, internal reorganization, rehabilitation, and revitalization—it remains an insufficient challenge. It is all possible. Where will the funds come from and what will they be used for? They will come from our own pockets and serve our own interests. As we give we shall gain; we are, after all, giving to our own. How will the mandate be implemented? The President's parliamentary skills will see the bills through a cooperative Congress. Where will the personnel come from? Well, perhaps not entirely from the expected sources. The slowing down of defense contracts will release engineers. But what do engineers know about children's education? Not too much, perhaps, but they can learn. Everything is possible. Nothing is too difficult.

Yet while the plans are being made, whole armies of young people and an ever growing number of older people are quite literally flinging themselves into causes demanding immediate action. Some are well defined. The Civil Rights movement is one of these. Others are trivial or even meaningless. Still others are so ambiguous that it is hard to say what the issues are. In these causes they involve themselves bodily—in marches, sit-ins, sleep-ins, and other mass efforts that invite danger, defeat, and death. The clergy coming from churches that have slumbered comfortably while their congregations grew and building funds mounted are now picketing or standing in silent prayer in politically precarious places, inviting insult and arrest and bodily injury. And in a country that is outraged by the mistreatment of individual children, small Negro children, protected by sullen marshals or glumly acquiescent school administrators, take risks few people would ask of adults.

There is a sense of movement in the country—yes. But the country is suffering from a profound moral malaise that has its source in our unexpected wealth and affluence, in our uncertainty as to whether life has been enhanced or made valueless by the threat of thermonuclear war, in our uneasiness at knowing about the humiliation, the deprivation, the misery, the ill health, and the outright hunger suffered by some one-fifth of our own people and perhaps four-fifths of the peoples of the world. The admonition, "And why beholdest thou the mote that is in thy brother's eye, but perceivest not the beam that is in thine own eye," is as cogent today as it was when it was directed to the multitude gathered on the plain. Listening, we think of Boston attempting to reform Alabama, or Arkansas, or Mississippi. Yet the world has changed irrevocably since these words were spoken to the people out of all Judea and Jerusalem, and from the sea coast of Tyre and Sidon. For now no part of the body politic, which now includes all the peoples of the earth, can be healed unless all the body politic is treated. We cannot fence off Little Rock, Oxford, Selma, or the green campus at Berkeley and by doing so ignore Vietnam, Cyprus, or Ruanda-Urundi.

In spite of the size and spread of our existing foreign commitments, in spite of the outflow of gold, in spite of the support we have gingerly and uncertainly given the United Nations, the people of the United States still are hoping to build the future of the United States as if the country was as separate from the rest of the world as this continent was before the first voyage of Columbus. Yet we are in the world as we never have been before. Where in the past we had new millions of immigrants from virtually all the world, today we have millions of men overseas. Our children write us from India, Tanganyika, and Thailand, and we plan study programs for them in Rome, Nairobi, and Tokyo. But we have not yet really taken our place as a nation among nations, recognizing that each is essential to the safety of all. We are attempting to make a moral comeback in a game whose rules have altogether changed.

I believe we are still a people who are deeply and genuinely moved only by causes that we think are right, practical, and so difficult as to be rightly called "impossible." The impossible, that is, that will take a little longer. Faced by too great a disparity between our expressed ideals and our mode of behavior, we become cynical, self-indulgent, distrustful, apathetic, frightened, and open to corruption. We become, in fact, dangerous to ourselves and to the world. Faced only by tasks that are narrowly defined, only a few men and women will throw themselves into the fight, avid for action and certain that action—any action—is better than the apathy of the bystander. The New Deal with its massive preoccupation with poverty, misery, and lack of opportunity at home was a last fling at isolationism. And yet at the height of the New Deal years, when the United States cautiously stood back from efforts to stabilize an increasingly unstable world, thousands upon thousands of young Americans passionately debated the meaning for the world of the Spanish Revolution and a few hundred slipped out of the country and threw themselves into the actual battle lines. Even then isolation was losing its meaning for the generation that so soon afterward was flung into the battles of a whole world divided against itself. During the war the translation from a domestic upheaval to a struggle for larger goals was not so difficult. There were still enemies who could be fought on beaches, on islands, on the seaways, and on land that was already deeply scarred by old battles.

Today this translation from home to the world is far more difficult.

In his inaugural address, President Johnson said of the great society:

> It is the excitement of becoming—always becoming, trying, probing, falling, resting, and trying again—but always gaining.
>
> In each generation—with toil and tears—we have had to earn our heritage again.
>
> If we fail now, then we will have forgotten in abundance what we learned in hardship: that democracy rests on faith, freedom asks more than it gives, and the judgment of God is harshest on those who are most favored.
>
> If we succeed, it will not be because of what we have, but what we are; not because of what we own, but what we believe.

And in the President's address on United States policies in Vietnam, in which he spelled out American aims abroad, he spoke of this generation's dream:

> It is a very old dream. But we have the power and now we have the opportunity to make that dream come true.
>
> For centuries, nations have struggled among each other. But we dream of a world where disputes are

settled by law and reason. And we will try to make it so.

For most of history, men have hated and killed one another in battle. But we dream of an end to war. We will try to make it so.

For all existence, most men have lived in poverty, threatened by hunger. But we dream of a world where all are fed and charged with hope. And we will help to make it so.

We have not yet acted on the implications of these words. They echo in our minds, but we have not yet taken them into our hearts. Yet it will not avail us to answer the needs or to right the injustices within the United States as long as we are unwilling to act with full responsibility in the wider world. We shall still see ourselves—and our picture of ourselves matters at the present time—in the likeness of a man who sits calmly on his own doorstep nursing a minor injury, while outside his fence his neighbors are engaged in a desperate battle where every man is needed.

Given our own beliefs and our assessment of our own strength, we shall be unmanned by low level goodness, taking pride in righting wrongs in some part of the Union, living in too small a part of the larger world to hold our own part of that world together. We can take heart by singing: "Triumph we must, For our cause it is just." But the cause can no longer be stated in terms of black and white, darkness and light. Essentially, there is no enemy within or outside our own gates.

Today every nation is faced by the same crucial problems: How to use its resources for the benefit of all its people; how to live at peace in the world; how to do its share in bringing the world's population into balance; how to make safe the air, the earth, and the waters of the earth for new generations; how to bring under control the powers of life and death that are now irreversibly in man's hands. Each nation is now irrevocably the keeper of the children of all nations. If we fail—if any nation fails—neither we nor any other people will be here to carry on the human adventure begun so long ago, its beginnings lost in unrecorded history, and just now emerging into the light of man's knowledge of what it is and what it may become.

As a people, it has taken us almost four centuries to weld ourselves into what is now—almost—a united nation. Much of what we have accomplished has come about through the pressures of the outside world. Strong, wealthy, and powerful, we must now turn toward the rest of the world ready to accept a responsibility that is bound not to the duties, the loyalties, and the hopes of earlier years, but to the whole world, the only world in which we can act today and carry out our highest hopes for the future. We have no other.

BIBLIOGRAPHICAL APPENDIX

★

THE BROADER the canvas on which one works the greater will be one's obligations. If I write an article on the fire-walking ceremony of Bali, I need only acknowledge and list articles on fire-walking in Fiji and Tahiti and India, perhaps a dozen in all. If I write a book about a tribe upon which nothing has been written before, I may have only the verbal help given me by a missionary or a trader to recognize. But in a study like this, all that one has read and heard, brief comments made on someone else's paper at an almost forgotten scientific meeting years ago, a violent argument over a cup of coffee at midnight, a footnote in a book the very title of which is forgotten, the memory of the tone in a teacher's voice as he said: "No man is under any obligation to tell all the truths he knows at once," or the sudden insight that follows watching a schoolteacher discipline a child—all enter in. Acknowledgment is impossible, in the sense that one states gratefully all the help that one has received. Bibliography is likewise impossible, for no publisher would tolerate the list and the war would be over before each title could be tracked down. What I have done is to try to do several things—to give the references for books or theories to which I specifically refer, to give the researches of my own which lie back of some particular statement, to list articles of my own where I have dealt more fully with aspects lightly touched in the pages of this book, and to tell over those special moments of insight or indebtedness which are still green in my memory.

There are certain basic acknowledgments to be made: to my parents, who reared me to be a social scientist, and my grandmother, who set me taking notes on younger children's behavior when I was eight; to Franz Boas, who taught me anthropology; to Ruth Benedict, Lawrence K. Frank, John Dollard, and Erich Fromm, who helped to formulate the idea of character structure as used in this book; to Erik Erikson, whose understanding of the relationship between the body and the process of character development lies inexplicitly behind much of this book; to Geoffrey Gorer and Kurt Lewin for long and illuminating discussions of the peculiarities of American culture; and finally to my husband, Gregory Bateson, for all I have learned, in general, from collaborative work, and for what I have learned in particular about American culture—from his comment—and about differences between American and English culture.

For help in the preparation of the manuscript, I have to thank the Julius Rosenwald Fund and the American Museum of Natural History.

BIBLIOGRAPHY — 1942
REVISED

(Arranged to correspond to numbers in chapters)

★

CHAPTER I
(Introduction — 1942)

1. 1925-26. Samoa (Auspices of National Research Council)

   1928-29. Manus Tribe, Admiralty Islands, New Guinea (Auspices of Social Science Research Council)

   1930. An American Indian Tribe (Auspices of Mrs. Elmhirst's Committee, American Museum of Natural History)

   1931-33. New Guinea: Arapesh, Mundugumor, Tchambuli Tribes (Auspices of Voss Fund and South Seas Exploration Fund, American Museum of Natural History)

   The following three trips were under the auspices of Voss Fund and South Seas Exploration Fund, American Museum of Natural History, in conjunction with Committee for Research in Dementia Praecox, 33rd Order of Masons, Scottish Rite Fund, and Social Science Research Council

   1936-38. Bali

   1938. New Guinea: Iatmul Tribe

   1939. Short return visit to Bali

2. MEAD, MARGARET. On Behalf of the Sciences. *In* Symposium: "Toward an Honorable World." *Wilson College Bulletin,* Vol. 3, No. 4, pp. 19-29, 1940.

3. LOEB, EDWIN M. Mentawei Social Organization. *American Anthropologist,* Vol. 30, No. 3, pp. 408-433, 1928.

4. LYND, ROBERT S., and HELEN M. LYND. Middletown: A study in Contemporary American Culture. New York, Harcourt, Brace, 1929.
———. Middletown in Transition: A Study in Cultural Conflicts. New York, Harcourt, Brace, 1937.

5. WARNER, W. LLOYD, and PAUL S. LUNT. The Social Life of a Modern Community. (Yankee City Series, Vol. 1.) New Haven, Yale University Press, 1941.

6. ROSTEN, LEO C. Hollywood: The Movie Colony; the Movie Makers. New York, Harcourt, Brace, 1941.

7. ALLEN, GRANT. The British Barbarians: A Hill-Top Novel. New York, Putnam's, 1895.

8. MEAD, MARGARET. War Need Not Mar Our Children. *The New York Times Magazine*, pp. 13, 34, February 15, 1942.

9. MEAD, MARGARET. Youth Would Be Valiant. *National Parent-Teacher*, Vol. 36, No. 2, pp. 14-16, 1941.

10. For an example of the type of detailed study of culture which provided the background for this study, see:
MEAD, MARGARET.
Living with the Natives in Melanesia. *Natural History*, Vol. 31, No. 1, pp. 62-74, 1931.
More Comprehensive Field Methods. *American Anthropologist*, Vol. 35, No. 1, pp. 1-15, 1933.
Kinship in the Admiralty Islands. Anthropological Papers of The American Museum of Natural History, Vol. 34, Pt. 2, pp. 138-358, New York, 1934.
Native Languages as Field-Work Tools. *American Anthropologist*, Vol. 41, No. 2, pp. 189-205, 1939.
The Mountain Arapesh. II. Supernaturalism. Anthropological Papers of The American Museum of Natural History, Vol. 37, Pt. 3, pp. 319-451, New York, 1940.
BATESON, GREGORY, and MARGARET MEAD. Balinese Character: A Photographic Analysis. Special

Publications of The New York Academy of Sciences, II. New York, 1942; reissued 1962.

11. MEAD, MARGARET. —From the South Seas (Containing Coming of Age in Samoa, Growing Up in New Guinea, and Sex and Temperament). New York, Morrow, 1939. (See Introduction to book; also concluding chapter of each of the three parts.)

★

CHAPTER II

(Clearing the Air)

1. BATESON, GREGORY. Morale and National Character. *In* Civilian Morale, Second Yearbook of the Society for the Psychological Study of Social Issues, Goodwin Watson, Editor. Boston, Houghton Mifflin, 1942. Pp. 71-91.

2. MEAD, MARGARET. Social Change and Cultural Surrogates. *Journal of Educational Sociology*, Vol. 14, No. 2, pp. 92-109, 1940.

3. MEAD, MARGARET.
An Anthropologist Looks at the Teacher's Role. *Educational Method*, Vol. 21, No. 5, pp. 219-223, 1942.
The Student of Race Problems Can Say. . . ," *Frontiers of Democracy*, Vol. 6, No. 53, pp. 200-202, 1940.

4. MEAD, MARGARET. Educative Effects of Social Environment as Disclosed by Studies of Primitive Societies. *In* Environment and Education, E. W. Burgess, Editor. (Human Development Series, I. Supplementary Educational Monographs, No. 54.) Chicago, University of Chicago Press, 1942. Pp. 48-61.

5. For a discussion of racism, see:
BENEDICT, RUTH F. Race: Science and Politics. New York, Modern Age, 1940. Reprinted 1959, Compass C42, New York, Viking.

6. DOLLARD, JOHN. Caste and Class in a Southern Town. New Haven, Yale University Press, 1937. 3rd ed., 1957, Anchor A95, Garden City, Doubleday.

★

CHAPTER III

(We Are All Third Generation)

1. I owe my understanding of the significance of these chronological ties to discussions with Kurt Lewin and John G. Pilley.
2. MEAD, MARGARET. Conflict of Cultures in America. *In* Proceedings of the 54th Annual Convention of the Middle States Association of Colleges and Secondary Schools . . . 1940. Philadelphia, Middle States Association . . . , 1940. Pp. 30-44.
3. WARNER, W. LLOYD, and PAUL S. LUNT. The Social Life of a Modern Community. (Yankee City Series, Vol. 1.) New Haven, Yale University Press, 1941.
4. LOWIE, ROBERT H. Plains Indian Age-Societies: Historical and Comparative Summary. Anthropological Papers of The American Museum of Natural History, Vol. 11, Pt. 13, pp. 877-984, New York, 1916.
5. Cf. Samuel Butler's definition: That vice is when the pain follows the pleasure and virtue when the pleasure follows the pain.
6. BATESON, GREGORY, and MARGARET MEAD. Balinese Character: A Photographic Analysis. Special Publications of The New York Academy of Sciences, II. New York, 1942. Reissued 1962.
7. I owe my classification of the American attitude toward the "founding fathers" to a conversation with Dr. Ernst Kris, in which he was commenting on the way

in which Americans, apparently, want a strong father, although, in actual fact, they always push their fathers aside.

★

CHAPTER IV

(*The Class Handicap*)

1. MEAD, MARGARET. Has the "Middle Class" a Future? *Survey Graphic*, Vol. 31, No. 2, pp. 64-67, 95, 1942.

2. The "class analysis" has been developed and elaborated by Professor W. Lloyd Warner and his associates, and may be explored in its various aspects in the Yankee City Series (The Social Life of a Modern Community, Vol. 1. New Haven, Yale University Press, 1941); in Deep South, by Allison Davis, Burleigh Gardner, and Mary Gardner (Chicago, University of Chicago Press, 1941); and in Children of Bondage, by Allison Davis and John Dollard (Washington, American Council on Education, 1940). See also Dollard's Caste and Class in a Southern Town (New Haven, Yale University Press, 1937).

3. One of the fullest discussions of the middle-class character structure in Germany may be found in Erich Fromm's Escape from Freedom (New York, Farrar & Rinehart, 1941).

MEAD, MARGARET. On the Institutionalized Rôle of Women and Character Formation. *Zeitschrift für Sozialforschung*, Vol. 5, No. 1, pp. 69-75, 1936.

4. Terms used by Warner and his associates.

5. *Xiphorus Helleri* males.

6. MEAD, MARGARET. Material Conditions Affect our Character Structure. *In* Panel Discussion: "The Perils

of Democracy," 15th Annual Meeting, American Adult Education Association. *Journal of Adult Education,* Vol. 12, No. 3, pp. 269-277, 1940.

★

CHAPTER V

(The European in Our Midst)

1. MEAD, MARGARET. Our Educational Emphases in Primitive Perspective. *American Journal of Sociology,* Vol. 48, No. 6, pp. 633-639, 1943.
2. MEAD, MARGARET. Growing Up in New Guinea. New York, Morrow, 1930. Reprinted 1962, Apollo A-58, New York, Morrow.

★

CHAPTER VI

(Parents, Children and Achievement)

1. MEAD, MARGARET. Broken Homes. *Nation,* Vol. 128, pp. 253-255, February 27, 1929.
2. MEAD, MARGARET. Culture and Personality. *American Journal of Sociology,* Vol. 42, No. 1, pp. 84-87, 1936.
3. MEAD, MARGARET. Character Formation in Two South Sea Societies. *In* Transactions of the American Neurological Association, Sixty-Sixth Annual Meeting . . . 1940. Richmond, Va., William Byrd Press, 1940. Pp. 99-103.
   Administrative Contributions to Democratic Character Formation at the Adolescent Level. *Journal of the National Association of Deans of Women,* Vol. 4, No. 2, pp. 51-57, 1941.

★

CHAPTER VII

(*Brothers and Sisters and Success*)

1. MEAD, MARGARET. The Family in the Future. *In* Beyond Victory, Ruth Nanda Anshen, Editor. New York, Harcourt, Brace, 1943. Pp. 66-87.
2. HERZOG, HERTA. Why People Like the *Professor Quiz* Program. *In* Radio and the Printed Page, by Paul Lazarsfeld. New York, Duell, Sloan & Pearce, 1940.

★

CHAPTER VIII

(*Are Today's Youth Different?*)

1. MEAD, MARGARET. Democracy's Scapegoat: Youth. *Harper's Magazine,* Vol. 182, No. 1088, pp. 132-136, 1941.
2. BATESON, GREGORY. Radical Youth. Memorandum prepared for the Committee for National Morale. (Unpublished manuscript.)
3. MEAD, MARGARET. Social Change and Cultural Surrogates. *Journal of Educational Sociology,* Vol. 14, No. 2, pp. 92-109, 1940.
   Growing Up in New Guinea. New York, Morrow, 1930. Reprinted 1962, Apollo A-58, New York, Morrow.
4. MEAD, MARGARET. Sex and Temperament in Three Primitive Societies. New York, Morrow, 1935. Part I. Reprinted 1963, Apollo A-67, New York, Morrow.
5. MEAD, MARGARET. Youth Would Be Valiant. *National Parent-Teacher,* Vol. 36, No. 2, pp. 14-16, 1941.

★

CHAPTER IX

(The Chip on the Shoulder)

1. DOLLARD, JOHN, and others. Frustration and Aggression. New Haven, Yale University Press, 1939.
   See also:
   BATESON, GREGORY. The Frustration-Aggression Hypothesis. *Psychological Review,* Vol. 48, No. 4, pp. 350-355, 1941.
2. BATESON, GREGORY. Equilibrium and Climax in Inter-Personal Relations. Paper read at Conference of Topologists, Smith College, Northampton, Mass., December 31, 1940-January 2, 1941.
3. The same type of responsive, unpatterned aggressiveness is found among the Iatmul of New Guinea, where little boys are taught their aggressiveness by women. See:
   BATESON, GREGORY.
   Music in New Guinea. *The Eagle* (St. John's College, Cambridge, England), Vol. 48, No. 214, pp. 158-170, 1934.
   Naven. Cambridge, University Press, 1936. 2nd edition, 1958, Stanford, Stanford University Press.
4. BATESON, GREGORY. Morale and National Character. *In* Civilian Morale, Second Yearbook of the Society for the Psychological Study of Social Issues, Goodwin Watson, Editor. Boston, Houghton Mifflin, 1942. Pp. 71-91.

★

CHAPTER X

(*Fighting the War American Style*)

1. BATESON, GREGORY, and MARGARET MEAD. Principles of Morale Building. *Journal of Educational Sociology*, Vol. 15, No. 4, pp. 206-220, 1941.

★

CHAPTER XI

(*Are Democracy and Social Science Compatible Each with Each?*)

1. KRIS, ERNST. Some Psychoanalytic Comments on Propaganda and Morale. Paper read at a meeting of the Psychologists' League, New York, February 7, 1942.
2. MEAD, MARGARET. —From the South Seas. New York, Morrow, 1939. Introduction.
3. MEAD, MARGARET. On Behalf of the Sciences. *In* Symposium: "Toward an Honorable World." *Wilson College Bulletin*, Vol. 3, No. 4, pp. 19-29, 1940.
4. LASSWELL, HAROLD D. The Contribution of Freud's Insight Interview to the Social Sciences. *American Journal of Sociology*, Vol. 45, pp. 375-390, 1939.
5. BATESON, GREGORY. Problems of Applied Science and Manipulation. Paper read at First General Meeting of the Society for Applied Anthropology, Harvard University, May 3, 1941.
6. MEAD, MARGARET. The Comparative Study of Culture and the Purposive Cultivation of Democratic Values. *In* Science, Philosophy and Religion, Second

Symposium, Lyman Bryson and Louis Finkelstein, Editors. New York, Conference on Science, Philosophy and Religion, 1942. Pp. 56-69.

See also comments by Gregory Bateson, Social Planning and the Concept of Deutero Learning. *Ibid.*, pp. 81-97.

★

CHAPTER XII

(*If We Are to Go On*)

1. ROSTEN, LEO C. Hollywood: The Movie Colony; the Movie Makers. New York, Harcourt, Brace, 1941.

2. My understanding of this aspect of shame in America I owe to a conversation with Helen Lynd, who was stressing our lack of techniques for handling shame.

3. MEAD, MARGARET. Warfare Is Only an Invention —Not a Biological Necessity. *Asia,* Vol. 40, No. 8, pp. 402-405, 1940.

4. FROMM, ERICH. Escape from Freedom. New York, Farrar & Rinehart, 1941.

★

CHAPTER XIII

(*Building the World New*)

1. ALEXANDER, FRANZ. Educative Influence of Personality Factors in Environment. *In* Environment and Education, E. W. Burgess, Editor. (Human Development Series, I. Supplementary Educational Monographs, No. 54.) Chicago, University of Chicago Press, 1942. Pp. 29-47.

2. BENEDICT, RUTH. Patterns of Culture. Boston,

Houghton Mifflin, 1934. Reprinted 1961, SE 8, Boston, Houghton Mifflin.

MEAD, MARGARET. Sex and Temperament in Three Primitive Societies. New York, Morrow, 1935. Reprinted 1963, Apollo A-67, New York, Morrow.

3. GORER, GEOFFREY. Japanese Character Structure and Propaganda: A Preliminary Survey. New York, Institute for Intercultural Studies, 1942 (mimeographed). See also Geoffrey Gorer's Themes in Japanese Culture. *Transactions of The New York Academy of Sciences,* Ser. 2, Vol. 5, No. 5, pp. 106-124, 1943.

4. ERIKSON, ERIK H. Hitler's Imagery and German Youth. *Psychiatry,* Vol. 5, No. 4, pp. 475-493, 1942.

★

CHAPTER XIV

(These Things We Can Do)

1. FRANK, LAWRENCE K. World Order and Cultural Diversity. *Free World,* Vol. 3, No. 1, pp. 389-395, 1942.

My original sense of the possibilities of orchestrating different cultural forms I owe to the writings of Randolph Bourne and Horace Kallen.

And Keep Your Powder Dry was a pioneer venture. In 1942 no anthropologist had attempted to write about a major complex culture using the model of the whole culture that had been developed through the study of small primitive societies. No anthropologist had worked out a style of disciplined subjectivity, a way of combining the objectivity obtained by studying an alien culture and the articulate awareness of ethical involvement necessary for studying one's own. I had to work out these problems for myself; I was fortunate in having the intellectual support of those to whom I expressed my indebtedness in the Bibliographical Appendix of the first edition.

Today, twenty-three years later, much has changed.

During World War II, as the applied science of national character was in the process of formulation, we learned how to work on the modern cultures with whose fate our lives were bound up and in doing so we learned how to build complex research groups made up of members of several cultures, including the one being studied. With practice we also learned how to phrase our findings. This was something I merely did intuitively in this book. But later, as more anthropologists worked on the problem in various cultures, we came to recognize the necessity of writing about a culture and a people in a vocabulary that would be acceptable both to its own members and to members of other cultures.

Somewhat more slowly, in the studies carried out in the postwar period, we came to recognize the specific hazards of a description in which a culture was presented in terms of the multilevel awareness necessary for insight and understanding. We experienced the difficulties that are bound to occur when a people's conscious cultural formulations are juxtaposed to cultural trends that ordinarily, in that culture,

327

are out of consciousness—especially the confusion that results from a continual shift in the level of discussion. But gradually we learned to hold the level of discussion constant and to discuss cutural perceptions of reality and cultural fantasy (perceptions that are reflected, for example, in responses to projective materials) in separate contexts.

With the publication of national character studies, we experienced the criticism and opposition both of those who were ambivalent to their native culture (immigrants to the United States, for example, who deeply repudiated their own first culture) and of others who were ambivalent to the culture they were in the process of acquiring. As yet we have not fully learned how to come to grips with the difficulties posed by their affectively toned objections. I can foresee, but I cannot avert, certain objections that will be made on these grounds to my description of contemporary American character.

In addition, we have experienced the difficulties that arise when, through a series of confusions that are in part a result of historical accident, the recognition of national character is linked to political racism. The difficulties grow out of the general assumption, explicit or implicit, that any theory of personality which involves the recognition of characteristics (whether these are innate or acquired through early learning) that may be constant throughout life is necessarily racist in tendency. This viewpoint may be, though it is not always, associated with the belief that a theory of personality is consonant with a democratic ethic only if it allows for infinite modification by learning throughout life. In this combination, opposition to theories about cultural character that take cognizance of innate constitution-temperament is allied with opposition to theories about cultural character that imply the importance and the essential irreversibility of early childhood cultural experiences.

Commitment to a theory of infinite malleability throughout human life may take various forms. It is expressed in the persistent emphasis Soviet Russians place on the effects of environmental influence. It is also expressed in the persistent refusal by Americans to recognize that long cultural deprivation as it is experienced by any ethnic group is, in fact, depriving. Such a commitment is a very understandable response to the misuses made of conceptions of constitutional type in Nazi thinking (as, for example, in the work of Jaensch during the Nazi period). It is also an understandable response to the attitudes sometimes attributed to Jung. And in the whole contemporary discussion of the problem two points stand out clearly. One is the unassailability of the ethical position taken by those who have resisted the misuse and distortion of concepts that, in distorted forms, have contributed to the denigration of all members of a particular human group. The second is the relationship of this commitment to a fundamental optimism about the feasibility of rapid social and cultural change.

It is necessary to clarify the cultural preferences and the generous motives underlying the contemporary insistence on the infinite malleability of man. The difficulties growing out of confusion about what is involved obfuscate our ability, on the one hand, to consider objectively the clues to the origins of cultural difference provided by differences in temperament and, on the other hand, to study in detail the processes by which recognizable differences in cultural behavior appear in different institutional settings.

In the existing climate of opinion, I feel it necessary to restate my own position. On the basis of my own work and that of others, I believe there is convincing evidence for the existence of differences in temperament as well as in intelligence and for the existence of temperamental differences that crosscut sex differences and sex differences that crosscut temperamental differences. There is also convincing evidence for the existence of universal processes that are subject to individual differentiation within but not among human groups (that is, tribes, races, and ethnic groups). These universal processes, reflecting man's long evolutionary history, are the dynamic expression of certain species-characteristic relationships that involve man's superior brain, long infantile dependency, and peculiar developmental rhythm. They are shaped profoundly by culture and are subject to individual differences in intensity, but they are discernible in all human groups, whatever their social and cultural patterning may be.

The conversations and exchanges to which I referred in the original bibliographical appendix have gone on. They have included friends not mentioned earlier and over the years they have been amplified by new voices, notably Alex Bavelas, Ray L. Birdwhistell, Gotthard C. Booth, Lyman Bryson, Nicolas Calas, Eliot D. Chapple, Edith Cobb, Elsa Frenkel-Brunswik, Anthony Garvan, Clemens Heller, Jules Henry, Everett Hughes, Marie Jahoda, Clyde Kluckhohn, Robert Lamb, Dorothy Lee, Nathan Leites, Martin Loeb, Margaret Lowenfeld, David McClellan, Rhoda Metraux, Philip Mosely, Lois and Gardner Murphy, Talcott Parsons, David Riesman, Erwin Schuller, Frank Tannenbaum, Edmond Taylor, and Martha Wolfenstein. Some conversations have been stilled by death. But these are my colleagues and friends who have specifically influenced my thinking about American national character, chosen for thanks from among the larger number of my colleagues and friends who have contributed to my scientific understanding of the field of culture and personality.

Certain ongoing and other newer collaborative efforts have been particularly important in my thinking about American culture. I should like to mention with gratitude a number of books written or studies made by those with whose work I have been in close intellectual contact. Among these are Geoffrey Gorer's *The American People* (1948), for the revised edition of which he wrote a new chapter (1964); Gregory Bateson's contribution to *Communication: The Social Matrix of Psychiatry* (1951), written in collaboration with Jurgen Ruesch; Ruth Benedict's *The Chrysanthemum and the Sword* (1946), which was addressed to American action; Ray Birdwhistell's analysis of micro-cultural differences, as exemplified in his paper, "Family Structure and Social Mobility" (1958); Erik Erikson's *Child-*

hood and Society (1950); Everett Hughes' work on American institutional forms; Robert Lamb's interrupted work on American cities; Martin Loeb's work on the core culture; Rhoda Metraux's unpublished study of certain aspects of American character in *A Report on National Character* (1951), and her ongoing analysis of American imagery; David Riesman's *The Lonely Crowd* (1950) and *Faces in the Crowd* (1952); Frank Tannenbaum's work on American culture, particularly "The Balance of Power in Society" (1946); Martha Wolfenstein's *Disaster* (1957); and *The Movies* (1950), by Martha Wolfenstein and Nathan Leites.

I have also added to the earlier bibliography a short list of books and articles related to the applied science of national character. Three of these, *The Study of Culture at a Distance* (Mead and Metraux, eds., 1953), "National Character" (Mead, 1953), and *Childhood in Contemporary Cultures* (Mead and Wolfenstein, eds., 1955), contain extensive references to other relevant work.

BIBLIOGRAPHY — 1965

1. NATIONAL CHARACTER AND ITS
CRITICS: SELECTED REFERENCES

*ALEXROD, SIDNEY. Infant Care and Personality Reconsidered: A Rejoinder to Orlansky. *In* Psychoanalytic Study of Society, II. New York, International Universities Press, 1964. Pp. 75-132.

BENEDICT, RUTH. The Chrysanthemum and the Sword. Boston, Houghton Mifflin, 1946.

———— The Study of Cultural Patterns in European Nations. *Transactions of the New York Academy of Sciences,* Ser. 2, Vol. 8, No. 8, pp. 274-279, 1946.

———— The Family: Genus Americanum. *In* The Family: Its Function and Destiny, Ruth Nanda Anshen, Editor. New York, Harper, 1949. Pp. 53-64.

*BERGER, MORROE. "Understanding National Character"—and War. *Commentary,* Vol. 11, No. 4, pp. 375-386, 1951.

DEUTSCH, KARL W. Nationalism and Social Communication. New York, Wiley, 1953.

DUIJKER, H. C. J., and N. H. FRIJDA. National Character and National Stereotypes. New York, Humanities Press, 1961.

*ENDLEMAN, ROBERT. The New Anthropology and Its Ambitions. *Commentary,* Vol. 8, No. 3, pp. 284-291, 1949.

ERIKSON, ERIK H. Childhood and Society. New York, Norton, 1950. 2nd ed. rev., 1963.

*GOLDMAN, IRVING. Psychiatric Interpretations of Russian History, A Reply to Geoffrey Gorer. *American Slavic and East European Review,* Vol. 9, No. 3, pp. 151-161, 1950.

* Critical comments are starred.

GORER, GEOFFREY. The Concept of National Character. *In* Science News, No. 18. Harmondsworth, Middlesex, England, Penguin Books, 1950. Pp. 105-122.

———— and JOHN RICKMAN. The People of Great Russia. New York, Chanticleer Press, 1950. Reprinted 1962, N-112, New York, Norton.

*INKELES, ALEX. Some Sociological Observations on Culture and Personality Studies. *In* Personality in Nature, Society, and Culture, Clyde Kluckhohn, Henry A. Murray, and David M. Schneider, Editors. New York, Knopf, 1953. Pp. 577-592.

*———— and D. J. LEVINSON. National Character: The Study of Modal Personality and Sociocultural Systems. *In* Handbook of Social Psychology, 2 vols., Gardner Lindzey, Editor. Cambridge, Mass., Addison-Wesley, 1954. Pp. 977-1020.

*KARDINER, ABRAM. Psychosocial Synthesis: Reply to Mead. *Science,* Vol. 130, p. 1728, December 25, 1959.

———— and others. The Psychological Frontiers of Society. New York, Columbia University Press, 1945.

KLINEBERG, OTTO. A Science of National Character. *Journal of Social Psychology,* Vol. 19, first half, pp. 147-162, 1944.

LEITES, NATHAN. Psycho-Cultural Hypotheses about Political Acts. *World Politics,* Vol. 1, No. 1, pp. 102-119, 1948.

*LINDESMITH, A. R., and A. L. STRAUSS. A Critique of Culture-Personality Writings. *American Sociological Review,* Vol. 15, No. 5, pp. 587-600, 1950.

LINTON, RALPH. The Concept of National Character. *In* Personality and Political Crisis, A. H. Stanton and S. E. Perry, Editors. Glencoe, Ill., Free Press, 1951. Pp. 133-150.

*LITTLE, KENNETH L. Methodology in the Study of Adult Personality. *American Anthropologist,* Vol. 52, No. 2, pp. 279-282, 1950.

LOWIE, ROBERT H. The German People: A Social Portrait to 1914. New York, Farrar and Rinehart, 1945.

———— Toward Understanding Germany. Chicago, University of Chicago Press, 1954.

MEAD, MARGARET. The Study of National Character. *In* The Policy Sciences, Daniel Lerner and Harold D. Lasswell, Editors. Stanford, Stanford University Press, 1951. Pp. 105-132.

———— National Character. *In* Anthropology Today, A. L. Kroeber, Editor. Chicago, University of Chicago Press, 1953. Pp. 642-667.

*———— The Swaddling Hypothesis: Its Reception. *American Anthropologist*, Vol. 56, No. 3, pp. 395-409, 1954.

*———— Ruth Benedict. *Science*, Vol. 129, p. 1514, June 5, 1959.

*———— Letter in Reply to Kardiner. *Science*, Vol. 130, pp. 1728, 1732, December 25, 1959.

———— National Character and the Science of Anthropology. *In* Culture and Social Character: The Work of David Riesman Reviewed, Seymour M. Lipset and Leo Lowenthal, Editors. New York, Free Press of Glencoe, 1961. Pp. 15-26.

———— Anthropology: A Human Science: Selected Papers, 1939-1960. (Insight Book, No. 22.) Princeton, Van Nostrand, 1964.

———— Continuities in Cultural Evolution. New Haven, Yale University Press, 1964.

———— and RHODA METRAUX. The Anthropology of Human Conflict. *In* The Nature of Human Conflict, Elton B. McNeil, Editor. Englewood Cliffs, N.J., Prentice-Hall, 1965. Pp. 116-133.

———— and RHODA METRAUX, eds. The Study of Culture at a Distance. Chicago, University of Chicago Press, 1953.

———— and MARTHA WOLFENSTEIN, eds. Childhood in Contemporary Cultures. Chicago, University of Chicago Press, 1955.

*ORLANSKY, HAROLD. Infant Care and Personality. *Psychological Bulletin*, Vol. 46, No. 1, pp. 1-48, 1949.

*RIESMAN, DAVID. Psychological Types and National

Character: An Informal Commentary. *American Quarterly*, Vol. 5, pp. 325-343, Winter, 1953.

*SHUB, BORIS. The Soviets Expose a Baby. *New Leader*, pp. 11-12, June 17, 1950.

WALLACE, ANTHONY F. C. Culture and Personality. AS 1. New York, Random House, 1961.

*WOLFE, BERTRAM D. Swaddling and the Russians. *New Leader*, p. 20, May 21, 1951.

*——— The Swaddled Soul of the Great Russians. *New Leader*, pp. 15-18, January 29, 1951.

2. AMERICAN STUDIES: SELECTED REFERENCES

American Case Histories. *In* Mental Health and Infant Development, II, Kenneth Soddy, Editor. New York, Basic Books, 1955. Pp. 17-170.

ARENSBERG, CONRAD M. American Communities. *American Anthropologist*, Vol. 57, No. 6, pp. 1142-1162, 1955. See references for studies published prior to 1955.

BARKER, R. C., and H. J. WRIGHT. The Midwest and Its Children. Evanston, Ill., Row Peterson, 1955.

BIRDWHISTELL, RAY L. Family Structure and Social Mobility. *Transactions of The New York Academy of Sciences*, Ser. 2, Vol. 21, No. 2, pp. 136-145, 1958.

BOORSTIN, DANIEL J. The Americans: The Colonial Experience. New York, Random House, 1958.

BRYSON, LYMAN. The Drive toward Reason in the Service of a Free People. New York, Harper, 1954.

CASH, WILBUR J. The Mind of the South. New York, Knopf, 1941. Reprinted 1960, New York, Random House.

FRANK, LAWRENCE K. The Cost of Competition. *In* Society as the Patient. New Brunswick, N.J., Rutgers University Press, 1948. Pp. 21-36.

GALLAHER, ART. Plainville Fifteen Years Later. New York, Columbia University Press, 1961.

GARVAN, ANTHONY B. Architecture and Town Planning in Colonial Connecticut. New Haven, Yale University Press, 1951.

GESELL, ARNOLD, FRANCES ILG, and others. Infant and Child in the Culture of Today. New York, Harper, 1943.

GINZBERG, ELI, and DOUGLAS W. BRAY. The Uneducated. New York, Columbia University Press, 1953.

——— and others. The Ineffective Soldier, 3 vols. New York, Columbia University Press, 1959.

GORER, GEOFFREY. The American People. New York, Norton, 1948. Rev. ed., 1964.

HANDLIN, OSCAR. The Uprooted. Boston, Little Brown, 1951.

——— Race and Nationality in American Life. Boston, Little Brown, 1957.

HENRY, JULES. Culture against Man. New York, Random House, 1963.

HOLLINGSHEAD, AUGUST B. Elmtown's Youth: The Impact of Social Classes on Adolescents. New York, Wiley, 1949.

KIMBALL, SOLON T., and MARION PEARSALL. The Talladega Story. University, Ala., University of Alabama Press, 1954.

KLUCKHOHN, CLYDE. The Evolution of Contemporary American Values. *Daedalus*, pp. 78-109, Spring, 1958.

——— and FLORENCE KLUCKHOHN. American Culture: Generalized Orientations and Class Patterns. *In* Conflicts of Power in Modern Culture, Seventh Symposium, Lyman Bryson, Editor. New York, Conference on Science, Philosophy and Religion, 1947. Pp. 106-128.

LAMB, ROBERT K. Entrepreneurship in the Community. *Explorations in Entrepreneurial History,* Vol. 2, No. 3, pp. 114-127, 1950.

LANTIS, MARGARET, ed. The U.S.A. as Anthropologists See It. *American Anthropologist,* Vol. 57, No. 6, pp. 1113-1295, 1955.

LASSWELL, HAROLD D. Power and Personality. New York, Norton, 1948.

———— The Political Writings. Glencoe, Ill., Free Press, 1951.

LERNER, MAX. America as a Civilization. New York, Simon and Schuster, 1957. See also for very comprehensive references on American life.

McCLELLAND, DAVID C. The Achieving Society. Princeton, Van Nostrand, 1961.

MEAD, MARGARET. The American Family as Seen by an Anthropologist. *American Journal of Sociology*, Vol. 53, No. 6, pp. 453-459, 1948.

———— Male and Female. New York, Morrow, 1949. See Appendix III for references by Margaret Mead, 1927-1948, on American culture.

———— The Comparative Study of Cultures and the Purposive Cultivation of Democratic Values, 1941-1949. *In* Perspectives on a Troubled Decade: Science, Philosophy and Religion, 1939-1949, Lyman Bryson, Louis Finkelstein, and R. M. MacIver, Editors. New York, Harper, 1950. Pp. 87-108.

———— The School in American Culture. Cambridge, Harvard University Press, 1951.

———— Outdoor Recreation in the Context of Emerging American Culture Values. *In* Trends in American Living and Outdoor Recreation. (Reports to the Outdoor Recreation Resources Review Commission, No. 22.) Washington, U.S. Government Printing Office, 1962. Pp. 2-65.

METRAUX, RHODA. American National Character Structure. *In* A Report on National Character, Rhoda Metraux, Editor. New York, Columbia University Research in Contemporary Cultures, 1951. Pp. 21-53. (Mimeographed)

MILLS, C. WRIGHT. White Collar. New York, Oxford University Press, 1951.

———— The Power Elite. New York, Oxford University Press, 1956.

MURPHY, LOIS B., and collaborators. The Widening World of Childhood: Paths toward Mastery. New York, Basic Books, 1962.

MYRDAL, GUNNAR. An American Dilemma. New York,

Harper, 1944. Reprinted 1962, New York, Harper and Row.

PARSONS, TALCOTT. Age and Sex in the Social Structure of the United States. *American Sociological Review*, Vol. 7, No. 5, pp. 604-616, 1942.

POTTER, DAVID. People of Plenty. Chicago, University of Chicago Press, 1954.

RIESMAN, DAVID. The Lonely Crowd. New Haven, Yale University Press, 1950. Reprinted 1961, Y41, Yale University Press.

———— Faces in the Crowd. New Haven: Yale University Press, 1952.

———— The Study of National Character: Some Observations on the American Case. *Harvard University Library Bulletin*, Vol. 13, pp. 5-24, Winter, 1959.

———— and NATHAN GLAZER. The Lonely Crowd: A Reconsideration in 1960. *In* Culture and Social Character: The Work of David Riesman Reviewed, Seymour M. Lipset and Leo Lowenthal, Editors. New York, Free Press of Glencoe, 1961. Pp. 419-458.

RUESCH, JURGEN, and GREGORY BATESON. Communication: The Social Matrix of Psychiatry. New York, Norton, 1951.

STOUFFER, S. A., and others. Studies in Social Psychology in World War II, 4 vols. Princeton, Princeton University Press, 1949-1950.

TANNENBAUM, FRANK. Darker Phases of the South. New York, Putnam, 1924.

———— The Balance of Power in Society. *Political Science Quarterly*, Vol. 61, No. 4, pp. 481-504, 1946.

———— Slave and Citizen: The Negro in the Americas. New York, Knopf, 1947.

———— A Philosophy of Labor. New York, Knopf, 1951.

VIDICH, ARTHUR J., and JOSEPH BENSMAN. Small Town in Mass Society. Anchor Book A216. Garden City, New York, Doubleday, 1960.

WARNER, W. LLOYD. American Life: Dream and Reality. Chicago, University of Chicago Press, 1953.

———— The Living and the Dead. (Yankee City Series, Vol. 5.) New Haven, Yale University Press, 1959.

———— ROBERT J. HAVIGHURST, and MARTIN B. LOEB. Who Shall Be Educated. New York, Harper, 1944.

———— and J. O. LOW. The Social System of a Modern Factory. (Yankee City Series, Vol. 4.) New Haven, Yale University Press, 1947.

———— and PAUL S. LUNT. The Social Life of a Modern Community. (Yankee City Series, Vol. 1.) New Haven, Yale University Press, 1941.

———— and PAUL S. LUNT. The Status System of a Modern Community. (Yankee City Series, Vol. 2.) New Haven, Yale University Press, 1942.

———— and LEO SROLE. The Social Systems of American Ethnic Groups. (Yankee City Series, Vol. 3.) New Haven, Yale University Press, 1945.

WEST, JAMES. Plainville, U.S.A. New York, Columbia University Press, 1945. Reprinted 1961.

WHYTE, WILLIAM F. Street Corner Society. Chicago, University of Chicago Press, 1955.

WOLFENSTEIN, MARTHA. Disaster: A Psychological Essay. Glencoe, Ill., Free Press, 1957.

———— and NATHAN LEITES. The Movies: A Psychological Study. Glencoe, Ill., Free Press, 1950.